A Wordsworth Chronology

F. B. PINION

G.K.HALL&CO.

70 LINCOLN STREET, BOSTON, MASS.

Published 1988 in the United States of America and Canada by
G. K. HALL & CO.
70 Lincoln Street
Boston, Massachusetts 02111

First published 1988 by
THE MACMILLAN PRESS LTD
Houndmills, Basingstoke
Hampshire RG21 2XS

Printed in Hong Kong

Library of Congress Cataloging-in-Publication Data
Pinion, F. B.
A Wordsworth chronology.
Bibliography: p.
Includes index.
1. Wordsworth, William, 1770–1850—Chronology.
I. Title.
PR5887.P56   1988   821'.7   87–25208
ISBN 0–8161–8950–1

To Harold and Charlyn Orel

Contents

List of Maps

General Editor's Preface

Most biographies are ill adapted to serve as works of reference – not surprisingly so, since the biographer is likely to regard his function as the devising of a continuous and readable narrative, with excursions into interpretation and speculation, rather than a bald recital of facts. There are times, however, when anyone reading for business or pleasure needs to check a point quickly or to obtain a rapid overview of part of an author's life or career; and at such moments turning over the pages of a biography can be a time-consuming and frustrating occupation. The present series of volumes aims at providing a means whereby the chronological facts of an author's life and career, rather than needing to be prised out of the narrative in which they are (if they appear at all) securely embedded, can be seen at a glance. Moreover, whereas biographies are often, and quite understandably, vague over matters of fact (since it makes for tediousness to be forever enumerating details of dates and places), a chronology can be precise whenever it is possible to be precise.

Thanks to the survival, sometimes in very large quantities, of letters, diaries, notebooks and other documents, as well as to thoroughly researched biographies and bibliographies, this material now exists in abundance for many major authors. In the case of, for example, Dickens, we can often ascertain what he was doing in each month and week, and almost on each day, of his prodigiously active working life; and the student of, say, *David Copperfield* is likely to find it fascinating as well as useful to know just when Dickens was at work on each part of that novel, what other literary enterprises he was engaged in at the same time, whom he was meeting, what places he was visiting, and what were the relevant circumstances of his personal and professional life. Such a chronology is not, of course, a substitute for a biography; but its arrangement, in combination with its index, makes it a much more convenient tool for this kind of purpose; and it may be acceptable as a form of 'alternative' biography, with its own distinctive advantages as well as its obvious limitations.

Since information relating to an author's early years is usually scanty and chronologically imprecise, the opening section of some volumes in this series groups together the years of childhood and adolescence. Thereafter each year, and usually each month, is dealt with separately. Information not readily assignable to a specific month or day is given as a general note under the relevant year or month. The first entry for each month carries an indication of the day of the week, so that when necessary this can be readily calculated for other dates. Each volume also contains a bibliography of the principal sources of information. In the chronology itself, the sources of many of the more specific items, including quotations, are identified, in order that the reader who wishes to do so may consult the original contexts.

NORMAN PAGE

Introduction

The principal sources for this chronology are the Wordsworth letters and journals. Other significant quarries are indicated in the Bibliography. Mark L. Reed's chronology has been consulted for revision, and to it I owe a number of items from sources which have been unavailable to me; infrequent differences are based very occasionally on the old evidence, more importantly on the recently published love-letters of William and Mary Wordsworth.

For an author who lived eighty years, and was active almost to the end, a chronology of restricted length demands much greater selectivity than would be given to one of the inheritors of unfulfilled renown such as Keats. There is an enormous amount of recorded evidence from which to draw, but insufficient at certain periods for an even chronological treatment. Sometimes, as with Dorothy's Alfoxden journal, one can offer no more, if due proportions are to be observed, than the characteristic or the specifically significant; at times of crisis or special interest, the information given is more intensive and detailed, whenever possible.

The child *is* father of the man, and this means that the younger Wordsworth cannot be fully understood without knowledge of his whole life, and of the way he reacted to the dominant issues and movements of his age. On the available evidence, the life and even the personality of the maturer Wordsworth are more interesting than those of the earlier. To appreciate him we need to be familiar with his loyalties to friends and relatives, the latter including at least as many Hutchinsons as Wordsworths. We need to know his concern for his children and grandchildren, for Hartley Coleridge, 'Keswick' John, and the orphaned Southeys. We must recognise how much he knew of contemporary affairs at home and abroad, how much his experience of the French Revolution coloured his thinking, and how closely related he was to many of the principal figures of the day in the world of politics, religion, and art. The testimony of his frequent visits to London impresses not only by his numerous friendships but also by the revelation of his influence, resistant or progressive, unduly alarmist or wisely prescient.

Wordsworth was so much devoted to causes, as well as to his immediate kin, his nephews and grandchildren, and numerous other relatives and friends, that his chronology demands a high degree of selective inclusiveness, particularly for the second half of his life, in any attempt to achieve continuity of interest and biographical integration.

Close attention to the later years provides ample explanation for Wordsworth's failure to continue *The Recluse*. Although he chose to depend too much on travel for poetry, the number of incidental poems and passages, sonnets notably, in which (taking their subjects into account) he reached levels of excellence beyond his scope during the *Lyrical Ballads* period is higher than is customarily allowed. Yet he speaks from experience when he counsels Moxon to seek independence by staying in business, to let the Muses pursue him rather than give up his time to their pursuit. His sense of proportion remains a challenge to values: he is more interested in persons than in books, and, though his anxiety for younger dependants made him more circumspect with money, he is still the poet who held that by 'getting and spending' we 'lay waste our powers'; he is shocked to discover how much Scott had succumbed to ambition for worldly grandeur.

The complication or tediousness of Wordsworth's correspondence on financial or political matters makes it necessary to subordinate these subjects to more personal and literary entries. Links between his life and poetry, though not presented exhaustively, are not neglected; such inclusions prove to be more numerous than might be expected.

It must be remembered that there is not always sufficient evidence to guarantee the complete accuracy of dating. Letters and journals are sometimes wrongly dated, such errors not being limited, one suspects, to the demonstrable; this applies perhaps more often to Dorothy than to others. Dates, of course, may be entirely missing; or the critical information may be limited to the days of the week, as with Mary Wordsworth's letter of probably 8–9 April 1850.

A valuable supplement to the chronology is provided in 'Persons of Importance in Wordsworth's Life'. No one among them, not even Crabb Robinson, is as important as Dorothy Wordsworth or Mary Hutchinson/Wordsworth or Sara Hutchinson or Coleridge. The sketches, however, besides providing contexts for many entries, can reveal deeper implications; just how far, for instance,

Wordsworth differed from the Tractarians is high-lighted when Robinson's comments are considered in conjunction with the career of F. W. Faber.

Far too many places, foreign especially, are mentioned for notes. The locations of most of the foreign towns or cities will be more familiar or discoverable to many readers than places of very local interest, and for this reason four maps have been provided of relevant areas in England and Scotland. This restricted choice is based on the frequency and relative importance of the references. Three of the maps are transferred from *A Wordsworth Companion* (London and New York, 1984), a work in which my major interest has been the assessment of Wordsworth's writings. Attention must be called to the situation of Park House farm; unfortunately my relief at finding a Park House very near Eusemere on Jefferys' 1770 map of Westmorland made me overlook all I had read in the letters about the location of Tom Hutchinson's farm in Cumberland, two miles north of Eusemere.

Despite the traditional spelling of Wordsworth biographers, and the baptismal evidence (which, I am kindly informed by the Revd K. E. Wood of Grasmere, is clearly not very authoritative in the parish register), I have observed the prevailing modern orthography for Wordsworth's daughter Catharine. This preference is based on the frequency of the 'a'-form compared with the 'e'-form in the letters, as well as on the testimony of her gravestone. The anachronistic use of 'Dove Cottage', 'Dora's Field', and '*The Prelude*' seems not only convenient but necessary.

List of Abbreviations

The list set out below indicates abbreviations which, once introduced, are used consistently, except where their significance could easily have been forgotten or where a personal reference is demanded. Other abbreviations such as De Q or Q (for De Quincey and Quillinan) are employed whenever the context makes the reference clear. The general aim has been to avoid a text which is too acronymically demanding.

Persons

CW	Christopher Wordsworth (W's brother)
D	Dorothy (W's sister)
H	Hutchinson
HCR	Henry Crabb Robinson
IF	Isabella Fenwick
JW	John Wordsworth (W's brother)
MW	Mary Wordsworth
RW	Richard Wordsworth (W's brother)
STC	Samuel Taylor Coleridge
W	William (the poet) or Wordsworth

Places

DC	Dove Cottage (used anachronistically)
RMt	Rydal Mount

Publications

Ex	*The Excursion*
L	*The Letters of William and Dorothy Wordsworth*; for the numbers, e.g. *L*1, *L*5, see the Bibliography.
LB	*Lyrical Ballads*
Pr	*The Prelude* (1850 edition)
SHL	Sara Hutchinson's letters; see the Bibliography.

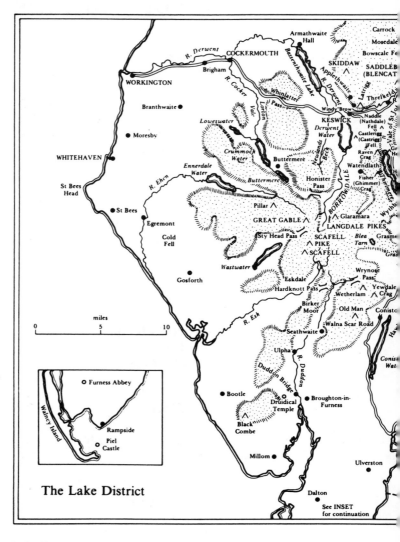

(a) The Lake District

NB: (1) The Park House farm tenanted by Thomas Hutchinson is about 2½ miles north of Eusemere.

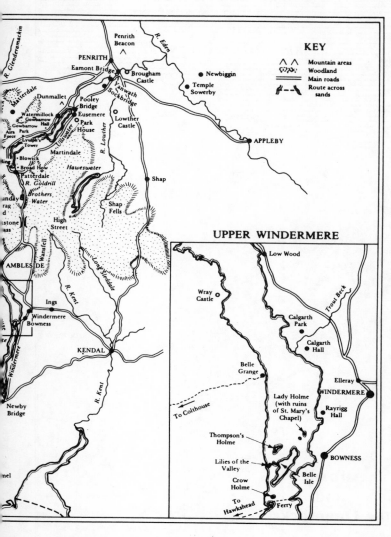

KEY

∧∧ Mountain areas
〰〰 Woodland
═══ Main roads
🐎--🐎 Route across sands

UPPER WINDERMERE

(2) Hallsteads on Skelly Neb is on the lake side of the road almost opposite Gowbarrow Hall.

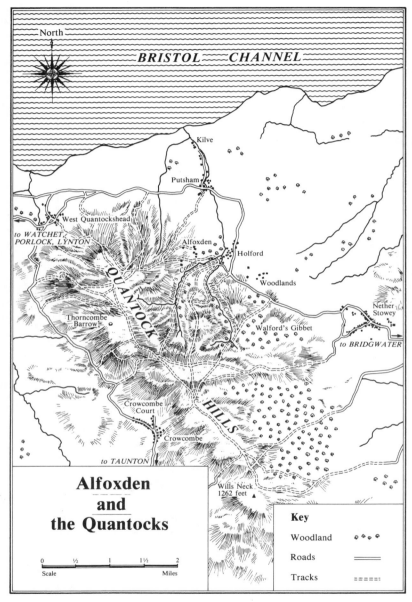

(b) Alfoxden and the Quantocks

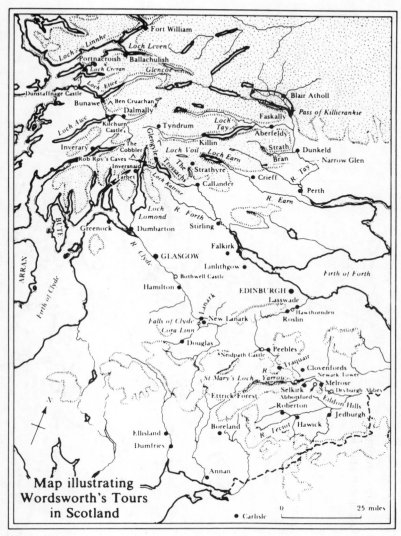

Map illustrating
Wordsworth's Tours
in Scotland

(c) Scotland

xix

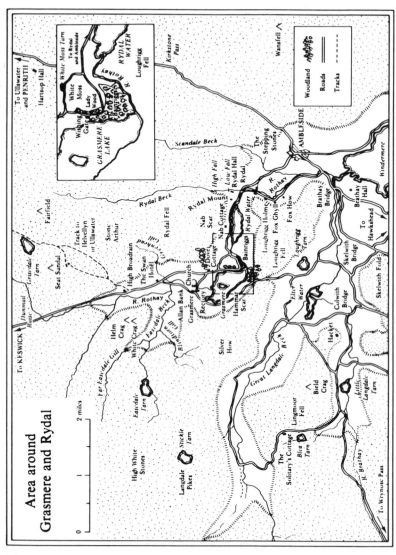

(d) Grasmere and Rydal

xx

A Wordsworth Chronology

Early Years
1770–1787

W's great-grandfather had come from Yorkshire, and bought property at Sockbridge near Penrith. His son Richard became the Receiver-General for Cumberland, and in 1745, when the Young Pretender and his supporters invaded England from Scotland, took refuge, with money and important documents in his possession, in or near Patterdale, at the head of Ullswater, while his wife kept watch over their home.

Richard, the elder of his sons, seems to have lost his favour; he became the Collector of Customs at Whitehaven. The Sockbridge estate passed to John, who served his legal apprenticeship at Penrith, and became the 'law-agent' of Sir James Lowther (Earl of Lonsdale from 1784), a political magnate and owner of much property, including an extensive estate near Penrith, the new town and harbour of Whitehaven, and a large house at Cockermouth, the tenancy of which John secured some time before he married Ann Cookson in February 1766. Additional work came to him as bailiff and recorder of Cockermouth, and as coroner at Millom near the Duddon estuary, more than thirty miles to the south. Ann was the daughter of a linen-draper at Penrith, her mother being one of the Crackanthorpes of Newbiggin Hall. At the time of her marriage she was little more than eighteen, and John Wordsworth, twenty-four. They had five children:

Richard	b. 19 August 1768	d. 19 May 1816
William	b. 7 April 1770	d. 23 April 1850
Dorothy	b. 25 December 1771	d. 25 January 1855
John	b. 4 December 1772	d. 5 February 1805
Christopher	b. 9 June 1774	d. 2 February 1846

For W's early recollections of the Derwent, which ran below the terrace at the bottom of their garden, see *Pr* i, 269–300; for the view across the river to his father's field and the road which seemed to ascend like a 'guide into eternity', see *Pr* xiii, 142–51.

On one of his rides, when staying with his grandparents at Penrith, he was taken by their servant James to the hills near Penrith Beacon (which had flared for the last time in 1745, as a warning against invaders, when W's great-grandfather fled to Patterdale); leading his pony, he lost sight of 'honest James' and was frightened by letters cut in the turf, marking as he supposed the site of the gibbet where the corpse of a murderer had been hung (*Pr* xii, 208–61). In the 1805 version of *The Prelude* he says he was not six years old at the time.

In 1776 he began to attend the grammar school near Cockermouth Church. A memorable experience came when he was taken to his Uncle Richard's at Whitehaven, and his sister Dorothy wept with delight at seeing the sea for the first time on their way down to the town from Moresby; cf. W's note to his poem 'Oh a High Part of the Coast of Cumberland' and, for another example of D's sensibility, 'To a Butterfly' ('Stay near me – do not take thy flight!'); see also the testimony of 'The Sparrow's Nest'. The sonnet 'Address from the Spirit of Cockermouth Castle' affords vivid recollections of W's escapades.

His mother died in March 1778, probably from pneumonia, caught while on a visit to a friend in London, where she slept in a cold, damp room; for W's recollection of her, see 'Catechising' (*Ecclesiastical Sonnets* III, xxii), *Pr* ii, 267–8 and v, 256–93. For a period the children (the older perhaps not for the first time) were transferred to their grandparents at Penrith, where, as pupils in the same school, D and W became friendly with Mary Hutchinson. In the summer D was sent to live with her mother's cousin, Miss Elizabeth Threlkeld, at Halifax in Yorkshire, where she remained until May 1787. W was moody and difficult at times, once slashing a family portrait, after daring Richard to do so, and on another occasion thinking of suicide when he saw some foils in the attic.

Mrs W had inculcated a love of fairy tales and adventure stories in her children, and, whenever they were at Cockermouth, their father encouraged their reading. One of the earliest books W treasured was a 'slender abstract' of *The Arabian Nights* (*Pr* v, 460–76). In June 1779, just before the end of the first half-year term, he and Richard were taken to Hawkshead Grammar School, in preparation for full-time education there after the summer holiday. This was mainly a boarding-school, some boys living in the headmaster's house, others in the village. So successful was it, particularly in the teaching of mathematics, that boys were sent to it from long distances, one of W's friends, Robert Greenwood (the 'Minstrel of the Troop', *Pr* ii, 168), coming from Ingleton in north-west Yorkshire. Through its sixteenth-century founder Edwin Sandys it had close connections with St John's College, Cambridge.

W and RW were fortunate to live in Hawkshead with Ann Tyson, an elderly woman who had had much experience with children and in household management when she was with the Knott family of Coniston in her youth; they owned an iron-foundry in Furness and another in a part of Scotland to which she accompanied them for their summer holidays. W had not been long at Hawkshead when he joined a throng by the shore of Esthwaite to see a drowned man brought to the surface; he attributed his lack of fear to having seen such sights in the fairy world of romance (*Pr* v, 426–55). For his adventures while he was at Hawkshead, see *Pr* i, 301ff., *Pr* ii, and 'Nutting'.

Hawkshead was a market centre, where W made many acquaintances. His grave, thoughtful looks interested a pedlar, who told him many of his experiences; he probably chatted with the old dame commemorated in *Pr* ii, 33–46; and he came to know the village schoolmaster who was partly the original of his 'Matthew'. He was only 'a little boy' when he took a lad of his own age, an itinerant conjuror's assistant, to admire the view from the 'station' above the Windermere ferry-house; see his note to 'Lines' ('Nay, Traveller! rest'). Once he climbed over Wrynose Pass with a local angler to fish near the source of the Duddon (cf. the opening paragraph of his introductory note to *The River Duddon*).

Usually the W boys spent Christmas with their father at Cockermouth, and their summer holiday at Penrith. It was probably in the summer of 1781, when RW was detained by illness at Hawkshead, that W, staying the night with his escort at Patterdale, took a boat and rowed into the middle of upper Ullswater (*Pr* i, 357–400). At home, both at Christmas, and when he was there in the summer, he read a good deal (cf. *Pr* v, 477–90); later he remembered the fascination of such books as *Gulliver's Travels*, *Don Quixote*, *Gil Blas*, and Fielding's novels. His father persuaded him to commit to memory long passages of Shakespeare, Milton, and Spenser. Just before Christmas 1783, as he was returning on horseback from Millom, John W lost his way in mist and darkness on Cold Fell, where he had to spend the night with hardly any shelter from the freezing cold. He was very ill when he reached home, and died on 30 December; (for W's eager anticipation of Christmas with his father, see *Pr* xii, 287ff.).

In January 1782 John joined his brothers at school and with Ann Tyson, who in the autumn of 1783, or earlier, moved to Colthouse just outside Hawkshead. (Christopher W joined them in August 1785, at the beginning of RW's last term.) The boys had considerable freedom. W would climb dangerous crags in Yewdale to destroy ravens' eggs, a practice encouraged annually by local farmers, because lambs were often the ravens' prey; he was present when one of his school companions had to be rescued. Sometimes he walked round Esthwaite Water with his friend John Fleming of Rayrigg Hall, Windermere, before school began at 6 a.m. (7 a.m. in the winter). Once he walked as far as the brow of a 'steep barrier', and saw Grasmere Vale and its lake, thinking how happy he would be living there (*The Recluse* I, i, 'Home at Grasmere', 1–55). Excursions with companions by boat on Windermere and by horse to distant Furness Abbey are described in *Pr* ii. His visit to Ings Chapel, the church on the Kendal road to which he refers in 'Michael', was probably made on foot. The skating scene (*Pr* i, 425–63) combines memories of cliff scenes by Windermere, where there was skating in 1785, with recollections of skating on Esthwaite, where it was more common.

The appointment of a young headmaster, William Taylor, at the opening of 1782 was important for W, for he lent him books of poetry, particularly of the later eighteenth-century writers, and encouraged him to write; W's 'Lines Written as a School Exercise at Hawkshead' belong to 1784–5, and indicate how much his religious attitude to the universe owed to the Newtonian enlightenment of his head teacher. As Taylor lay dying in June 1786 he called the senior pupils, including W, to his bedside (cf. lines in W's account of his visit to Taylor's grave at Cartmel in the summer of 1794, *Pr* x, 532–44). W continued to write verse, 'Anacreon' (Hawkshead, 7 Aug 1786) and 'Beauty and Moonlight' expressing his love of Mary Hutchinson; 'A Ballad' is dated 23 and 24 March 1787. His most important poem is 'The Vale of Esthwaite', much of which he wrote in the summer of 1787, when he was reunited with D at Penrith, after an interval of nine years.

1787 (continued)

July (late)   D writes from Penrith to her friend Jane Pollard of Halifax. She is delighted to be with her brothers. W and Christopher (CW) seem very clever; John (JW) is to be a sailor; RW, who has spent one night with them, is articled to his cousin Richard W, an attorney at Branthwaite near Cockermouth. Remarks and innuendos from their relatives have made them all unhappy. Her brothers have had to stay a week after term at Hawkshead 'owing to the ill-nature' of their uncle Christopher Cookson ('Kit'). The servants, including James, are 'insolent' (*L*1, 4–5). Their fortunes are discussed at the table, but little is likely to come from the Earl of Lonsdale. (He had paid their father nothing; his debt is now reckoned at £4700; litigation instituted by Richard W of Whitehaven and Uncle Kit is still proceeding.) D estimates that their fortune amounts to about £600 each, enough for her brothers' education; John says £200 will suffice to fit him out, and the rest can go to W, who wishes to be a lawyer.

5 August   W, JW, and CW return to Hawkshead. W is 'obliged' to return, undoubtedly by Uncle Kit (*L*1, 8).

October   W returns to Penrith about the 6th (Saturday), after completing the poem 'Dear native regions', based on an image first developed with a similar thought in 'The Vale of Esthwaite', from an observation of sunset made when he was thirteen, resting with school-friends in a boat under sycamores on the edge of Coniston Water (cf. *Pr* viii, 458–75). Ann Tyson has bought silk and velvet to make him a coat for Cambridge.

  After three weeks at Penrith, during which D is busy preparing his clothes, W leaves, most probably, as expected, with William Cookson, the uncle D loves, for St John's College, Cambridge, where Cookson is one of the clergy-fellows. With John Myers, W's cousin, also bound for St John's, they stay three or four days with Myers' married sister at York. On the way south W hears for the first time a woman utter blasphemy, and sees her abandoned 'to open shame' and 'pride of public vice' (*Pr* vii, 382–93).

30 October   Reaches St John's, where he is entered as a sizar (with a reduction in fees).

6 November   He is made a Foundress Scholar, perhaps owing to his uncle's influence.

December   Obtains first class in his examinations. (For his recollections and change of attitude and interests at Cambridge, see *Pr* iii.)

1788

January   JW sails for Barbados.

June   College examinations: W awarded a second class. (Perhaps he pays his first visit to London before returning to the Lake District. *Pr* vii, 65–8 suggests it could have been in the spring, at the end of the Lent Term; the 1805 version, however, states that it was 'at least two years' before his stay there in 1791.) On his way north, this year or next, he visits Dovedale in Derbyshire. From Kendal he walks to the Windermere ferry, then to Colthouse.

July   Altogether he stays several weeks with Ann Tyson during the summer; hers is the one home he loves. See *Pr* iv, especially for the magnificent dawn view, after a dance, which makes him a 'dedicated spirit'.

August and later   The dates for his visits to Penrith, Whitehaven, and elsewhere are uncertain. During this vacation (rather than a year later) he probably enjoys walks with D along the Eamont to Brougham Castle (*Pr* vi, 195–223) and with Mary Hutchinson to Penrith Beacon (*Pr* vi, 224–36 and xii, 261–6). His poetical efforts are devoted to *An Evening Walk*.

Late September or early October   During another stay at Colthouse, as he climbs the Sawrey road from Windermere ferry, he encounters the emaciated discharged soldier, looking ghastly in the moonlight as he leans exhausted against a milestone (*Pr* iv, 370–469).

17 October   William Cookson marries Dorothy Cowper at Penrith, and D departs with them to live at the rectory, Forncett, Norfolk.

October (later)   W leaves for Cambridge, whether from Penrith or Colthouse is uncertain; Cf. *Pr* vi, 1ff.

November (early)   D and the Cooksons, after two weeks in Newcastle, visit W at Cambridge on their way to Forncett.

December   W unclassed, after failing to take the whole examination. He has neglected university studies increasingly during the year, and devoted much time to reading the poets.

1789

March   By this time RW has left Cumberland for London, and joined the legal office of Parkin and Lambert in Gray's Inn. W has probably begun the study of Italian under the distinguished scholar Agostino Isola; at some earlier period he has embarked on French and German. These studies are private, undoubtedly to further W's interests in poetry.

June   W again unclassed for not having taken the whole examination; his distaste for certain branches of mathematics has grown. He probably spends some time with D at Forncett before travelling north.

June   There are reasons for thinking that the visit to Dovedale which W attributes to this summer took place in 1788; his visits to some of the Yorkshire dales (cf. *Pr* vi, 190–4) are as probable at least as Mary Moorman's suggestion that he spent some time also with Tom Hutchinson, Mary's brother, on the farm where Tom assisted his uncle at Sockburn-on-Tees in County Durham. (The Hutchinsons had been orphaned since the death of their father, a Penrith tobacco merchant; when their great-aunt died in 1788, Mary and Sara H had gone to live with their uncle at Sockburn.)

August   During this month (and again during the following) W is at his uncle's at Whitehaven. In between he probably stays with his married cousin Mary Smith (from Whitehaven) at Broughton-in-Furness.

September (mid)   With Ann Tyson and CW at Colthouse, where he stays about a month, working at times, as he had done earlier, no doubt, on *An Evening Walk*. (This is his last visit to Ann, who gives up her boarding business at the end of the year.)

October (mid)   On his way back to Cambridge, W makes a brief call on Uncle Kit at Penrith.

December (end)   In London, probably for Christmas and the New Year, W can be expected to meet RW. Evidently he meets JW, for years later he told Samuel Rogers how he bought a copy of the sonnets by William Bowles when they first appeared (in 1789), and had annoyed the brother who was drowned at sea by stopping to read them as they walked in London.

1790

3 January   By this date JW has joined *The Earl of Abergavenny*, a large new merchant ship belonging to the East India Company, and commanded by his cousin John Wordsworth from Whitehaven.

June   W is unclassed in his college examinations, but placed among those who show 'considerable merit' in the subjects for which they have been examined.

Such is his enthusiasm for 'picturesque' scenes that W may have already bought William Gilpin's *Observations* relative to the Lake District (1786) and his comparable volumes on the Highlands of Scotland. (1788). Gilpin's description in the first of these may have encouraged W's visit to Dovedale. At this time his interest has turned to *Travels in Switzerland* by William Coxe, Fellow of King's College, Cambridge. W and his college friend Robert Jones, a keen mountaineer from the north of Wales, have decided to make a tour in the Alps, following Coxe's route extensively but in reverse.

July
10   (Sat) W and Jones spend the first night of their journey at Shooter's Hill. W has avoided seeing RW in London lest he should think their scheme 'mad and impracticable' (*L1*, 37).
12   At Dover, after spending the night at Canterbury.
13   They reach Calais on the eve of the Day of Federation (a

celebration of the Revolution on the first anniversary of the storming of the Bastille).

27   After walking, each carrying a bundle of 'needments' on his head, and staying nights at Ardres, Lillers, Arras, Péronne, then a village near Coucy-le-Château, Soissons, Château-Thierry, Sézanne, followed by a village near Troyes, Bar-le-Saune, Châtillon-sur-Seine, Saint-Seine-l'Abbaye, and Nuits-St-Georges (after passing through Dijon), they reach Chalon-sur-Saône.

29   They board a boat which takes them down the Saône to Lyon with a party of *fédérés* returning from the Champ de Mars celebrations in Paris.

30   They reach Lyon.

August

4–5   (Wed–Thurs) After two or three days on the road, and one night in a nearby village, W and Jones stay two days as guests at the Monastery of the Grande Chartreuse, where they contemplate the 'wonderful scenery' (*L1*, 33). See *Pr* vi, 332–429.

10   After staying at a town in Savoy, and moving on to Geneva and Lausanne, they reach Villeneuve at the head of Lake Geneva.

12   Reach Chamonix from Martigny, and stay for views of Mont Blanc and the glaciers.

16   They reach Brig after returning to Martigny and making their way up the Rhone valley.

17   After climbing the Simplon Pass they are amazed to hear they have crossed the Alps. Lower down they pass through the Gondo Gorge in three hours of memorable but exhausting conditions. W spends a sleepless night at the Spittal (an eight-story building; cf. D's journal for the 1820 'Tour on the Continent', 9 Sep. See *Pr* vi, 517–648.

19   Along Lake Maggiore ('Locarno's Lake').

22   Following a night at a village by Lake Como, and another night near Gravedona, W and Jones are separated as they head north among the woods on the western side of the lake; cf *Pr* vi, 649–726 and *Descriptive Sketches*, 77–153.

29   At Lucerne, after moving north via the Splügen Pass, reaching the Rhine, and making an indirect route to the Reuss valley and Lake Uri. (See *Descriptive Sketches* for the sunset, the

'pictured fane of Tell', and other scenes on the tour. The poem is based as much on literary influences and descriptions as on actual recollections. For stylistic improvements and impressions W was indebted to English poets and French writers, including Ramond de Carbonnières, who had added his observations to his translation of William Coxe's *Travels*.)

30   W and Jones stay the night at a village by the Lake of Zurich.
31   To the church and convent of Einsiedeln (cf. *Descriptive Sketches*, 540–52).

September
 6   (Mon) Via Glarus and Appenzell they reach the Lake of Constance, where W begins a long letter to D (a previous one, which is lost, was completed at the Grande Chartreuse). See this for further details of the tour up to 14 September. W plans to be in England by 10 October.
10   After following the Rhine to the Falls at Schaffhausen, they return via Baden to Lucerne, where they stay the night.
13   They reach Grindelwald.
14   W resumes his letter at a village on the road to Lauterbrunnen, where they stay the night.
16   The letter is concluded at Berne. They stay the night at Avenches, perhaps intending visits to Rousseau's haunts by the Bieler See, certainly some excursions about the Lake of Neuchâtel, before making for Basle and the Rhine.
22   They leave Basle in a boat they have purchased there.
28   After an easy passage down the Rhine, they reach Cologne, where they spend the night.

October   When W and Jones reach England (by Calais, he told his nephew–biographer late in life) is uncertain. How W spends his time on reaching England is unknown; in the letter concluded at Berne he had said that he did not need to be at Cambridge before 10 November, and hoped he could stay two or three weeks with D at Forncett. He may have gone back to college in October.

December   He seems to have left Cambridge early this month for Forncett, for (in a letter of 23 May 1791) D writes that he was 'with us six weeks in the depth of winter', when the weather was mild and they walked together a great deal.

1791

January At Cambridge, while waiting to take his final examinations, W (so he told his nephew–biographer) reads Richardson's *Clarissa*. He is awarded a pass degree. On the 28th his uncle Richard sends him £60.

c. 25 May After four months of *'strenua inertia'* in the City (*L*, 49; for his activities, see *Pr* vii), he departs from London, leaving nearly all his books there (probably with RW). He is to stay at Jones's home in north Wales (Plas-yn-Llan, Llangynhafal, near Ruthin). His uncle at Whitehaven has just sent him £20.

26 June D, writing to Jane Pollard, states that W is so happy in the Vale of Clwyd with Jones and three of his sisters that he is likely to remain there all the summer. (For his excursions and climbs, see the letter of dedication to Jones which W prefixed to *Descriptive Sketches*; the ascent of Snowdon which is recalled at the opening of *Pr* xiv almost certainly belongs to this period.)

3 August W writes to his ex-Cambridge friend William Mathews from Jones's home. He is sorry that he cannot read Italian poets as he would like, for lack of a dictionary and grammar, and that he has not brought his Spanish grammar with him, so that he can keep up with his Spanish; he has read hardly any modern literature except *Tristram Shandy* and a few papers from *The Spectator*.

September He leaves Wales to see John Robinson, probably at the latter's home in Isleworth. (A collateral descendant of the wife of W's grandfather Richard, Robinson had great influence; he was part-owner of *The Earl of Abergavenny*, which was named after his son-in-law, and he was M.P. for Harwich, where he thought he could obtain W a curacy.) W has deemed it better to see him in person, and explain that he is too young for ordination. He leaves London for Cambridge.

23 September Writing to Mathews from Cambridge, he says that if he had no obligations to relatives he would not mind wandering about the country, as Mathews, dissatisfied with teaching, thinks of doing; it would be better than 'vegetating on a paltry curacy'. (D had written – L1, 52 – that W's 'pleasures are chiefly of the imagination'; he is 'never so happy as when in a beautiful country'.)

9 October   Still at Cambridge, where CW is entered for Trinity College. On the advice of his uncle William, W is to study Oriental Languages.

November
7 (Mon) RW writes to his uncle at Whitehaven, asking him to send £40 for the support of W, who is in London and advised to live in some less expensive country than England before his ordination; W wishes to go to France. (Later, most probably in November, W informs D at Forncett that he is resuming his study of Spanish, and that his object during the winter is to learn French so that he can be a travelling companion to some young gentleman in the summer.)
26 He has been at Brighton since the 22nd, waiting to sail for France. On the 23rd he writes to Mathews, saying that he is on his way to Orléans, and will study Oriental Languages when he returns to England. He has called on Mrs Charlotte Smith, the poet and novelist. Departs for Dieppe in the evening.
27 Reaches Dieppe (morning); (evening) Rouen.
30 Arrives at night in Paris, after waiting two hours in Rouen for a diligence.

December
5 (Mon) After attending sessions of the National Assembly (assisted by an introductory letter from Mrs Smith to a deputy) and the Jacobin Club, and visiting various well-known parts of Paris, including places made famous by the Revolution (cf. *Pr* ix, 34–80), W leaves for Orléans (which he reaches the next day).
18 Having been disappointed to find that Helen Maria Williams, the poet and writer on Revolutionary France to whom Charlotte Smith had given him an introduction, had left Orléans before he arrived, W is pleased to make the acquaintance of Mr Foxlow, a local cotton-manufacturer, who promises that he and his wife will introduce him to the best society in Orléans when they return after a few days in the country. (In this way he probably meets Annette Vallon, on a visit to her brother, a lawyer's clerk in Orléans.)

1792

February and later   Early (?) in February W leaves Orléans for Blois to be near Annette, a Catholic and Royalist; they are passionately in love. At Blois he is lodged in a house with 'military officers'; (there were many waiting to join the *émigrés*, as they do when France declares war on Austria in April).

W, a democrat at heart, becomes friendly with Michel Beaupuy, an idealist army captain who believes in the principles of the Revolution (cf. July). Humble, courteous, scholarly, and philosophical, he discusses political theory with W on long walks by the Loire and in wooded country, making it real with a range of illustrations from ancient history to the poverty of French peasantry in the present.

W is a democrat, not a revolutionary; he is shocked when he hears that French troops are quartered in the Grande Chartreuse (this affects his presentation of it in *Descriptive Sketches*, on which he is now working, and in *The Prelude*), and grieved to see ancient buildings which have been destroyed by Revolutionary forces. (For W's general impressions of this period, and later, see *Pr* ix, 81ff., a diffuse account which was at first, i.e. in 1805, much extended by the inclusion of 'Vaudracour and Julia', a well-known story in France which W heard from Beaupuy. How much it is irradiated by the memory of his romantic infatuation thirteen years earlier is conjectural.)

19 May   W informs Mathews that he intends to be ordained in the coming winter or spring.

28 May   D's letter to RW shows that a curacy for W at Harwich is still possible.

June   Uncle Kit inherits the Crackanthorpe estate at Newbiggin; (a few weeks later he legally adopts the surname of 'Crackanthorpe').

July   Beaupuy leaves Blois to defend his country against the Austrians on the Rhine.

3 September   Writing to RW from Blois, W refers to his return and to staying in London a few weeks to attend to his 'publication' (*L*1, 81). He awaits a remittance of £20. (Late in life he said he was in

Orléans during the Paris massacres of 2–6 September. He almost certainly left Blois some time in September, following Annette, unhappy and in disgrace at home, to Orléans. Whether he returned to Blois is unknown.)

October   At Orléans he continues his work on *Descriptive Sketches* (cf. the reference to the Loiret tributary and October clouds, 624–6; the note of rejoicing in the birth of Liberty which follows expresses W's feelings after hearing of the French victory against the Prussians at Valmy on 20 September). Late in the month he leaves for Paris, where, in the course of his city walks he sees the Temple where Louis XVI is imprisoned, the palace which has been stormed, and the Place du Carrousel, a recent scene of carnage. At night thoughts of the September massacres fill him with fear. The next day (probably the 30th) a copy of Louvet's denunciation of Robespierre is thrust at him by a hawker (see *Pr* x, 1–120). (He could have met James Losh, a fellow-Cumbrian, in Paris, but there is no evidence that he did.)

December (early)   Having little money, W providentially, as it seemed later (for had he stayed he would have 'made common cause' with Girondins who were executed), leaves for England, either at this time or earlier; cf. *Pr* x, 120–236.

15 December   Birth and baptism of Anne-Caroline Wordsworth at Orléans.

22 December   D's statement (all that remains of her letter) that W is in London and writes to her regularly suggests he has been there some time. Most probably he is staying at Staple Inn with RW and the latter's Cockermouth friend J. L. Wilkinson. It seems likely that about this time he reaches an agreement on the publication of his two poems.

1793

29 January   W's *An Evening Walk* and *Descriptive Sketches* are published in two small quarto volumes by Joseph Johnson of St Paul's Churchyard. By this time W has probably told Wilkinson the story of Vaudracour and Julia, which he thinks of writing as a novel.

1 February   France declares war on England.

11 February   England declares war on France, and W is shocked.

16 February   D and CW at Forncett wish that W had had a friend to advise him on his poems before publication; they contain graphic scenes, but are often faulty in expression. Godwin's *Political Justice* is published.

(W may have already begun his reply to Richard Watson, Bishop of Llandaff, who spent most of his time as an absentee bishop, his home being Calgarth Park near Windermere. After the execution of Louis XVI on 21 January, Watson had added a criticism of the Revolution to a reprint of his sermon on 'the Wisdom and Goodness of God' in making both rich and poor. W's defence of the Revolution occupied him for several weeks, but was never finished or published; it shows some acquaintance with Godwin's *Political Justice*. Perhaps the rising reaction against any form of Jacobinism, and the outbreak of *popular* risings in France against the repression of the Revolutionary government steadily cooled W's ardour.

The fact that he did not visit Forncett is significant. He had undoubtedly disclosed his relations with Annette, and offended his uncle. There seems to be no further question of his entering the Church.)

20 March   Two letters of this date from Annette, one to W, the other to D, have been preserved; they were intercepted before they left Blois. (Had war not broken out between France and England, W might have married Annette as he intended.)

Spring(?)   It is probably during this period that W forms the habit of dining with Samuel Nicholson of Cateaton Street, and going with him afterwards to hear Joseph Fawcett, an eloquent dissenting preacher who draws large audiences to his chapel in Old Jewry. (In his note to *The Excursion* W states that Fawcett lacked the 'strength of character to withstand the effects of the French Revolution', and was in some respects the original of his Solitary.)

June (late?)   Though a patriot, W is appalled to find his own country supporting reactionary interests against the drive for freedom in France. Such feelings recur on the Isle of Wight whenever he sees the fleet at anchor or hears its cannon (cf. *Pr* x, 236–330). He is with a school-friend, William Calvert (steward of the Duke of Norfolk at Greystoke Castle near Penrith), who has invited him to be his holiday-companion. W hopes to become a tutor to some young gentleman, but will travel with Calvert to northern Wales if he finds no employment in the meantime, and then meet D and her friend Jane Pollard at Halifax, to which he has been invited by Mr and Mrs Rawson (formerly Elizabeth Threlkeld) during their visit to London.

July (late?)   After about a month on the island, he and Calvert are crossing Salisbury Plain when C's horse runs away, and his carriage (a whiskey) is overturned and broken in a ditch. C rides north, while W, after visiting Stonehenge and forming impressions which he was to work into poetry, makes his way towards south Wales.

August   After passing through Bath and Bristol, and taking a boat no doubt to Chepstow, he walks up the Wye valley to Tintern Abbey. He is most probably familiar with William Gilpin's *Observations on the River Wye* (1782), and his enthusiasm is still for the picturesque (cf. the opening and ll. 72–83 of 'Lines', which he composed after revisiting Tintern Abbey in 1798). At Goodrich Castle he meets the little girl of 'We are Seven'. Much further along the Wye, probably between Builth Wells and Rhayader, he walks and talks with a wild rover, the original of Peter Bell. (The statement W made to George Venables, as recorded in *Kilvert's Diary*, 28 Sep 1870, may seem more convincing than the recollection prefixed to 'Peter Bell', which states that W walked *down* the Wye valley from Builth almost to Hay with this vagabond, but see the entry for 19 Aug 1810.) What sight-seeing W did on his way north is not known; as much as he could, one suspects. D at Forncett has heard from him by the 30th; he is happy with Jones in that 'most delicious of all Vales, the Vale of Clwyd' (*L1*, 109).

September   He probably stays there several weeks, making various outings and climbs; much time is spent composing his Salisbury Plain poem.
    (The story that he returned to France and witnessed the execution of Gorsas on 7 October is based on Carlyle's *Reminiscences*. It seems most improbable: W had hardly any money, and the risk of entering enemy country, especially to

consort with Girondin friends, was far too great. Had he done so, it seems incredible that he, D, and their friends left no statement on the subject. W probably told Carlyle that he had known Gorsas, the first of the Girondin deputies to be executed.)

December W stays with relatives in the Lake District; he is at Whitehaven for Christmas.

1794

January He is at or near Keswick, staying with school-friends, Calvert at Windy Brow and John Spedding at Armathwaite Hall just north of Bassenthwaite.

17 February With D at Mr Rawson's, Halifax, after a separation of more than three years. He has no prospect of employment, and cannot think of the Church or law. Has read no Spanish for three years, but will resume Italian immediately, and teach D the language. He cannot afford to take his M.A. degree.

10 March Uncle Richard sends 5 guineas to D at Halifax.

April W and D travel by coach to Kendal, whence they walk, picnicking near Low Wood, Windermere (cf. 'There is a little unpretending Rill'), and taking what was to become a favourite walk round Rydal Water and over White Moss to Grasmere, where they stay the night. (The next day they walk to Keswick, and up to Windy Brow, Calvert's farm-house, where W can stay as long as he is unemployed. He revises, and adds to, *An Evening Walk*; D makes a fair copy of 'Salisbury Plain'. She is delighted with the views and the tenant family with whom they are staying.)

21 April After more than two weeks at Windy Brow (three nights at the Speddings'), D replies to Mrs Christopher Crackanthorpe's reproofs, chiefly against 'rambling about the country on foot'. She thinks W sufficient protection, enjoys meeting his friends, has revised her French, and begun reading Italian. They expect to stay a few more weeks.

23 May From Whitehaven (where they stay several weeks, first

probably at their uncle's, then with their cousin John's wife) W
writes to Mathews, who has proposed collaboration in a monthly
publication; W cannot afford to live in London, and he thinks it right
to declare that he belongs to 'that odious class of men called
democrats', completely opposed to contemporary forms of political
suppression such as imprisonment and transportation (cf. *Pr.* xi,
52–73).

28 May   Uncle Richard has been staying with his attorney son
Richard at Branthwaite, and is very ill. (He dies almost three weeks
later.)

8 June   Writing from Whitehaven to Mathews, W deplores the
executions that continue in France; he is all for freedom of opinion,
but against any form of speech intended to inflame passion. He
knows (from what has happened in France) that 'the multitude walk
in darkness' and need enlightenment. He gives a number of plans
for the proposed monthly miscellany, suggesting it be called 'The
Philanthropist'. Calvert's brother Raisley (whom he has probably
met at Keswick) has offered him a share of his income.

c. August   For some weeks D and W stay with cousins, both from
Whitehaven, Mrs Smith at Broughton-in-Furness, and Mrs Barker
further south at Rampside, with Piel Castle in view (cf. the opening
of 'Elegiac Stanzas Suggested by a Picture of Peele Castle'). Early in
the month W is crossing the Leven estuary, after a visit to William
Taylor's grave at Cartmel, when he hears the welcome news that
Robespierre is dead (guillotined Monday 28 July; cf *Pr* x, 481ff.).
Shortly afterwards W probably stays with Raisley Calvert, who is
very ill, and again either at the end of the month or early in
September.

28 September   After a further period of some length in the
Broughton–Rampside region, W returns to Windy Brow, where
Raisley is so ill that he wishes to travel to Lisbon. Knowing that he
cannot do so unaided, W writes to William Calvert, asking if he can
be given the necessary financial assistance to accompany Raisley. At
the latter's request, he tells WC the terms of his brother's will,
including a legacy of £600 to himself (W).

October

9 (Thurs) They start for Lisbon, but the strain of travel is too much for Raisley.

10 W returns with Raisley to Keswick, and writes to RW. He has explained to Raisley that he and his brothers owe their widowed aunt at Whitehaven over £400 for sums lent by their uncle. Raisley wishes his legacy to be set aside to enable W to pursue his aims, literary or otherwise, and assist him in time of need; W asks his brother to give the required assurances.

13 RW assures W that he will readily enter into a bond to this effect.

c. 17 W informs RW that Raisley has decided to leave him £900, with a penalty of £400 to secure it from the claims of his late uncle's representatives.

23 Raisley signs the will which leaves £900 to be invested for W's use and benefit, with power to invest any portion he wishes for the benefit of his sister D.

7 November W tells Mathews he wishes to be in London; cataracts and mountains are good occasionally, but will not do for constant companions (*L1*, 136). He is too busy caring for his sick friend either to enjoy them or study. Mathews has found employment with a newspaper, and W wonders whether he can find him similar work, but only with a paper in opposition to the present Government.

December (late) He is at Penrith with Raisley, who gets weaker daily.

1795

c. 9 January Raisley Calvert dies.

12 January After the funeral, at Greystoke, W makes for Newcastle, where D has been staying with friends.

16 January She expects him to be in London in two or three weeks.

February It is not known how long W has stayed at Newcastle, or whether he spends some time with the Hutchinsons at Sockburn, a pastoral farm (within a loop of the Tees) which Tom has rented from his uncle Henry at Stockton-on-Tees.

27 February   W has tea at William Frend's with James Losh and prominent radicals including William Godwin.

March to April   He has become friendly with Godwin, whom he calls on or breakfasts with occasionally. During the later part of this period D is at Sockburn with her old Penrith friends Mary and Margaret Hutchinson.

May to early August   The many friends W meets or makes include Mathews, Francis Wrangham, and Basil Montagu, a law student and contemporary of W at Cambridge, with whom W lives for some months at Lincoln's Inn. His wife had died, and he has maintained himself and his two-year-old son by borrowing money and taking pupils. Subject to bouts of intemperance when depressed, he finds W an excellent counsellor and influence. He had lived with Wrangham, curate of Cobham, where they had both taught pupils whose fathers had business in the West Indies. As a result of visiting Wrangham with Montagu and John Pinney, a graduate studying law with the latter, W receives an offer from Pinney of a rent-free house named Racedown Lodge, in Dorset, with the provision that John and his brother can stay there during shooting and coursing seasons. When their father, a Bristol sugar merchant, hears of this letting (as he assumes it to be) he invites W to stay with him.

(For W's conflict of thought, as a result of reading and discussing political theory when the struggle for liberty in France has produced extreme reactionary measures against radicals and reformers in England, see *Pr* xi, 173–320, bearing in mind that it was by degrees in the next year or so that W weaned himself from the extreme forms of Godwin's political philosophy.)

c. 18 August   W leaves for Bristol.

September
3   (Thurs) Writing to Jane Pollard, who has recently married Mr Marshall, a Leeds linen-manufacturer, D, who seems to have been staying with the Rawsons of Halifax since she left Sockburn (probably early in May), is excited at the prospect of joining W at Racedown. With income from Calvert's legacy, £50 p.a. for the maintenance of little Basil Montagu, possibly another child, and W's expectation of having Mr Pinney's son as a pupil, everything seems promising. She is to join W at

Bristol, where she is invited to stay with the Pinneys, before proceeding with Basil to Racedown.

c. 22　D arrives in Bristol.

25　£250 of the Calvert legacy is received by RW. (Altogether £525 is paid by the end of the year, another £250 by the end of 1796, with completion of payment as late as August 1798.)

c. 26　After staying 'at least five weeks' in Bristol, where he has been pleased to meet the poet Robert Southey, but has seen too little of Samuel Taylor Coleridge, a man of great talent, W leaves for Racedown with D and probably little Basil: they arrive about midnight.

October

1　(Thurs) W lends Montagu £300 for an annuity investment.

4　Coleridge marries Sara Fricker at Bristol.

November

14　(Sat) Southey marries Edith Fricker, sister of Coleridge's wife. (Southey and Coleridge's 'pantisocracy' planning belongs to the early part of the year.)

19 or 20　W walks to Lyme, hoping to see one of Mathews' friends.

20　W and Wrangham had proposed writing an imitation of Juvenal, and W sends him a satirical passage which Wrangham can insert in his poem if he pleases; it contains the line 'Must honour still to Londsdale's [*sic*] tail be bound?' He has revised 'Salisbury Plain' until it is almost another work.

30　D informs Mrs Marshall that one of Annette's letters has reached them since they came to Racedown. They shop at Crewkerne, and hope Montagu will visit them before Christmas. The peasants are miserably poor.

December The Ws find the country delightful; they have a pleasant house, a library with Italian books, and a good garden, where W (D notes) 'handles the spade with great dexterity' (*L1*, 163). It is clear that he knows Joseph Cottle, the Bristol bookseller and publisher, and has hopes of doing business with him. John Pinney and his brother Aza[riah] come for Christmas.

1796

7 January   John Pinney departs for Bristol.

10 January   Aza Pinney departs for London.

(During January W lends £200 to Montagu's friend Charles Douglas, and Joseph Cottle sends W a copy of Southey's *Joan of Arc*; he is clearly interested in W's Salisbury Plain poem.)

March
  6   (Sun) John Pinney and his brother Aza leave after a month at Racedown, during which they have spent time walking, riding, hunting, coursing, and cleaving wood – the last a desirable occupation (D thinks) in a part of the country where coal is so dear. They take a copy of W's revised poem 'Adventures on Salisbury Plain' for Cottle.
  7   D writes to Mrs Marshall. She and W were very disappointed Montagu had not come, and hope to see him in the summer. She is working hard on her Italian. Basil is a blooming open-air boy and her perpetual pleasure. W congratulates Francis Wrangham on his recent appointment as vicar of Hunmanby near Bridlington, and tells him he is determined to continue the Juvenal satires. He has been hewing wood and rooting up hedges. Basil is making more physical than moral progress; for one thing, he 'lies like a little devil' (*L1*, 168).
 21   W tells Mathews they plant cabbages, into which, according to one of his London friends, they will be transformed. He has returned to reading, and attempts to write satires. He hopes M has kept the list of his books, and asks him to call at Montagu's to ensure they are securely sent on to him. They are expensive, and should include 'Gilpin's tour into Scotland, and his northern tour, each 2 vol.' Godwin has sent him a copy of his second edition of *Political Justice*, and he thinks the preface badly written.

1 April   Burial of Margaret Hutchinson (died of consumption) at Sockburn.

13 May   Coleridge refers to W as a 'very dear friend', 'the best poet of the age', 'a Republican and at least a *Semi*-atheist'; (he had been much impressed by *Descriptive Sketches* – cf. *Biographia Literaria*, iv – and has probably read the manuscript of 'Adventures on Salisbury Plain').

June   W pays a lengthy visit to London, where he meets Godwin, Montagu, John Stoddart, and James (or John) Tobin.

2 July   Montagu and Charles Douglas sign a promissory note for £220 due to W on 1 January 1797 in return for the £200 already lent to Douglas.

c. 9 July   W returns to Racedown.

(For the change in his views since settling at Racedown with D, her influence, and the influence of Nature – including the renewal of close contact with people, and time to reflect on incompatibilities of abstract reasoning and life – see *Pr* xi, 321–70. From the sense of 'genuine knowledge', based upon awareness of human feelings as much as on reason, W's reflections lead to a rejection of the view that individual liberty can be pursued independently of concern for others (cf. *Pr* xi, 223–44). The plan of *The Borderers*, begun most probably not later than August, develops from this train of thought. That one of the active germs for the story of the play was the crime of Fletcher Christian as leader of the mutiny on *The Bounty* is suggested by the two October entries.)

19 September   Birth of Hartley Coleridge.

23 October   W denounces as a forgery letters in *The Weekly Entertainer* which purport to come from Fletcher Christian in exoneration of Captain Bligh. (How great W's interest must have been can be seen from the following facts: FC was a senior pupil at Cockermouth school when W attended it; his brother Edward was head of Hawkshead Grammar School when W was a pupil there, and Edward's defence of Fletcher in 1794 had been supported by W's uncle Canon Cookson of Forncett and by his cousin Captain John W of Whitehaven. For the principal link with *The Borderers*, cf. the second scene of Act iv.)

24 October   W is 'now ardent in the composition of a tragedy' (*L1*, 172).

November (end)   Mary Hutchinson arrives with her brother Henry from Sockburn. (The next morning he departs to join his ship at Plymouth.)

December   RW buys a hundred yards of linen and three of cambric, W to pay half the cost (see 19 Mar 1797).

24 December   Joseph Gill, the Pinneys' overseer at Racedown, buys a diary for D at tenpence.

26 December   In his own diary, he notes that the snow at Racedown is very deep.

1797

c. 25 February   Sending Wrangham some long-promised Juvenalian verses, W indicates that he has no wish to take more pupils; (he and D never had more than one). The first draft of *The Borderers* is almost finished.

March
15   (Wed) Montagu unexpectedly arrives, before the Ws have risen.
19   D informs RW that no shirts are ready, the linen arriving only the previous week. W has gone to Bristol with Montagu for 'a week or ten days'; she is happy with Mary H. John W has written, saying how sorry he is not to be on board his cousin John's ship, the new *Earl of Abergavenny*; (the previous one had been bought by the Government in April 1795). In the evening D writes to Mrs Marshall, congratulating her on the health and activity of her little boy. The system she and W follow in educating Basil is simple (and Rousseauistic); it is based on the evidence of the senses and on curiosity, not on books, though B knows his alphabet; punishment takes the form of natural consequences. W will be in Bristol about a fortnight; his absence is a loss, for he is 'the life of the whole house'.

End of March(?)   After parting with Montagu in Bristol, W stays with the Coleridges at Nether Stowey, where he meets Thomas Poole, who thinks (like STC) that W is the greatest man he ever knew.

April   Perhaps W completes 'Lines Left upon a Seat in a Yew-tree',
a poem which, though begun in 1787, gives the direction of his
thought and poetry in 1797. In contrast to the unfruitfulness of the
self-centred and morbid, W emphasizes the loveliness in life and the
world around which springs from 'labours of benevolence'. Perhaps
he works on 'The Old Cumberland Beggar', more probably on 'The
Ruined Cottage' (the story of Margaret which was incorporated in
Book I of *The Excursion*). Later, the religious love in which he walked
with Nature during adolescence (*Pr* ii, 357–8, 394–418) becomes
deepened and more defined through the influence of Coleridge's
religious philosophy, best summed up in 'the one Life within us and
abroad' of his 1795 poem 'The Eolian Harp'.

May
3   (Wed) RW wishes to have full details of W's financial
    transactions with Montagu and Douglas, and advises him not
    to rely too much on memory.
7   W provides this information, and states that Robinson W
    (son of their deceased uncle Richard, and now Collector of
    Customs at Harwich) is pressing for payment of debts, as he
    is getting married and wants to buy a house.
28 D writes to RW on this subject, and says that W hopes the
    relevant part of Robinson W's letter will be read to Montagu.
    The tragedy, which he hopes R. B. Sheridan, manager of
    Drury Lane Theatre, will consider, is almost finished.
(During the month W works perhaps on 'A Somersetshire
Tragedy', a story of love and murder, based on the life of John
Walford and his execution at the place of his crime 'amidst the
beautiful scenery of the Quantock Hills'. Tom Poole had told the
story and written a moving account of it. W's poem was destroyed
by his grandson Gordon W, who said it had little merit. At this
time, or earlier, W writes the first two cantos of 'The Three
Graves', a poem continued by STC; Mary Hutchinson copies part
of it.)

June
4   (Sun) Mary H, leaving for home via London, takes four shirts
    and a letter from W on the Robinson W issue for RW; she
    also takes a copy of the last forty-five lines of 'The Ruined
    Cottage', the first part of the poem to be written.
6 or 7   S. T. Coleridge arrives; the first thing read is 'The Ruined

Cottage'. In the afternoon he reads at length from his play *Osorio*. (The next morning W reads *The Borderers*. STC stays most, if not all, of the time until the 28th.)

12 D tells Mary H how great her (MH's) loss is in not seeing STC; his conversation 'teems with soul, mind, and spirit' (*L1*, 188).

28 W and D accompany him on his way home (at Nether Stowey).

July

4 (Tues) Writing to Mary H, D describes the waterfall they have discovered in a steep wooded dell above Alfoxden House park. (Subsequent to this, during the two weeks at Stowey, W hears that Alfoxden is to let, and applies for tenure.)

7 Charles Lamb reaches Stowey from London for his holiday with the Coleridges. (He stays a week, and is taken to Alfoxden, where he sees the waterfall; cf. 'This Lime-tree Bower my Prison', written by STC in the arbour of Poole's garden after his wife Sara has accidentally scalded his foot.)

12 An agreement, witnessed by Thomas Poole, is signed for the letting of Alfoxden House to W by John Bartholomew for a year from last Midsummer, at £23, including taxes. The house, which is furnished, is leased to Bartholomew by the Revd Lancelot St Albyn's widow, guardian of his son, a minor.

13 W and D move into Alfoxden with Basil and STC.

17 John Thelwall, who had been imprisoned in 1794 for his revolutionary views, and has corresponded with STC, reaches Stowey just after Sara's return from Alfoxden to 'superintend the wash-tub'.

18 She takes him to Alfoxden in time to call STC and W for breakfast.

21 They all walk back to [Nether] Stowey. Thelwall wishes to retire from politics and settle in the country.

August Suspicion of W soon arises in the neighbourhood from his dark complexion and his living with a woman who 'passes for' his sister and has a child. When they are seen examining a brook, probably with STC (who had chosen the subject to give unity to a poem with scope for 'description, incident and impassioned reflections on men, nature, and society' – a theme he passed on to W for *The Recluse*), they are thought to be French spies. Visitors to Alfoxden increase suspicion, and a Government detective is sent to inquire and observe. (Of the stories connected with this abortive security mission, the most amusing is STC's, to the effect that, while he and W were discussing Spinoza by a sand-dune on the shore, the detective in concealment thought they were talking about himself, 'Spy Nosy'. Thelwall's association with the Ws did not help, and continued rumour resulted in the owner's refusal to allow the Alfoxden sub-lease to be renewed when the year's tenancy expired.)

10 September   James Tobin, Aza Pinney's partner in his Bristol business, arrives with Thomas Wedgwood. (They leave on the 15th. About the middle of the month Charles Lloyd stays a few days at Alfoxden after visiting the Coleridges.)

November (early)   STC, W, and D make an excursion to Porlock and Lynmouth, thence to the Valley of the Rocks, which suggests to the imaginative STC an absurdly impracticable way of jointly writing an imitation of Gessner's *Death of Abel*; see STC's prefatory note to 'The Wanderings of Cain'.

13 November   STC and W, while walking to Watchet, discuss a ballad subject; W, who had been reading Shelvocke's *Voyages*, contributes some leading ideas. (Cf. his note to 'We are Seven', recorded late in his life, in which he treats the two outings as one, in the spring of 1798; a footnote to the opening of Part IV of this 'ballad', 'The Rime of The Ancient Mariner', suggests that their walking-tour included Dulverton.)

20 November   *The Borderers* has been sent to 'the managers' of Covent Garden Theatre.

November (end)   On the advice of one of its principal actors, to whom the play was sent, W travels to London with D to alter it 'for the stage'. They stay with the Nicholsons of Cateaton Street, leaving Basil with his father at Alfoxden.

December
8   (Fri) The decision of Covent Garden Theatre is awaited. D has seen Mrs Siddons at Drury Lane Theatre in *The Merchant of Venice* and Garrick's *Isabella*.

13   *The Borderers* having been refused, the Ws cut short their London visit, planning to leave on the 15th. W and James Tobin call on Godwin.
31   W and D have remained in Bristol, perhaps staying part of the time with Cottle's parents.

1798

January
3   (Wed) Return to Alfoxden from Bristol.
6   Montagu is at Bristol, on his way to London, with five shirts for RW.
20   D's journal begins.
23   W and D walk together (afternoon). The sea blue, but gloomy red at sunset; audible on the top of the hills, but not in summer.
25   W and D have tea at Poole's. Observing the sky on the way back, W composes 'A Night-piece' extempore.
27   They observe moonlight effects in the wood; 'the manufacturer's dog makes a strange, uncouth howl'.
29   W walks to the top of the hill to view the sea. 'Nothing distinguishable but a heavy blackness.'
30   He calls D into the garden to see 'a singular appearance', a semi-circle of colours, more vivid than a rainbow, that becomes a complete circle around the moon, and fades away in a few minutes.
31   They set out for Stowey by moonlight. A violent storm forces them to shelter under hollies in the wood. First Venus is seen, then Jupiter, as the sky clears; black hawthorn hedges glitter with millions of diamond drops; the road to Holford glitters like a stream.

February
1   (Thurs) They visit Mr Bartholomew at Putsham.
3   Walk with STC over the hills before dinner (at five o'clock). D never saw such 'a union of earth, sky, and sea'.
4   Walk almost to Stowey with STC.
5   Walk to Stowey with STC.
6   To Stowey over the hills.

7   Finding the way to Putsham dirty, they change course, up the smaller coomb to Woodlands, to the blacksmith's and the baker's, and through Holford.

9   W gathers sticks for fuel.

10 To Woodlands and the waterfall.

14 W not well enough to walk far; he and D gather sticks in the wood.

16 Through the wood to fetch eggs from the coomb; carry large bundles of sticks back.

17 W walks to Bartholomew's with STC. On his return, he and D go to the coomb for more eggs.

21 STC calls in the morning (and on the next).

23 W walks with STC (morning).

26 STC, and Mr and Mrs Cruikshank of N. Stowey, call (morning). D and W walk back most of the way with STC after dinner; they lie down, and sit down, to view the prospect. Poole calls in their absence.

27 W and Basil accompany D through the wood on her way to Stowey (evening). STC returns with her in bright moonlight.

(Probably W's account of his meeting the discharged soldier – cf. Sep–Oct 1788 – is written during this month.)

March

3   (Sat) W lies under the trees while D goes to the shoemaker's; afterwards they visit the 'secluded' farmhouse (in the coomb?) for eggs.

5   As on the previous Friday, they gather fir-apples (cones) for fuel. To the baker's and the shoemaker's. They find Poole in the parlour when they return, and have tea together. D sends Mary Hutchinson the Margaret section of 'The Ruined Cottage', reporting that, with the Pedlar section, it has now reached 900 lines; W has been ill, but insists on getting up early; he can versify much more easily, but has difficulty in keeping pace with his thoughts.

6   Walks in the wood with D on her way to see STC (evening). W writes to James Tobin, announcing that they leave Alfoxden at Midsummer; it has been let to the Cruikshanks. He fears being published, and is 'easy' now about the theatre; if he undertakes another play, it will be 'purposely' written, either for reading or for the stage. He has written 1300 lines of his projected poem (*The Recluse*, including 'The Ruined Cottage');

it will contain 'pictures of Nature, Man, and Society', and will accommodate anything he knows (*L*1, 212).

7   He and D have tea at STC's. They notice one last leaf on the top of a tree, dancing round and round in the wind, as in Coleridge's 'Christabel' (I, 49–52). W has received a loan of £10 from Cottle, and asks him to forward without delay a copy of Erasmus Darwin's *Zoonomia* (1794–6).

8   STC comes to Alfoxden after dinner.

9   Clear and sunny again; a very warm day, perhaps the day on which W composes 'To my Sister' ('It is the first mild day of March'). The Coleridges come to stay at Alfoxden.

10   After sauntering in the park in the morning, and observing groups of people – children playing in the sun, and adults 'quietly drinking in the life and soul of the sun and air' – STC, W, and D take an evening walk to the top of the hill.

11   A cold day; the children go down towards the sea, W and D to the hill-tops above Holford. From Alfoxden W writes (STC sitting at the same table) to James Losh, telling him about their plan to visit Germany to learn German and 'natural science', and inviting him and his wife to join them and the Coleridges in this enterprise. Josiah and Thomas Wedgwood have settled an annuity of £150 on STC.

12   Tom Poole dines with them (and on the next day).

13   In his letter to Cottle, STC asks him on behalf of W what he would offer to publish (a) *Osorio* and *The Borderers*, (b) 'Salisbury Plain' and 'The Ruined Cottage'.

16   W, D, and STC take a short walk in the park; W very ill, but well enough in the evening to join in a walk to Putsham.

18   The Coleridges leave. W and D walk half way to N. Stowey with them; a hail-shower makes them shelter under hollies as they return. W writes 'A whirl-blast from behind the hill'.

20   STC dines with them.

21   They have tea at the Coleridges'.

23   STC brings his completed ballad, 'The Rime of the Ancyent Marinere'.

24   STC, the Chesters, and Ellen Cruikshank call. To the coomb for eggs (evening).

25   To STC's for tea. Reach Alfoxden at 1 a.m.

26   Meet Tom Wedgwood at STC's after dinner.

27   Dine at Poole's.

29   STC dines at Alfoxden.

April
2 (Mon) A high wind. STC arrives to escape the smoke in his cottage, and stays all night.
3 W, STC, and D walk to Crowcombe 'to make the appeal' (to a friend of the owner of Alfoxden?). D leaves W there, and parts with STC at the top of the hill.
4 To the seaside (afternoon); a heavy shower makes them shelter under firs at Putsham.
5 STC to dinner.
6 D walks part of the way home with him (morning). She and W attempt to find the source of the brook in the 'lesser Coombe', but the cold evening makes them give up.
7 They discover it before dinner, and return by the hill-tops, with a grand view.
12 W writes to Cottle, telling him he has added rapidly to his 'stock of poetry', and inviting him to come and hear it. He and STC have decided not to publish their tragedies, but concentrate on a volume of poems, to raise money for their projected visit to Germany.
13 To Stowey (evening), W at Poole's, D at STC's; both sup at STC's.
14 Books, including Godwin's memoirs of his wife Mary Wollstonecraft, author of *Vindication of the Rights of Woman*, arrive from Tobin in London.
15 To Crowcombe, where they walk about the squire's grounds, observing Nature's atonement for the disfiguration caused by artificial ruins, hermitages, etc. (the cult of the picturesque).
20 W and D walk up the hill dividing the coombs (evening) and return along Crowcombe road, by the thorn and the 'little muddy pond'. 'Peter Bell' begun; ('The Thorn' seems to have been completed).
26 William Shuter is staying at N. Stowey; W visits him to 'have his picture taken'.

May
5 (Sat) W sends RW details of money received from the Calvert legacy, and from Montagu in respect of the loan from that legacy.
6 D expects the painter (Shuter) and STC; her journal entry suggests they did not arrive.
9 W thanks Cottle for Charles Lloyd's works, three volumes of

Massinger, and £13 6s. 6d. He has yet to read Lloyd's novel (*Edmund Oliver*, which presents an episode in STC's life with mischievous intent). He returns Darwin's *Zoonomia* (the source of the basic story in 'Goody Blake and Harry Gill'), and is determined to finish the Salisbury Plain poem, though he has to set it aside for another project (*Lyrical Ballads*).

16   W, D, and STC, after the birth of his second son Berkeley on the 14th (B died on 10 Feb 1799 while his father was in Germany), set off to visit the Cheddar Gorge; they sleep at Bridgwater.

17   They visit the gorge and caves, and sleep at Cross, near Axbridge. With this entry – wrongly dated – D's Alfoxden journal ends.

18   W goes on to Bristol, hoping to meet Lloyd and help to bring about some reconciliation between him and STC; Lloyd, however, has left for Birmingham, where his father, a Quaker banker, lives.

Shortly afterwards William Hazlitt visits STC at Stowey, and is brought to Alfoxden, where D gives him free access to W's manuscript poems for *Lyrical Ballads*. He stays overnight; next morning STC reads 'The Idiot Boy' aloud in the park. The next day W, returning from Bristol, after seeing a performance of 'Monk' Lewis's melodrama *The Castle Spectre*, finds them at Stowey; the following day at Alfoxden, they hear him read 'Peter Bell' in the open air. On his return in the evening, Hazlitt gets into a metaphysical argument with W, which results in two more poems for *LB*: 'Expostulation and Reply' and 'The Tables Turned'. (For H's recollections, see his essay 'My First Acquaintance with Poets'.)

Cottle comes down to Alfoxden in his gig, at W's invitation, to discuss final plans for *LB*; he may have returned to Bristol with the manuscripts by the end of May or very early in June.

June

11   (Mon) Hazlitt's visit ended, he and STC reach Bristol in the evening.

12   W is in Bristol; he sups with James Losh and his wife at Shirehampton near Bristol. Perhaps he sits for a portrait drawing by Robert Hancock about this time.

13   He becomes the Loshes' guest until the 16th. D writes to her aunt Mrs Rawson of Halifax. She and W intend to stay with a

family in a cheap part of Germany for a year at least; she expects the Coleridge family to go. Basil will have to remain in England; solitude has made him selfish, and he will be better with children of his own age.

25 The Ws leave Alfoxden for Bristol, staying first with the Coleridges.

July

2 (Mon) They leave N. Stowey for Bristol.

3 D's letter to Mrs Rawson (begun 13 June) is completed.

8 W and D visit James Losh, who is receiving medical treatment at Bath.

10 They cross the Severn and walk to Tintern Abbey.

11 To Monmouth and Goodrich Castle.

12 They begin the return journey, staying at Tintern.

13 By boat to Chepstow, thence to Bristol in a small vessel. The last twenty lines of W's Tintern Abbey poem (the final composition of which began after leaving the abbey; it had no doubt been the subject of much thought during the previous three days) are composed as they walk down into the city (where the whole poem is written out for the first time shortly afterwards, and handed to Cottle for inclusion in *LB*).

c. 15 W and D move to Shirehampton, probably occupying the Loshes' cottage, while they are in Bath.

August

3 (Fri) STC in Bristol or Shirehampton.

c. 4 He, W, and D set off on a walking tour to visit John Thelwall at Liswyn Farm on the Wye near Brecon. (They return after about a week.)

13 RW receives the remainder of W's legacy from Calvert.

27 W and D reach London after travelling a few days on foot, by waggon, coach, and post-chaise, having seen the presence-chamber at Blenheim, and looked round colleges at Oxford.

28 W writes to Cottle, who has promised him 30 guineas for his share of *LB*, inviting him to sell his (W's) copies of Gilpin's *Tours* (to Scotland, and to the Lakes). W has borrowed money from Josiah Wedgwood for his stay in Germany.

September

14 (Fri) W and D leave London with STC and John Chester for Yarmouth (which they reach the next day at noon). By this time copies of *LB* have been read in London.

16 Sail for Hamburg.

18 Reach the mouth of the Elbe at 10 a.m. (For impressions of Cuxhaven, their stay in Hamburg, and events until Goslar is reached, see D's journal.)

21 W and STC are taken by Victor Klopstock to see his brother the poet Friedrich Klopstock, with whom W converses in French for over an hour, chiefly on poetry.

23 D too unwell to visit churches (Sunday).

26 W and D dine with V. Klopstock and his wife, their niece, and the poet and his wife. F. Klopstock and W talk animatedly the whole afternoon.

28 The greasy-faced landlord overcharges W by more than 4 guineas.

30 STC and Chester depart for Ratzeburg.

October

1   (Mon) W buys a copy of Bürger's poems and of Percy's *Reliques*.

3   He and D leave Hamburg in the evening, travelling by diligence to Upper Saxony. W is glad to leave a 'miserable' place, where shopkeepers and innkeepers impose on foreign visitors.

5   They reach Brunswick (Braunschweig), where they dine and stay overnight.

6   By poor roads to the ancient city of Goslar, at the foot of the Hartz Mountains. (End of D's journal).

14 or 21 December   D and W have received STC's hexameters, beginning 'William, my teacher, my friend! Dear William and dear Dorothea!' and ending 'but I am lonely and want you!' The winter has been severe, and W has written much poetry, including some Lucy lyrics and narrative description of boyhood experiences (skating, the 'stolen' boat episode, 'Nutting'). They hope STC will be persuaded to live with them in the Lake District.

1799

February

3 (Sun) Their stay at Goslar has been unexpectedly prolonged owing to the winter and bad roads. Progress has been made with the language; it would have been greater if only they could afford to entertain.

23 They leave Goslar on foot.

27 At Nordhausen, after walking in hilly wooded country, often on roads deep in water or mud, via Claustal, Osterode, and Scharzfeld, the last ten miles by post-waggon. By this time W has 'pruned' 'Peter Bell' and done further work on his Salisbury Plain poem.

(No clear consistent evidence survives of the Ws' movements for several weeks, or whether they meet STC, who moved from Ratzeburg to Göttingen in February.)

April

20 or 21 (Sat or Sun) They meet STC in Göttingen. He finds them depressed, anxious to be in England, and disappointed that he cannot think of leaving Tom Poole.

25 At Hamburg.

May

c. 1 (Wed) They reach Yarmouth, after a crossing of two days and nights from Cuxhaven, and begin their journey to Sockburn-on-Tees, where they will stay with the Hutchinsons until December.

23 Writing to RW on his own debts and financial expectations, W thinks his connection with the London publisher Johnson has been damaged, and sales of *LB* reduced, by Cottle's failure to accept his advice (to transfer the edition and the copyright to Johnson).

June

2 (Sun) He expresses regret in a letter to Cottle that the latter has contracted for the sale of *LB* by the London booksellers Arch. Reminds him that of the 30 guineas promised only £10 has been paid.

24 Acknowledges receipt of the £5 he had requested from Cottle;

tells him his view that the archaisms in 'The Ancyent Marinere' had not helped sales of *LB*, and that he has not heard from STC.

July

4 (Thurs) D writes to Poole, clearly hoping for news of STC. Poole is asked to write if he hears of a suitable place for W, who wishes to live in pleasant country near a good library.
27 W receives the remainder of Cottle's debt, but refuses interest.

1 August John W's ship reaches England. (At Sockburn W has helped the Hutchinsons with their farm work. By the end of the summer he completes the two-part autobiographical poem on his boyhood, most of which was retained in the first two books of *The Prelude*.)

September

2 (Mon) W invites Cottle to come north, so that they can tour the Lake District.
10 STC has heard from W, who is ill and seems unhappy; he suspects that Montagu has left him in financial difficulties; W will not think of returning to Alfoxden. About this time STC urges him to work steadily on *The Recluse*, and write a blank-verse poem particularly for those who, after the failure of the French Revolution, have given up hope of social amelioration.

October

12 (Sat) STC is delighted that W's autobiographical poem is to be 'addressed' to him.
22 Cottle leaves Bristol with STC for the north of England.
26 They reach Sockburn.
27 They begin their tour with W.
30 After two days at and around Barnard Castle, Cottle, afflicted with rheumatism, parts from his companions at Greta Bridge, to return home. W and STC proceed by coach to Temple Sowerby, where they are joined by JW, who has been at Newbiggin Hall, attending the funeral of Christopher Crackanthorpe ('Uncle Kit').
31 With JW, they call on the Revd Thomas Myers, the widowed husband of W's aunt, at Barton (a large parish including Sockbridge); to Bampton for the night.

November

1 (Fri) By Haweswater and Long Sleddale to Kentmere.

2 To Windermere (Bowness) and across to Hawkshead (Ann Tyson had died in May 1796).

3 By the head of Windermere to Rydal and Grasmere, where they stay at Robert Newton's inn, near the church.

5 They climb Helvellyn; at Grisedale Tarn JW leaves them for Ullswater and Newbiggin. W thinks of building a house at Grasmere, JW being ready to give him £40 to buy the ground.

8 W and STC leave Grasmere for Keswick. They stay near Ouse Bridge, at the foot of Bassenthwaite.

11 After two days in which they visit Cockermouth and places in and around Keswick, they leave for Lorton (where they look at a huge yew; see Sep 1804), Crummock Water, and Buttermere (where they meet Mary Robinson of the Fish Inn; cf. 16 Aug 1803).

12 They climb by Scale Force over into Ennerdale, where W hears the story of 'The Brothers'.

14 They leave Wastdale for Borrowdale.

15 To the Lodore Falls, the Druids' Circle, and Threlkeld (below Saddleback).

16 To Matterdale, Aira Force, and Ullswater.

18 STC leaves W at Eusemere (home of the Clarksons) and proceeds on his way to Scotch Corner (then to Sockburn, where he stays a week and falls in love with Sara Hutchinson).

26 W arrives at Sockburn, where he finds Mary Hutchinson the 'solitary housekeeper'; she is overjoyed to see him. He has probably made preliminary arrangements for renting the house at Grasmere which was eventually known as 'Dove Cottage' from its having been 'The Dove and Olive Branch' inn.

December

17 (Tues) W and D set out from Sockburn for Grasmere by early-morning moonlight, riding on horses and accompanied by George Hutchinson to a point eight miles beyond Richmond; they see the setting, and hear from a peasant the story, of 'Hartleap Well'; sleep at Askrigg.

20 After staying overnight at Sedbergh, then at Kendal, they reach Dove Cottage. The weather has been wintry, but they have not been deterred from visits to waterfalls in Wensleydale,

and they have bought and ordered furniture at Kendal from the £100 left to D by Uncle Kit.

27   Both have caught colds. D has been busy trying to make a cold and almost empty house comfortable; W has been skating on Rydal Water, and has begun 'The Brothers'.

1800

January   JW arrives (and stays most of the time until 29 Sep).

February   Mary H comes at the end of the month and remains five weeks.

March   Lines in an early version (on three full moons since the Ws' arrival at Grasmere) show that W is working on the first book of *The Recluse*, 'Home at Grasmere'.

April   STC arrives on the 6th and stays exactly four weeks, during which he discovers that Greta Hall, Keswick, is to let (cf. 'Home at Grasmere', 659–61); W and he agree to prepare a two-volume edition of *LB*, the second to consist of new poems. W contemplates writing a novel.

May
4   (Sun) STC leaves for home, taking copies of poems for the new edition of *LB*. (At Bristol he makes arrangements for printing by Biggs and Cottle, and proof-reading by Humphry Davy, chemist at the Pneumatic Institute, Clifton. Longman of London is to be the publisher.)
14   D begins her Grasmere journal, after W and JW set off for Yorkshire; her intention is to write it until their return, for W's pleasure.
24   RW receives £100 plus interest from Charles Douglas (cf. 2 July 1796).
27   D meets the beggar woman, then her family on the Ambleside road; (from her description W writes 'Beggars' in March 1802).

June
7   (Sat) W returns (JW, the next day). They have stayed with

Tom and Mary Hutchinson (now at Gallow Hill near
Scarborough), after visiting Yordas, a cave near Ingleton, and
Gordale Scar.

19   W and Mr Sympson, the aged but active curate of Wythburn,
     fish in Thirlmere.
21   They fish with JW at Rydal Water.
29   The Coleridges arrive and stay, STC until 23 July, the
     remainder until the 24th, before moving into Greta Hall.
     (During this period STC is ill, but he and D, W advising,
     prepare copies of poems for the new *LB*. Most probably the
     meeting with the angler of the fourth poem in 'Poems on the
     Naming of Places' takes place during STC's stay.)

July
20   (Sun) STC meets Mr and Miss Sympson at Dove Cottage.
21   W's poem 'The Farmer of Tilsbury Vale' (incident and
     character as described by Thomas Poole) appears in *The
     Morning Post*.
27   D makes a copy of 'Ruth'.
29   W sends Davy revised copies of poems for *LB*, and promises
     the preface in a few days.
31   STC comes to Grasmere, where he copies poems for *LB* (and
     stays until 2 Aug).

August
 1   (Fri) D copies 'The Brothers'.
 6   W returns after four days with STC at Keswick.
 8   Walks with D via Watendlath in the evening to Greta Hall
     (where more copying for *LB* follows).
14   They call at Mirehouse, home of W's school-friend Spedding,
     on the edge of Bassenthwaite below Skiddaw.
17   Return to Grasmere. W has composed 'The Seven Sisters' in
     recent days.

September
 1   (Mon) W reads 'To Joanna' and 'The Fir Grove' (an early
     version of 'When, to the attractions of the busy world') to
     STC, who had arrived the previous evening; they bathe in
     the lake. (W had found that the grove, Lady Wood, where he
     was wont to compose as he paced up and down, had been
     John's pacing-ground.)

3   W, JW, and STC, on his way to Keswick, ascend Helvellyn with Mr Sympson.

6   The Ws breakfast with James Losh and his wife at Ambleside. The Clarksons dine with the Ws.

9   Mr Marshall, husband of D's great friend Jane of Halifax, calls. W and JW walk round Rydal Water and Grasmere with him; after dinner they row out with D to the island in the middle of Grasmere.

13   W engaged in writing his preface (suggested by STC) for the second edition of *LB*. Robert Jones, the college friend with whom he toured the Alps, calls (and stays for nearly two weeks, part of the time at Dove Cottage; for his traits, cf. W's poem 'A Character', written about this time).

14   Birth of Derwent Coleridge.

26   When W and D return from accompanying Jones on his departure with STC to Keswick, they meet a leech-gatherer on his way to Carlisle. (See D's postscript for her journal entry of 3 Oct, and the transformation of setting and subject in 'Resolution and Independence', which W wrote in May–June 1802.)

29   W and D accompany JW to Grisedale Tarn, where they have their last sight of him in the Lake District, as he makes his way on the first stage of his journey south, to take command of *The Earl of Abergavenny*, after his cousin's retirement.

30   Charles Lloyd, now living at Brathay near Ambleside, dines with the Ws.

October

4   (Sat) STC arrives, and reads the second part of 'Christabel'.

5   He reads it in the morning, and the Ws are even more delighted. W and D busy writing an addition to the preface. W ill in the afternoon, as he has often been, mainly as a result of composition.

6   Agreed not to include 'Christabel' in *LB*; (towards the end of the year W informs his publisher that it would have been discordant with his own poems). The completed 'Christabel' is to be published with 'The Pedlar'.

7   STC returns to Greta Hall.

10   W sits up late, writing 'Point Rash Judgment'.

11   After dinner he and D walk up Greenhead Gill in search of a

sheepfold; (he has the poem 'Michael' in mind as a replacement for 'Christabel').

18 Works in vain all the morning at 'The Sheepfold' ('Michael'); lies down until the evening, sleepless and unable to work.

22 STC calls before dinner, and John Stoddart at tea-time.

27 D takes food to W in the fir grove, where she had previously walked and found it an excellent shelter from the wind.

29 John Stoddart arrives (and stays until 4 Nov).

November

11 (Tues) W works at 'The Sheepfold'. He has been continually ill, in wintry weather. They have often met the Lloyds, and become acquainted with Charles's sister Priscilla, Christopher W's fiancée.

18 The Ws at Greta Hall. W and STC set out towards Penrith to meet Sara Hutchinson.

22 She and the Ws reach Dove Cottage in the evening.

28 STC at Grasmere; he has a frightful dream, and W cries out aloud on hearing his scream.

December

9 (Tues) 'Michael' is finished.

18 'Michael' is sent to the printers, ll. 1–206 copied by STC, the rest probably by Sara H.

19 W sends ll. 71–3 for insertion in the fourth of 'Poems on the Naming of Places', and two single-word revisions of 'Michael'.

22 The volume of D's journal ends in the middle of a sentence, suggesting the loss of a volume before its resumption in October 1801.

1801

January

14 (Wed) W writes a long letter to the eminent Liberal statesman Charles James Fox. (This is to be forwarded, with letters written by STC to other important people, to JW in London; he will leave them with Longman, to be sent out with complimentary copies of *LB*.) W draws Fox's attention to the impoverishment of small landowners, and the breaking-up of their families, partly owing to the spread of industrialization.

He refers to 'The Brothers' and 'Michael' as poems which illustrate how small inherited estates (the property of 'Statesmen', as they are locally known) are rallying-points for family affection.

c. 25   The second edition of *LB* is published.

30   JW sees the review of *LB* which Stoddart is preparing for *The British Critic*, and thinks it too flattering, too obviously written by a friend. The Ws and Sara H are at Eusemere (Thomas Clarkson's home and farm) at the end of the month (and during the early part of Feb).

February (mid)   Sara H goes to Greta Hall to help the Coleridges.

February (late)   W writes to his friend Francis Wrangham, vicar of Hunmanby, regretting that he was unable to meet him when he called during his stay at Gallow Hill. He hopes he can lend Mary H books if ever he travels in that direction, and reports that STC is 'very unwell'. (For more than two years STC had been affected by opium and drink; he is now additionally afflicted with gout and rheumatic fever.)

27 March   W makes himself responsible for the repayment of the £30 advanced to STC by their publisher Longman. (Sara H leaves Dove Cottage late in the month.)

April

9   (Thurs) W writes to Poole, hoping he is pleased with 'Michael', for he had his character in mind when he wrote the poem. D sends him copies of the lines omitted from the poem by the printer, and of additional lines which W had considered inserting near the beginning of the second part.

27   W and D leave Greta Hall, after a stay of eight days, during STC's illness. A delightful walk home with a full moon over Helvellyn.

29   Writing on this visit, D tells Mary H that Mrs C is an excellent mother (breast-feeding Derwent) but incompatible with STC, chiefly because she lacks 'sensibility'. W is always ill when he tries to revise his poems, more so than when he writes new. 7 p.m. and the thrushes 'singing divinely' in the orchard (the small garden behind their cottage). W writes that he and D sat two hours during the morning, when it was 'burning hot'

outside, in 'John's firgrove'. The gate on the other side of the road from it (the Wishing-Gate) commands a beautiful view; it bears Sara's cypher, and Mary must come and carve hers. Significantly he sends her a copy of the Lucy poem 'I travell'd among unknown men', and ends 'God for ever bless thee, my dear Mary – Adieu.'

7 May STC comes to Dove Cottage (where he stays eight days, after which his eldest child Hartley is left in D's care for a period).

June Richard Sharp brings the poet Samuel Rogers to the Lake District, to meet STC and W.

c. 19 June Letter from Fox (dated 25 May), stating the pleasure he had in reading four poems (including 'The Idiot Boy') in the first volume of *LB*. On the poems to which W called his attention he merely says he is no friend of blank verse for subjects which are to be presented with simplicity.

July (early) W writes to Poole on STC, who has been ill ten months, hoping he can raise money to enable him to recuperate in the Azores.

12 August James Losh visits Dove Cottage, and stays the night.

6 September W witnesses the wedding of Laura Rush and Basil Montagu in Glasgow, after joining them and the Rush family on their way from the north of England; (he subsequently visits some of the Scottish lakes with Montagu and Sir William Rush).

October
10 (Sat) D's next surviving volume of her diary opens.
15 She and W dine with the Luffs, who have lodgings in Ambleside; their home is at Patterdale, near Goldrill Bridge.
16 Tom Hutchinson comes (and stays until the end of the month).
23 He and W ride to Hawkshead.
25 D and Tom ride to Legburthwaite (near the foot of Thirlmere), hoping to meet Mary H; as she does not arrive, they climb Helvellyn.
28 The Clarksons come.

November

9 (Mon) With Mary H, the Ws visit Greta Hall before the departure of STC for London.

10 Reach home at 9 p.m. D, full of anxiety for STC, eases her heart by weeping; 'nervous blubbering', W says. (Mary stays seven weeks at Grasmere.)

c. 21 W writes to RW (as he had in June) asking him to send all his (W's) books and (he begs this earnestly) any clothes he can spare.

23 Mary is making him a woollen waistcoat.

December

1 (Tues) Returning after collecting letters at Rydal, D and Mary are overtaken by two drunken soldiers who fight the mountains with their sticks (cf. the drunken sailor in Canto iv of *The Waggoner*). W works at his translation of 'The Prioresse's Tale' after reading Chaucer and Spenser in JW's volumes of Dr R. Anderson's *Works of the British Poets*.

6 Mary reads the first canto of Spenser's *The Faerie Queene* (cf. W's dedication of *The White Doe of Rylstone* to her).

11 The Luffs dine at Dove Cottage.

12 Thomas Clarkson calls before tea, and stays the night.

19 The Ws call at the Lloyds' (they are out), and dine with the Luffs (as on the 17th).

21 Hearing that STC is ill, W writes to him; he has resumed work on 'The Pedlar'.

29 After walking to Greta Hall on the 28th, the Ws and Mary proceed (a mile and a half with J. L. Wilkinson) to Threlkeld, then by a pack-horse route over the hills to an inn, probably at Dockray, after which they descend on a slippery road (where D is often obliged to crawl on all fours, and M falls several times) to Ullswater, and on in darkness to the Clarksons at Eusemere.

31 Mary leaves (probably to stay with her aunt at Penrith).

1802

January

3 (Sun) Mary brings letters from Sara and STC.

15 W and D dine at Yanwath with Thomas Wilkinson, a Quaker

who had found the property his friend Clarkson needed to build Eusemere; (he loved to garden in his grounds by the River Eamont).

17 They meet Mary at Penrith. (Whether she has returned to her home with her brother George or Tom in the interval is not clear.)

22 After staying five days with W and D at the Clarksons', she leaves. ('Dear Mary! there [at Stainton Bridge] we parted from her', D wrote in her journal.)

23 W and D leave Eusemere, walk along Ullswater, and past Grisedale Tarn (seeing nothing but mists and snow) to Grasmere.

29 'A heart-rending letter from Coleridge – we were sad as we could be' (D's journal). W writes to him.

31 W has slept badly, after overworking on 'The Pedlar'. He and D walk round the two lakes, part of the route dear to both because STC and D had walked that way with W when he first brought them to Grasmere. At the foot of Grasmere (the lake) they sit on the stone near Mary's name, which she had cut herself and which W now makes plainer with his knife. William Calvert dines with them.

February

1 (Mon) Box arrives from London, with W's books, and clothing as requested.

4 D working at Montagu's shirts for W.

14 W, who has been working hard at 'The Pedlar', rides in his blue spencer and '*new* pantaloons fresh from London' to see Mary at Penrith.

15 A letter from Annette Vallon arrives.

16 W returns at tea-time, having heard the story of Alice Fell related from experience, probably at Eusemere, by Robert Grahame of Glasgow, a slave-abolitionist friend of Clarkson.

22 Letter from Annette (and Caroline). Negotiations for peace between France and England have already begun. (They result in the Treaty of Amiens, March 1802, but war is resumed in May 1803.)

24 W writes to Annette (announcing his engagement to Mary?). Much business unripping his coats for the tailor's visit next day.

March

7   (Sun) W returns, after a visit to Calvert (at Greta Bank – the new name for Windy Brow) for a few days. D has 'stitched up *The Pedlar*' (which he thinks of publishing with *Peter Bell*).

12   He finishes 'The Singing Bird' ('The Sailor's Mother').

13   'Alice Fell', begun the previous evening, is finished in the morning; Grahame had urged him to write it for humanity's sake.

14   D's reminiscence during a conversation on butterflies make W interrupt his breakfast to write 'To a Butterfly' ('Stay near me – do not take thy flight!'). Tires himself, trying to alter it (evening, by the fire).

17   He finishes 'The Emigrant Mother'. After dinner D makes a pillow of her shoulder, and reads to him until her beloved sleeps.

19   STC arrives, looking half stupefied, after walking in wind and rain.

22   Another letter from Annette. W and D decide they will meet her, and he will 'go to Mary'.

23   He works at 'To the Cuckoo'.

24   D vows they will not leave the Lakes for Gallow Hill (i.e. when W marries).

26   He writes 'The Rainbow' ('My heart leaps up . . .').

27   W writes part of an ode (the first four stanzas of 'Intimations of Immortality').

28   These stanzas are read to STC at Keswick (echoes of them are found in his 'Dejection' ode).

April

4   (Sun) STC begins his verse letter to Sara H, and continues it far into the night; (it is revised to form 'Dejection: An Ode').

5   After eight days with the Coleridges in Keswick, where they dine with Calvert and the Wilkinsons, W and D proceed via Threlkeld to Eusemere.

7   W's birthday; he sets off, on a pony lent him by Calvert, from Eusemere to see Mary at her brother George's farm, at Bishop Middleham, beyond Bishop Auckland.

12   On the return journey, before and after passing through Staindrop, W composes 'Among all lovely things my Love had been', based on a recollection of taking D to see a glow-worm at Racedown, but inspired mainly by his love of M.

13   He reaches Eusemere in the evening.

15   After dinner and in a violent wind, the Ws leave the
     Clarksons; under the trees, by the side of Ullswater, they see
     a belt of daffodils reeling and dancing in the wind (cf. 'I
     wandered lonely as a cloud', written in 1804). Stay at the old
     inn, Patterdale, overlooking the lake.

16   On the bridge by Brothers Water, W writes 'The cock is
     crowing' (afterwards entitled 'Written in March'). Over
     Kirkstone Pass and down into Ambleside; call at the Luffs',
     but, hearing they have guests, do not stay. The same evening
     D writes a long letter to Mary, full of detail subsequent to W's
     arrival at Eusemere, and showing great concern for M's
     health. 'No fireside is like this. Be chearful in the thought of
     coming to it', she writes (*L1*, 352).

18   W writes 'The Redbreast Chasing the Butterfly' (observed the
     previous day).

21   STC comes and reads verses written to Sara H (cf. 4 Apr).

24   Evening, on the road to Rydal: STC, D, and W stop to see a
     primrose in the 'Glow-worm Rock' (cf. 'The Primrose of the
     Rock', completed long afterwards).

29   In John's Grove, as W and D rest in a trench, he imagines
     how sweet it would be if one could be thus in the grave,
     hearing the delightful sounds of earth, and knowing one's
     friends were near.

May

3   (Mon) W begins 'The Leech-Gatherer' ('Resolution and
     Independence'), undoubtedly a response to STC's 'Dejection'
     ode.

11   He finishes 'Stanzas Written in my Pocket-copy of Thomson's
     "Castle of Indolence"' (sketches of himself and STC).

21   After D has read Milton's sonnets to him, W writes two on
     Bonaparte (Napoleon I). So begins his attachment to the
     sonnet form, in which he was often supreme, especially on
     the subject of liberty and national independence.

24   Death of the Earl of Lonsdale.

June

12   (Sat) STC departs, after two days at Dove Cottage; D tells him
     they do not intend to live at Greta Hall (when W marries).

14   After receiving some criticisms of 'The Leech-Gatherer' from

Sara H, W is supported by D, who informs her that, when
she is not happy with the tendency or moral of any of his
poems, she should ask herself whether she has 'hit upon' the
right one; above all, she must not think that he writes for 'no
reason but merely because a thing happened' (*L1*, 367).

17   W adds a little to his ode ('Intimations').

18   Luff has brought a newspaper from Clarkson in which Lord
Lowther invites all who have claims for debts from his cousin
the Earl of Lonsdale (whom he succeeds) to write as soon as
possible. W writes at once to RW, urging immediate action.

20   W and D walk for a long time along their favourite walk,
above the cottage and along the east side of Lady Wood to
White Moss Tarn, talking about the disposal of their 'riches'.

21   W leaves for a short stay at Eusemere, in order to consult the
Revd Thomas Myers of Barton, and Dr Lowther, on the
Lonsdale debt.

22   The new edition of *LB* (with the enlarged preface) arrives.

July

4   (Sun) W finishes revising 'The Leech-Gatherer'.

8   D very excited. The horse is coming for their journey.

9   They set off to Keswick, on their way to Gallow Hill.

12   On foot via the Penrith road, the first six miles or more with
STC; they turn aside to explore the country near Hutton John
and Dacre on their way to the Clarksons at Eusemere.

14   Walk to Eamont Bridge, near Penrith, and travel by coach
over Stainmoor, Bowes Moor, and Gartherley, to Leeming
Lane, where they enjoy a good fire and supper at Scotch
Corner.

15   By post-chaise to Thirsk for breakfast, then on foot to
Rievaulx, where they find a good view of the abbey, and on
to Helmsley.

16   Via Pickering to Gallow Hill; Mary and Sara meet them seven
miles out.

26   After travelling with Mary over the Wolds, on the first stage
of their journey to Calais, D and W make their way to
Beverley and Hull.

27   Across the Humber to Lincoln.

29   After a stop at Peterborough, where they view the exterior of
the cathedral, and admire the west end, while the other

passengers dine (on the 28th), they reach London in the morning.

31 Leave London very early by the Dover coach (cf. 'Composed upon Westminster Bridge').

August

1 (Sun) Reach Calais at 4 a.m.

29 Leave Calais after frequent meetings with Annette and Caroline (cf. sonnets, especially 'It is a beauteous evening, calm and free').

30 Bathe, and then gaze across to France from Dover cliffs.

September

 7 (Tues) They dine with the Lambs (back from a holiday with the Coleridges at Keswick), and Charles takes them to Bartholomew Fair (cf. *Pr* vii, 675–721).

 9 With Christopher Wordsworth (CW), who has just arrived in London, they visit the Cooksons at Windsor, where his uncle William is in residence as a canon of St George's Chapel.

11 Returning to London, all three meet RW and JW, whose ship has recently arrived from China. (In the next ten days the whole family meets for the last time.)

22 W and D leave London for Gallow Hill (reached on the 24th).

October

4 (Mon) W and Mary (MW) are married at Brompton Church; D is too nervously excited and indisposed to attend. After breakfast, prepared by Sara H, W, M, and D begin their journey to Grasmere by post-chaise.

6 At Sedbergh D finds they are in the room where she and W spent an evening on their journey from Sockburn to Grasmere. They have travelled (first day) via Helmsley over the Hambleton Hills to Thirsk and Leeming Lane (the Great North Road from Piercebridge to Boroughbridge); (second day) via Middleham, Leyburn, and Wensleydale to Hawes. From Sedbergh they journey to Kendal and the church at Ings (built by Robert, not Richard, Bateman; cf. 'Michael', 255–70), and reach Dove Cottage (DC), where they view the garden by candlelight. W and D have been absent three months.

13   All go to Greta Hall with STC, on learning that Mrs C is away.
17   Thirteen neighbours are invited to tea at DC; W comes in just as it begins.
30   On his way to Keswick, W meets Stoddart and returns with him for dinner, after which S reads Chaucer to the Ws.

7 November   W begins translating Ariosto's *Orlando Furioso*.

December
D is ill at times. Sara H comes to DC and is ill; (she stays for a few weeks).
24   (Fri) On his way home from the south of Wales, STC calls with Tom Wedgwood, and learns that his daughter (Sara) was born the previous day.
30   He takes Wedgwood to see Luff at Patterdale (returning to DC via Kirkstone Pass the next day).

1803

January
1   (Sat) He misses D, who is at Greta Hall.
2   With W, MW, and Sara H, he walks half way to Keswick to meet her.
6   After being ill at DC, revisiting Luff, and being soaked in a tempest on the way back, STC is again at DC.
7   He walks to Greta Hall with Sara H.
16   D's journal ends.

February
2   (Wed) 'To Toussaint l'Ouverture' appears in *The Morning Post*; (more of W's political sonnets appear in the same paper from Jan to Oct).
23   W is satisfied with the settlement reached by RW and Mr Graham, one of Viscount Lowther's London firm of attorneys. (A claim for almost £10,400 had been submitted, including interest at £4336 1s. 10¼d., with legal costs for claims in 1794, and interest thereon, amounting to £1232 1s. 2d. RW had taken CW, and then JW, to Mr Graham, who had recommended a total payment of either £8000 or £8500, £3000 or £4000 to be paid soon – before JW left for China – and a

bond issued for the remainder with interest. £8500 was agreed on, £3000 being paid without delay, £1500 on 7 July, with two promissory notes for £2000 each at 5 per cent, redeemable on 7 July 1804. Of this nine-twentieths – £3825 – was invested by RW for W and D.)

28 March MW has been away almost a month at Penrith and Eusemere. Expected to return with Sara H on Friday.

28 April Sara leaves. (STC ill with rheumatic fever.)

May War between Britain and France is resumed as Napoleon's expansionist policy becomes more evident.

15 June D writes to RW for money; CW has been making her an annual allowance. She has spent nearly £20 on clothes in expectation of interest on her share of the £3000 paid by Viscount Lowther. W and M are expecting a child at the end of July.

18 June John W born prematurely.

17 July STC godfather at his christening. The baby has already been taken in his basket to the island in the lake. W and D expect to begin their Scottish tour with STC in about ten days. (Soon afterwards Hazlitt, who visits Grasmere from Keswick, paints W's portrait. Later in the month W meets Sir George and Lady Beaumont at Keswick. The Clarksons leave Eusemere about this time.)

August
9 (Tues) Samuel Rogers and his sister, on their way to the Highlands, have tea at Grasmere with the Ws and STC.
12 Using their recently acquired horse and jaunting-car, the Ws travel to Greta Hall, and hear from STC details of Sir G. Beaumont's generous gift to them. They discover that he and Lady Beaumont left Keswick an hour and a half before their arrival. The gift consists of property at Applethwaite, which Sir George bought, thinking that W might like to build a house there in order to live much nearer STC. On this day, or the next, the Ws inspect the property.
13 W walks with Rogers by Derwentwater, and D makes a copy of 'Resolution and Independence' for the Beaumonts.

14   After taking MW and Johnny seven miles on their way back
     to DC, W and D return to Keswick, their Scottish tour with
     STC starting the next morning.

16   Dine at Carlisle on the day Hatfield, the forger who posed as
     the Hon. A. A. Hope, M.P., and committed bigamy with
     Mary Robinson (see entry for 11 Nov 1799), is convicted; STC
     sees him in the gaoler's house. Sleep at Longtown.

17   Cross into Scotland, and reach Dumfries.

18   Visit the churchyard where Burns is buried. STC unwell.

20   After spending the previous night at Leadhills, they stop at
     Douglas Mill, a coach-inn where, on the same window-ledge
     as D uses to write to MW, W had written to D two years ago
     (cf. 6 Sep 1801). To Lanark; on their way to some of the Falls
     of Clyde, they catch sight of Robert Owen's mills at New
     Lanark.

21   Another view of the Falls (cf. 'Composed at Cora Linn').
     Sleep at Hamilton.

22   Reach Glasgow, after following the Clyde valley and visiting
     the castle at Bothwell.

23   Leave in the afternoon, their vehicle 'spreading smiles from
     one end of Glasgow to the other' (D's *Recollections*), and
     creating excitement among schoolboys, who long to ride.

24   From Dumbarton, where W and D have fine views from the
     castle, to Loch Lomond, staying the night at Luss.

25   View south from an island, over islands, with the castle on
     Dumbarton rock visible in the distance, mist giving it a
     ghostly appearance, and reminding D of Glastonbury Tor
     from Dorset hills. View of Ben Lomond over the lake, and,
     more exciting, of the famous Cobbler mountain above
     Arrochar. A walk after tea, then dinner, at Tarbet, where
     they sleep.

26   By boat to Rob Roy's Caves, then to Inversnaid. They follow
     a horse-track over to Loch Katrine; while they are debating
     whether to return, a man in Highland dress rides up, a more
     exciting picture than the lake. W walks to a farmhouse and
     finds accommodation.

27   Next morning, after hearing much on Rob Roy, who had
     owned the next farm, and was reputed to be buried there,
     they walk down to the ferry-boat. Too cold for STC to cross;
     he walks, and meets W and D after their crossing, which
     gives excellent views of the Trossachs. Return wet and cold
     to the ferryman's cottage for the night.

28 On the way back to Loch Lomond, they overtake two girls, the elder exceedingly beautiful (cf. 'To a Highland Girl'). One is the sister of the Inversnaid ferryman; the other, of his wife. The tourists dry their clothes and dine while waiting at the ferry-house for their boat. The hospitality they have received at the farm and the two ferrymen's cottages creates very favourable impressions of the Highlands. Return to Tarbet.

29 Heavy rain continuing, STC decides to send his clothes to Edinburgh, and make his way there; he leaves W and D a short distance beyond Arrochar.

30 They reach Inverary, and walk in the Duke of Argyll's pleasure-grounds; after dinner, to the castle.

31 To Loch Awe, near the head of which they sit long admiring a castle ruin which seems to cover the whole of the visible island, in front of Ben Cruachan, which they both had been thinking the grandest mountain they had ever seen. (See 'Address to Kilchurn Castle', the first three lines of which were composed at the time, the remainder years afterwards.) To an inn beyond Dalmally.

September

1 (Thurs) More views of Kilchurn Castle as they proceed towards the Pass of Brander below Ben Cruachan on their way to Bonawe, where they see the house to which Mr Knott, once a partner in the iron foundry there, brought his family for summer holidays, with Ann Tyson when she was young. Heavy rain, during which W and D spend much time in a boat on the upper part of Loch Etive, where they abandon any idea of reaching the road to the north for Glencoe.

2 By road down Loch Etive, which they cross by ferry (much to the consternation of their horse) to Loch Creran (where it runs away at the sight of another ferry-boat; eventually it is persuaded to swim over). To Portnacroish and on to the ferry-house inn near Ballachulish (where STC – as they learn later – had slept three nights earlier, after walking from the head of Loch Lomond to Glencoe).

3 To Glencoe, where, despite the grandeur of the mountains, they are disappointed not to find 'images of terror' (overhanging rocks and a gorge such as W describes in *Pr* vi, 621–40).

8 After travelling through Tyndrum and Killin, then by the side

of Loch Tay, to visit the historic Pass of Killiecrankie, and make a circular tour through Blair Atholl back to Faskally, they reach Dunkeld.

10　After passing through the Narrow Glen, the burial place of the legendary Ossian (cf. W's 'Glen Almain'), to Crieff the previous day, W and D proceed up the Strathearn valley past Loch Earn and Loch Lubnaig to Callander.

11　To the Trossachs (their horse and car being taken back to Callander) and Loch Katrine, where, with the mountains of Loch Lomond in view, they meet two women, one of whom greets then with 'What! you are stepping westward? (cf. W's poem 'Stepping Westward').

12　Call at Inversnaid ferry-house, cross Loch Lomond, then walk north to Pulpit Rock and Glenfalloch, down to Glengyle, and past the farmhouse where they had stayed, to the reputed burial-ground of Rob Roy.

13　From Loch Katrine over to Loch Voil; a harvest-scene, as they are descending, may have been in W's mind later when words in Thomas Wilkinson's *Tour in Scotland* suggested 'The Solitary Reaper'. At Strathyre, where they stay at 'the most respectable-looking house', D is asked the 'old' question, whether she is married; on hearing she is not, the 'woman of the house' answers, 'To be sure, there is a great promise for virgins in Heaven.'

14　Breakfast at Callander, and on to Stirling and Falkirk.

15　Linlithgow and Edinburgh, where they visit the castle. STC arrives home at noon.

16　To Arthur's Seat and the old parts of the city, mostly in rain. Then on to Roslin.

17　As they pass Hawthornden, they think of Ben Jonson's visit to the poet William Drummond. After breakfasting with Walter Scott and his wife at Lasswade, they visit Roslin Chapel, and proceed to Peebles.

18　To Neidpath Castle (cf. W's sonnet beginning 'Degenerate Douglas!') and Clovenford (near the Yarrow; cf. 'Yarrow Unvisited').

19　At Melrose, Scott meets them as he promised, and takes them to view the Abbey ruins.

20　To Dryburgh Abbey. In their lodgings at Jedburgh (cf. 'The Matron of Jedborough and her Husband') Scott recites part of *The Lay of the Last Minstrel* (published 1805).

21 After his session at Jedburgh Assizes as Sheriff of Selkirk, Scott walks with them in the Jed valley.
22 He travels with them to Hawick.
23 After walking with them, Scott leaves; they wish they could accompany him on a tour of the dales in the region, where 'in almost every house he can find a home and a hearty welcome' (D's *Recollections*). On their way home they soon pass Branxholm Tower, which reminds them of Scott's *Lay*.
24 After staying overnight at Langholm, they travel to Longtown, in the vicinity of which they look at 'the place on the sand near the bridge where Hatfield had been executed'.
25 They reach DC, finding 'Mary in perfect health, Joanna Hutchinson with her, and little John asleep in the clothes-basket by the fire'.

October
3 (Mon) W goes to Ambleside to join the Volunteers as part of the home defence against French invasions (cf. 'Lines on the Expected Invasion' and other October sonnets).
9 He calls on STC, after visiting the surgeon at Keswick on behalf of Joanna, who has been very ill. Tom Hutchinson has received notice to quit Gallow Hill.
14 W writes belatedly to thank the painter Sir George Beaumont for his gift of the Applethwaite estate; he is not likely to build a house there, as STC is planning to live abroad for his health; (Southey, whose wife is Mrs C's sister, has been persuaded to bring his family and occupy half of Greta Hall in anticipation). On Sunday, at Ambleside, the Grasmere Volunteers are to don their uniforms for the first time.
26 Hazlitt and W upset STC by their irreverence, W speaking disrespectfully of Paley, Ray, and Derham.

13 November   Writing to her friend Catherine Clarkson, who had left Eusemere for the sake of her health, D reveals that Tom H has taken Park House farm near Eusemere, and hopes C and Sara H will be neighbours next summer.

(It may be have been about this time that William Hazlitt left Keswick, where he had returned to complete a portrait of STC for Beaumont. According to the story W told Crabb Robinson, H was forced to flee by a mob for his attacks on women, making his way by moonlight, after being secreted at Greta Hall, to Grasmere, where W provided the money and clothes he needed to reach his destination. Towards the end of November John Thelwall calls, on his way to Edinburgh, where he is to lecture on elocution.)

25 December STC is at DC with Derwent for D's birthday; he had arrived on the 20th.

31 December W and STC walk up Greenhead Gill to the sheepfold, where W reads 'Michael'.

1804

4 January At a high point above Grasmere, STC hears from W 'the second Part of his divine Self-biography'.

14 January Lame with gout, stomach-sick, and haunted by ugly dreams, STC has remained at DC. W accompanies him almost to Troutbeck on his way to Kendal for London, where he hopes to arrange a health-cure period on the island of Madeira; (should he go, W will contribute £100 towards the cost). W has heard of Jeffrey's attack on his preface to *LB*, and on 'the Lake School' of poets (which included Lamb), in *The Edinburgh Review* of October 1802.

13 February W is busy continuing the poem of his early life, which is projected as an appendix to *The Recluse*. (About this time, and probably in subsequent weeks, W is engaged on his 'Ode to Duty', a subject suggested by STC, who in Dec 1803 had written on the need for duty and inclination to coincide: the law of moral reason must be our guide and impulse. From Sir G. Beaumont's at Dunmow he had written to W on 8 Feb 1804, telling him how blessed he – W – is, in that his 'Path of Duty lies thro' vine-trellised Elm-groves, thro' Love and Joy and Grandeur'.)

March
6 (Tues) W informs STC (now in London after his Dunmow visit, and hoping to go to Sicily) that he has finished another book of his poem, and that another will complete it. Writing to De Quincey the same day, he says that the subject of his completed book is his 'residence at the University' and that the poem is 'better [than] half complete: viz 4 books

amounting to about 2500 lines'. (Clearly he is uncertain about the development of this work; his intention had been to complete it in five books, ending with the ascent of Snowdon.) This poem, he tells De Q, is 'tributary' to an important moral and philosophical work on Man, Nature, and Society, of which only one book (probably 'The Pedlar') and 'several scattered fragments' (including the 1800 version of 'Home at Grasmere') have been written. He has also planned a narrative poem. He will be content if he lives to finish these three blank-verse works, the least important being that on his life (as he now plans it).

12   He stands as security for the repayment of £100 to William Sotheby, who has given a cheque for that sum to help STC in his travels.

25   D and MW have been making 'a complete copy' of W's poems, to be STC's 'companions in Italy'; they amount to about 8000 lines (*L1*, 458–9). Among them is 'Intimations of Immortality', probably completed about this time. STC, D informs Mrs Clarkson, is to stop at Gibraltar and Malta.

April
7   (Sat) W's birthday; he is working at the sixth book of his autobiographical poem (cf. *Pr* vi, 48–9). During the week Tom Hutchinson has probably settled in at Park House.

13   D's letter to Lady Beaumont is interrupted by one from STC, completed as he was about to sail; she includes W's sonnet written at Applethwaite with reference to STC ('Beaumont! it was thy wish . . .').

28   W attends a parade of the Loyal Wedgwood Volunteers near Gowbarrow Park, and dines with Luff, their captain. (From 1803 Captain Luff has been busy training a home-defence company of Volunteers known as Wedgwood's Loyal Mountaineers because they are financed by Thomas Wedgwood.)

29   W now in the seventh book of his poem.

May
5   (Sat) W and D climb over Grisedale Hause, above the tarn, to stay the night with the Luffs at Patterdale.

6   After riding to Lyulph's Tower (the Duke of Norfolk's shooting-lodge, built in the 1770s, and named after the Saxon

hero who gave Ullswater its name), W and D walk to Aira Force. She makes her way to Park House, while he walks via Matterdale to Keswick, to spend three days with the Coleridges and Southey.

8 D takes Sara H to see Eusemere, left with only a servant in charge. Thomas Clarkson is now in London, working for the passage of the bill to abolish slavery.

June

13 (Wed) W, D, MW, and Johnny travel in their jaunting-car to Greta Hall, where they are received with rapture by the children, Derwent especially. Hartley, nearly eight, pale and slender; Sara, eighteen months old, small, quick, and fairy-like.

14 From Greta Hall, W invites Walter Scott to Grasmere. He, MW, and Johnny proceed to Park House, D to DC, parting at Threlkeld.

17 W visits his cousin Captain W at Brougham Hall (the latter's home near Penrith).

23 D resumes her *Recollections* of the tour in Scotland, but makes hardly any progress. W returns to Grasmere, having heard of Lord Lowther's purchase of Eusemere. MW, who is expectant, is to stay at Park House three weeks longer.

July

18 (Wed) W has spent much of the last two days outdoors with Humphry Davy, who has left for Edinburgh.

20 W thanks Beaumont for the gift of Sir Joshua Reynolds' works; he has almost finished 'the life'. Regrets that at some earlier period Sir George's negotiations to buy land for a summer-house by Loughrigg Tarn had been balked.

25 The Coleridge children have been with the Ws since Sunday, nursery accommodation having been arranged at Fletcher's across the road. No letters from STC since his departure.

August

16 (Thurs) W's daughter Dorothy born at least three weeks before expected.

19 Mrs C and her children leave.

24 Sara H is D's 'assistant Nurse' (*L1*, 496).

29 Mrs C hears from STC; he has been very ill the whole way from Gibraltar to Malta, and expects to go to Sicily.
31 W informs Beaumont that his 'poetical labours have been entirely suspended' for two months; he is 'most anxious to return to them' (*L1*, 500).

September
16 (Sun) Dorothy's christening, for which MW's aunt and cousin, Elizabeth and Mary Monkhouse, have come over from Penrith. Sara H deputizes for Lady Beaumont as godmother.
23 Sara H returns to Park House, after helping her sister a month.
Late in September, and possibly early in October (MW having recovered), 'the first fine autumnal days' are 'seized' by D and W, who, after travelling to Keswick in their 'car', and taking the Southeys, Mrs Coleridge, and her sister Mrs Lovell to Buttermere, walk from Keswick via Whinlatter Pass to Lorton Vale, where they see 'the Patriarch of Yew trees' (cf. the opening of 'Yew-trees', probably written soon after this visit), thence to Ennerdale, which D wished to see for the sake of 'The Brothers', Wastdale, and the Duddon valley, which she thinks one of the wildest and most romantic of vales, and a perfect contrast to Wastdale. At Wastdale Head and Seathwaite they are most hospitably received. They find Basil Montagu and Lamb's friend George Dyer at Grasmere on their return. Small though it is for their increasing family, the Ws intend to remain at DC until they know where STC will live; the climate forbids his return to the north.

October
 6 (Sat) CW, now rector of Ashby, Norfolk, and Priscilla Lloyd are married in Birmingham. About this time two artists, Richard Duppa and Henry Edridge, seem to have visited W, the painter Edridge being delighted with the drawing of Applethwaite which Sir George Beaumont had sent W.
15 RW has been in the north for nearly two months, and has spent a few days at DC, possibly to discuss with W and D how much is due to their cousin Richard of Branthwaite in compensation for legal expenses in his unsuccessful claims of 1794 against the Earl of Lonsdale. W has resumed his poem (*The Prelude*).

29   Tom Monkhouse of Penrith, MW's cousin, is at DC, and promises to purchase stockings in London for W.

December
25   (Tues) Duppa has invited W to translate some of Michelangelo's sonnets for his biography of the artist. A circular moss-lined hut has recently been built to provide a summer retreat at the top of the Ws' 'little rocky orchard' (*L1*, 518).
31   Grasmere is frozen over, and all the Ws are on the ice, MW and D with the children on their knees being pushed on chairs by George Hutchinson (no longer a farmer) and W on their skates.

1805

January
2   (Wed) Tempted by the previous day's sunshine, they are driven in their Irish car by George H via Kirkstone Pass and along Ullswater to Park House.
5   M and D suffer from their cold journey (mainly as a result of hurrying up the steep Kirkstone ascent (because W was afraid of being late) and becoming overheated. (In later years W thought his trachoma, the eye-affliction from which he suffered recurrently for long periods, was initiated by this journey over Kirkstone. See his note to the poem 'To Dora', written in the spring of 1816 when he feared he might lose his sight.)
16   Hearing that Scott has forwarded a copy of *The Lay of the Last Minstrel* for D, W writes to him from DC, hoping that Scott will be able to visit his friends in Grasmere and Keswick in the summer. D sends Scott a copy of 'Yarrow Unvisited'. (Scott's poem did not arrive until March.)

February
Early in the month W writes to Richard Sharp in London, thanking him for the watch he had obtained for him, requesting him to write if he hears of suitable clerical employment for George H, and informing him that a Liverpool attorney is ruining the view at Grasmere by building a house which will be visible from every part of the Vale; (this 'temple of abomination' is the future

Allan Bank). JW has written from Portsmouth, in good spirits, and hopeful (about his trading prospects in Bengal).

11   (Mon) A letter from RW reporting the loss of John and his ship is brought from Rydal by Sara H at 2 p.m., when W and M are out walking; D is alone to bear the shock. In his reply to RW, W states that she and M are very ill. (Sara had heard the news at Kendal and hurried over, anticipating the letter, with the aim of giving all the help and comfort she could. On 5 Feb *The Earl of Abergavenny* had run into a westerly gale off Portland Bill; a Weymouth pilot had been taken on board but, when the wind dropped, the ship drifted and struck a rock in the Shambles. When this was cleared she was too waterlogged to reach the shore, and sank. Most of the crew, troops, and passengers were lost. John, supervising from the highest point of the ship – the 'hen coop' – was eventually swept overboard, and last seen struggling in the waves. Some weeks later his body was recovered, and buried at Wyke, near Weymouth.)

13   Southey, who also had heard the news on the 11th, and had sent his condolences, comes to DC at W's invitation, and stays two days.

16   W, who trembles to think what effect the news of J's death will have on STC, reports that Mrs C has heard news of her husband, back at Malta after three months in Sicily.

28 (or earlier)   After receiving an offer of financial help from Beaumont (who knew that the Ws had invested in J's last voyage), W sends his friend a summary of their financial history, disclosing that £1200 of the amount due to him and D had been lent to JW (for trading purposes; RW and CW had lent large sums to the same end). He does not know whether it has been insured, but expects it has.

March

7   (Thurs) Writing to Mrs Clarkson, MW speaks highly of W's exertions 'to comfort us', and states that John was the first who led her to everything she loves in the neighbourhood.

12   W (who has just heard from RW that the insurance is considerable) justifies acceptance of a banknote sent by Beaumont to cover any emergency, and thinks he will spend some of it on a few books he has long wanted. J's death has made him wonder whether human beings have *more of love* in

their nature than belongs to 'the great Cause and ruler of things' (*L1*, 556).

27   Letter arrives from STC dated 19 January, saying he will return in March, either 'by the Convoy, or overland through Trieste'.

Late in March or early in April, W visits his cousin John W, formerly captain of *The Earl of Abergavenny*, at Brougham Hall, and is much consoled by the details he hears concerning J's death.

11 April   After attempting to write a poem on J's virtues, and finding his feelings too strong for him to proceed, he has resumed *The Prelude*.

31 May   D finishes her *Recollections of a Tour made in Scotland*.

June
3   (Mon) W informs Beaumont that he finished his poem about two weeks ago. (It was published posthumously, the title being supplied by MW, from W's definition of it in his 1814 preface to *The Excursion* as the 'preparatory poem' to *The Recluse*. He describes it as 'a sort of portico to the Recluse' and 'part of the same building', which he hopes soon to begin. If he can write additionally 'a narrative Poem of the Epic kind', he will consider his life's task completed.) W composes 'Stepping Westward' while walking with D and little Dorothy in the green field by the Rothay river; cf. 11 Sep 1803.
6   W, D, and MW finish the moss-hut; (its primary purpose is to make DC less crowded).
8   He goes with a neighbour to fish at Grisedale Tarn, but recollection of parting with John (who often fished with him) there makes him return to write 'Elegiac Verses' ('The Sheepboy whistled loud').
11   At Patterdale with his fishing-tackle, after parting from M and D at Grisedale Tarn the previous day; (he returns three days later, after meeting Richard Sharp, who is on his way to Scotland).

July (last week)   Mrs Threlkeld and her daughter Elizabeth from Halifax begin their stay at DC. Mrs Clarkson, who has been under medical care at Bristol and elsewhere, returns to the Lake District about this time; she stays at Robert Newton's house overlooking the churchyard (leaving about 13 Oct).

August
Early in the month RW stays at DC, and decides to buy D a pony.
7 (Wed) W sends Lady Beaumont 'To the Daisy', a poem occasioned by reading one of J's letters, and including some expressions from it.
9 The Threlkelds leave, accompanied by D to Park House, where they stay two days, the former proceeding to the Crackanthorpes at Newbiggin, D returning on a pony, which is brought by W).
11 W walks with Thomas Wilkinson along the path the latter is developing by the Lowther river (*L*1, 646). Later he goes to Keswick, where he meets Walter Scott and Humphry Davy at Greta Hall.
12 They visit Watendlath and the Bowder Stone.
13 They set off for Patterdale.
14 They climb Helvellyn via Striding Edge, Scott having to pause often owing to his lameness, but making compensation with amusing stories. W tells the story which has recently come to light of Charles Gough, who had fallen to his death over the edge of Helvellyn, and of his dog, which had not deserted him for three months. (He was last seen on 18 April; his bones were discovered near Red Tarn on 20 July. On this subject W wrote 'Fidelity', and Scott, 'Helvellyn', neither poet knowing this result until long afterwards.)
15 With D and Mrs Scott they sail on Windermere.
26 The Ws are looking forward to a holiday near Sir George and Lady Beaumont at Coleorton, Leicestershire.

October (very early) D has her pony, and W can usually borrow one from a neighbour for MW; one of their rides is round Loughrigg Tarn.

9 October Another edition of *LB* is published.

November
3 (Sun) W and MW return from a three-day visit to Park House, W stopping a while at Ambleside to obtain the latest news of the war with France.

6   W accompanies D on her pony over Kirkstone to Patterdale, where they stay with the Luffs.

7   She sends Lady Beaumont a copy of W's new poem 'The Solitary Reaper'. W writes to Scott, particularly on the poetry of Dryden, whose works Scott is editing, and sends him a copy of 'Glen Almain'. They walk to the crag above Blowick for the view across the head of Ullswater; after dinner W discovers where he would like to build a house (Broad How). In the moonlight Mrs Luff's large white dog lies on the round knoll under the old yew-tree ('a beautiful and romantic image', D writes in her 'Excursion on the Banks of Ullswater'; W seems to have remembered it in *The White Doe of Rylstone*).

8   By boat with Luff to Sandwick, after which they walk and have a beautiful view of the church with its wall-enclosure and yew-tree. They climb on their way round to Patterdale and come to a ruin which was once a place of worship; last summer it saved an old man's life (cf. *Ex* ii, 730–895). The descent tires D.

9   News of Nelson's victory and death at Trafalgar reaches them at breakfast; they make inquiries at the inn, and D is shocked to hear there has been great rejoicing at Penrith. W being anxious that Wilkinson should negotiate the purchase of the property on which he could build a house at Patterdale, he and D set out on the Place Fell side of Ullswater, stopping again above Blowick for the view. Call at Eusemere; as the pony cannot carry both of them at the Eamont ford, W dismounts. Derwent Coleridge meets them at Park House. After tea W visits Wilkinson at Yanwath, and his cousin Captain W at Brougham.

11   Via the ford at Yanwath, to find Wilkinson digging with a spade in one of his fields (cf. W's poem 'To the Spade of a Friend'). Three delightful hours spent by the river and in the woods of Lowther Castle. Then to Penrith, where W and D read Admiral Collingwood's dispatches on the battle of Trafalgar.

12   Via Soulby Fell to Ullswater and by the main road to Patterdale. After tea with the Luffs, W rides as far as Brothers Water bridge. They reach DC at 11 p.m.

25   MW goes to Park House with her brother John from Stockton.

28   W follows.

29   D, after putting the children to bed, writes to Lady Beaumont.

She thinks of JW's first coming to DC, hopes that STC will not be captured by the French on his way home, and trusts that W will soon begin *The Recluse* in earnest.

December

14 (Sat) D has heard from Mrs C that STC is making his way home from Trieste via Vienna. W and M have been to Brougham Hall.

25 MW is still absent; expected to return, if the weather is favourable, with George and Joanna H on the 27th. The fiddler on his round arrives, the children of the neighbouring houses being in the kitchen, and Johnny is too shy to dance with any but D. She has made a copy of two-thirds of *The Prelude*. W is doing preparatory reading for *The Recluse*.

1806

January During the first two weeks W writes *The Waggoner*. MW had returned two or three days later than expected. Sara H is now staying with the Ws, who are anxious about STC's return. Charles Lamb buys editions of Chaucer, Spenser, Shakespeare, and Milton for W. The Lloyds have left Brathay for a few months in Birmingham. CW and Priscilla are at Lambeth, where he is chaplain to the Archbishop of Canterbury.

11 February W sends Beaumont a copy of 'Character of the Happy Warrior', composed after Nelson's death, and combining his virtues with those of JW. The death of Pitt (23 Jan) is a great loss, but W thinks he would have avoided 'grievous' mistakes, if he had given precedence to his country over the country under his administration. The question of landscape-gardening at Coleorton leads to a clarification of views expressed in W's letter of 17 October 1805.

March

2 (Sun) News from Mrs C, who has heard that STC had not travelled to Trieste, which was occupied by the French, but was at Naples on 26 December. Sara H's copy of *The Prelude* for STC is finished.

7   W applies to Montagu for money he needs to visit London;
    he owes his landlord two years' rent.
29 Just before departing for London, where he hopes the change
    will restore him, he writes to Thomas Wilkinson, stating that
    the price asked for the property he liked at Patterdale is too
    high (see 5 Aug).

April–May   In London, where he stays about eight weeks, with
CW and Priscilla, with Montagu (whose wife is ill), and, for much of
the time, with the Beaumonts in Grosvenor Square, W meets many
people, including the Lambs (to whom he reads *The Waggoner*),
Godwin, and the artists David Wilkie and Henry Edridge, who
probably sketches him during this visit. Samuel Rogers introduces
him to Charles James Fox, the leader of the Liberals, who does not
share W's strong anti-Bonapartism. W also visits his uncle William,
Canon Cookson, and his family at Binfield, not far from Windsor.
(Poems written as a result of his London visit: 'Stray Pleasures',
'Power of Music', 'Star-Gazers'; Beaumont's picture of Piel Castle in
a storm, which W saw at his house in Grosvenor Square, prompted
'Elegiac Stanzas', which was written not later than July.)

May
5   (Mon) W writes to De Quincey, hoping he will defer his visit
    to the north two of three weeks so that they can meet; (at the
    critical juncture, De Q's courage failed him).
25 W returns to Grasmere, having 'enjoyed himself highly' in
    London (*L2*, 31).
29 D requests RW to send £7, £5 from Sir George Beaumont and
    £2 from W and herself, to their old servant Peggy Marsh, of
    Racedown and Alfoxden, who married a blacksmith, and
    whose house at Hawkchurch near Axminster has been burned
    down.

June
2   (Mon) W hopes to tour the Border country with Scott for a
    month including the last week of June, the Beaumonts being
    expected at the end of July. D has sold her pony, and they
    have bought a cow.
c. 14   W composes 'Yes, it was the mountain Echo'.
15 Birth of the Ws' third child, Thomas.

c. 19   Robert Grahame of Glasgow calls with his wife and two daughters, and W dines with him at the Grasmere inn.

24   News of STC from Dr John Stoddart, King's Advocate in Malta: he had moved on to Rome when the French advanced on Naples. The Ws having no servant, Sara H has stayed on, helped by the young Hannah Lewthwaite, who had loved to assist ever since she had nursed Johnny (now with his aunt Joanna at Park House; the farm is unprofitable, and Tom Hutchinson is looking for another).

July   Owing to Sir George's ill-health, the Beaumonts cannot visit Grasmere; nor is Scott able to tour with W at the time proposed. MW is in poor health. To avoid whooping-cough, which is spreading at Grasmere, little Dorothy is taken to Park House. Accompanied by D and Hannah, she is carried by W until, at George Mackereth's, the parish clerk's, they meet a stranger, who carries her to the top of Grisedale Hause, where he leaves them; W carries her down to the Luffs', whence they travel the length of Ullswater by boat, the child screaming for half an hour to get out. Joanna has taken Sara's place at DC. During the month W adds 700 lines to *The Recluse*: (they could include the final passage of 'Home at Grasmere' which appeared as the 'Prospectus' of *The Excursion*, and, even more probably, passages which became part of Book IV of that work).

August
1   (Fri) The latest news of STC is that he was at Leghorn, waiting for a ship to England, and had lost all his papers, including the copes of W's poems. W feels that when he has discussed *The Recluse* with him, he will be able to 'go on swimmingly' (*L2*, 64). As DC is too small for the winter, and they have no alternative accommodation, he must accept the Beaumonts' offer of the Hall Farm house at Coleorton for six months.
5   W is embarrassed to hear that Wilkinson has bought Broad How, Patterdale, for him, after Lord Lowther had offered to pay the £200 difference between the price asked and the £800 W had offered.
18   Hearing that STC is in England, W cancels the tour with Scott. He and MW had spent a few days with their children at Park House, some of the time with Wilkinson, calling with

him at Lowther Castle to thank Lord Lowther for his
generosity, but finding him absent; later they visited the
Broad How property, which W thought 'most beautiful' (*L2*,
74).

21 He informs Beaumont that he will not build a new house, but
add two rooms to the old, at Broad How, if he does not move
south to be near STC.

September

8 (Mon) STC does not wish to meet his wife, W tells Beaumont.
(Perhaps about this time, either at Brathay Hall, home of the
artistic John Harden, or at the Lloyds', W meets John
Constable.)

13 Death of Charles James Fox; cf. W's 'Lines' ('Loud is the
Vale'), written on hearing that Fox was dying.

18 W writes to STC, suggesting they meet in London.

28 He proposes to collect his poems for a publication in the
winter. He has just learned that STC will be at Keswick in a
day or two, but, as STC has said nothing on the question
whether they should look for a house in or near Keswick, the
move to Leicestershire seems certain.

October

26 (Sun) After setting out by post-chaise with his family to see
the Beaumonts before they leave Coleorton, W is joined by
Sara H at Kendal, where STC's letter to her makes them wait
in the hope that he will come back, though he has left Penrith
for Keswick. He arrives in the evening, his former self hardly
recognisable; they are shocked and distressed by his state.

29 W and Sara leave him in the morning, MW and D having
stayed with him until their departure with the children the
previous morning. They had been prepared to return to
Grasmere, or take Belmount, a house near Hawkshead, but
STC would not hear of it; he would join them at Coleorton in
a month.

30 They reach Coleorton in the evening, one party by chaise, the
other by coach; (the Beaumonts remain until 3 Nov).

November

7 (Fri) W informs Wrangham that he can no longer collaborate
in Wrangham's satirical publication, and wishes his verses to

be destroyed; he is opposed to personal satire, and not keen to participate in the satire of public 'delinquents'. He urges STC to join them at Hall Farm, and bring Hartley, rather than give lectures in London.

10　Pleased with the site chosen for Lady Beaumont's winter-garden, he recommends Paper 477 of *The Spectator* on the subject. (For his thoughts on the setback suffered by the Coalition against Napoleon, see 'November, 1806'.)

24　Writing to Catherine (Mrs) Clarkson, D tells her that the farm supplies their needs; the dairy-maid, who makes their bread, and the bailiff live at the house. STC is to part from his wife, and take charge of Hartley and Derwent. (About this time W sends Wilkinson 'To the Spade of a Friend', composed, not written, at Yanwath probably during his visit in August.)

December

Early in the month W and D visits the ruins of Grace Dieu nunnery, and are delighted with the Charnwood scene. (In the sixteenth century the property passed into the hands of the Beaumonts, the dramatist Francis Beaumont being born there.) W has formed the habit of composing in the grove at Coleorton Hall or up and down the walk connecting the Hall with Hall Farm; (among the poems written during his stay are 'The Horn of Egremont Castle', 'Song at the Feast of Brougham Castle', and 'The Blind Highland Boy', the story told by George Mackereth of an event he had witnessed, thought to be written about Christmas for the entertainment of W's children). W spends much time in the selection and arrangement of poems for his forthcoming publications.

19　(Fri) STC expected with Hartley. D hopes he has given up drinking brandy, from which he will be 'tolerably safe' at Hall Farm, though he may be tempted by strong beer. W is busy planning the winter-garden in great detail.

21　STC arrives (afternoon), more like his old self, with Hartley.

27　The suspicion of an intimacy between W and Sara H begins to take root in STC's jealous, over-stimulated imagination.

1807

January

7　(Wed) W completes his reading of *The Prelude* to STC, who composes 'To William Wordsworth'; (some time during the winter STC's change of manner causes W to write 'A Complaint').

24 D informs Lady B that W usually visits the workmen in the winter-garden twice a day, and that STC does not take such strong stimulants as he did.

February (early) STC has hopes that the Ws will join him at Greta Hall; he believes his wife will move south, and that Southey may leave.

February (last week) W and the gardener visit Nottingham to buy plants.

March The Ws are still trying to find a house in the Lake District. The bill abolishing the slave-trade receives the royal assent (cf. W's sonnet 'To Thomas Clarkson').

April The Ws (and STC and Hartley, who afterwards stay in the west country) are in London for a month. After being at the Montagus' (Thornhaugh Street), they go to CW's at Lambeth towards the end of the month. W and Scott meet, and take Hartley to the Tower of London.

May
4 (Mon) Sara H goes to Mrs Clarkson's (Bury St Edmunds). W attends the Royal Academy exhibition.
6 The Ws return to Coleorton with Scott; (when he leaves for Scotland W and D accompany him to Lichfield).
8 W's *Poems in Two Volumes* published.

June
10 (Wed) After staying a few days longer at the request of the Beaumonts, who have returned, the Ws leave Coleorton for Halifax. They travel in two post-chaises to Nottingham, where they view the town and castle.
11 By coach to Sheffield, where they take a post-chaise, but have such a distressful journey, Thomas being ill, that they stay the night at Huddersfield.
12 At Halifax (where he makes a good recovery) they stay with the Rawsons and Threlkelds, and are joined by Sara H; D is delighted to see the places familiar to her in youth.

July

3   (Fri) They leave to stay with the Marshalls at New Grange, Kirkstall, Leeds.

6   MW, Sara, and the children proceed to Kendal by post-chaise. D and W are taken to Bolton Abbey, Wharfedale, and the neighbourhood, staying the night at Burnsall; (see 'The Force of Prayer' and *The White Doe of Rylstone*).

7   They walk to Gordale Scar and Malham Cove.

8   To Settle, Ingleton, and Kendal.

9   The whole party spend a day at Levens.

10 They return to Grasmere, where they find many changes. Among those who have died are Mr Sympson and George Dawson, 'the finest young Man in the vale' (*L*2, 158; cf. *Ex* vii, 38–291 and 695–890); the Bainriggs trees and the finest firs near the church have been cut down (cf. 'The Tuft of Primroses', 71–126). Soon after his return W rents Allan Bank, hoping to move in during the autumn.

13 He visits the Beaumonts, who are at Keswick; he stays until the 16th.

August

26 (Wed) By invitation, he meets Lord and Lady Holland at Low Wood Hotel (evening).

30 D informs Mrs Clarkson that her husband has spent a day with them, and comments on the manuscript of his forthcoming book on the slave-trade. Mr Crump has left the planning and planting of the grounds at Allan Bank to W. She has spent twelve days with the Beaumonts at Keswick, from about the end of July. While staying with MW and Joanna H at Eusemere (where the two Miss Greens, friends of the Ws, live) W and the Beaumonts have been the guests of the second Earl of Lonsdale, formerly Lord Lowther, at Lowther Castle.

September

2   (Wed) W and M return to DC with the Beaumonts (who live in the village, and stay another week).

18 W and M return from a week's tour, which began two days after the Bs' departure, and took them to Wastdale, Ennerdale, Whitehaven, and Cockermouth, where they look at the terrace-walk of W's birthplace.

October   W begins *The White Doe of Rylstone*, using 'The Rising of the North' in Percy's *Reliques* for the story.

18 October   He has obtained much useful information for his poem from a copy, sent by the Marshalls, of their friend Dr Whitaker's *History of Craven*. With her acknowledgment, D includes a copy of W's poem 'The Force of Prayer' to commemorate their Wharfedale visit.

4 November   Sudden arrival of Hartley Coleridge and De Quincey, who has accompanied Mrs C and her children north, leaving STC at Bristol, on his way to London, where he plans to lecture at the Royal Institution. They all stay the night. (De Q remains with the Ws several days, during which MW takes him to Easedale, where she stops to talk to a sister of the new nursemaid Sally Green; D, who has taken him to Esthwaite Water, introduces him to the Lloyds at Brathay, and W persuades him to join their excursion to Eusemere, MW planning to journey with Joanna and Miss E. Green to her rich uncle Henry and her eldest brother John at Stockton-on-Tees. W takes him to Penrith, probably through the Lowther woods; a few days later, when MW leaves, W follows him to Keswick. After staying again at DC, De Q returns south on the 12th.)

December
1   (Tues) After being delayed many days by heavy snow, W sets out for Stockton (where *The White Doe* is continued).
23   W and M, both 'in great favour' (*L2*, 185) with their uncle, return home just as Johnny and his sister Dorothy are going to bed.
28   D explains to Mrs Clarkson that when they rented Allan Bank they thought that STC would join them with Hartley and Derwent; they would not care for him now except as an occasional visitor. Jeffrey's attack on W's poems, in *The Edinburgh Review* (Oct), is too spiteful and senseless to affect wise, sensitive readers.

1808

January
3   (Sun) W has 'seized' the copy of Walton's *Compleat Angler* which Lady Beaumont has sent D; its imagery and sentiments

accord with his own 'train of thought' (*L2*, 186–7; cf. *Ecclesiastical Sonnets* III, v).

16 *The White Doe of Rylstone* completed.

18 In his letter to Scott, W shows considerable knowledge of Dryden and his period. He admires both Dryden and Pope, but says it will require 'yet half a century completely to carry off the poison of Pope's Homer' (*L2*, 191).

February

5 (Fri) The only good news heard of STC is that he has begun his lectures; D has no doubt that he still takes opiates.

c. 20 Writing to Sir George B, who has done a painting for *Peter Bell*, W draws a distinction between the *people*, who would like the poem, and the *public*, who would not. His statement that every great poet is a teacher, and he wishes to be regarded 'as a Teacher, or as nothing' arises from his concern for accuracy of original observation (not from moral issues); cf. *L2*, 194–5.

23 W leaves for London, hoping to bring back STC, who has broken down after two lectures.

March

15 (Tues) He breakfasts at the Lambs', and is introduced to Henry Crabb Robinson, foreign editor of *The Times*, and a friend of Mrs Clarkson.

23 D reports to W in London the loss of Sally Green's parents in a snowstorm on their way over from Langdale to Easedale.

28 She is already contemplating her campaign on behalf of the orphan Green children; Richard Watson, Bishop of Llandaff, has contributed 10 guineas.

31 She is upset that W has decided not to publish *The White Doe*; they need money to furnish Allan Bank, to keep two servants, and foster Sally Green.

April

3 (Sun) W, who has spent some time with the Beaumonts at Dunmow in Essex, leaves London for Grasmere, after visiting an exhibition of Sir Julius Angerstein's collection of pictures, dining with his publisher Longman, and hearing STC lecture twice. He has left his poem with STC.

8 Two days after reaching home, he is haunted by the vision of

Fleet Street in pure white snow, silent, with a few dusky pedestrians, and of St Paul's 'solemnised by a thin veil of falling snow', as he saw them after leaving STC at 7 a.m. on the 3rd (*L2*, 209). The memory makes him think of the blessings of an *exalted* imagination (for the significance of this, cf. *Pr* xiv, 188–205). He visits the Greens' grave, and begins composing the poem 'George and Sarah Green'.

11   He writes an appeal to Lady Holland for the Green children.
17   W feels exhausted after writing such appeals to influential friends. D intends to write a full account of this tragedy; (it was completed on 4 May, but not published before 1936).
19   W's letter to STC includes one of the best outlines of his aims in *The White Doe of Rylstone*.
25   W reports to Richard Sharp (now a West India merchant in London) the success of their appeal; all the Green children are in respectable homes, and MW is on the managing committee.

May (early)   STC negotiates satisfactory terms with Longman for the publication of *The White Doe*. W instructs L not to publish.

21 May   STC, who had promised to correct the proofs, protests.

Late in May, or early in June, W answers roundly and at great length some wild accusations he has received from STC: (1) arising from STC's annoyance with Stoddart for impounding all his books and papers at Naples as security for payment of customs and debt, and applied to some literary discussion in which W and Mrs Hazlitt (Stoddart's sister, her husband no lover of W) had taken part; (2) caused by suspicion of the Ws' friendship with the Lloyds (W thinks Charles mad); (3) that Sara's letters to him have been supervised by W and M, who had convicted her that his unhappiness was attributable to his attachment to her.

5 June   The move to Allan Bank (perhaps at the end of May) has been completed. Sara H has been suffering for a long period from a pulmonary ailment; MW is expectant, and has sprained her arm, and W has had to be kept out of the way. The work has been left consequently to the superintendence of D and MW's brother Henry, who has been with them a month, after obtaining his discharge from the Navy, and witnessing horrible brutality on a slave-ship. Overlooking the lake, and with a wonderful view of the Vale, W writes to Wrangham on the problem of education in large industrial centres, and of obtaining national education in a country where the Government is more interested in money than in morals.

July

3   (Sun) D writes to De Quincey, requesting him to obtain cheap copies of valuable books such as histories (including translations from the classics), Bacon's works, and Milton's prose works. Apart from the poets, W's library is 'little more than a chance collection' (*L2*, 257). (About this time the Ws spend a day with W's admirer John Wilson, at his cottage, close to the house he is having built at Elleray near Windermere.)

22 John Monkhouse brings his sister Mary from Penrith to stay at Allan Bank and relieve Sara H (whom he takes to Eusemere three days later).

August

1   (Mon) On the way to Eusemere with W and Mary Monkhouse, D is very ill at Ambleside; W meets John Wilson (with whom D and Mary M had been boating at the head of Windermere two days earlier), who insists that they travel by chaise. After dining with the Luffs, D and Mary proceed by boat, while W returns with the chaise.

4   After finding his letter of 20 June unposted, W thanks Scott for a copy of *Marmion*; he regrets Scott's censure of the dramatist Thomas Heywood in his Dryden notes, and praises *A Woman Killed with Kindness* highly.

30 The Convention of Cintra is signed (an agreement whereby French military forces in Portugal will be conveyed to France by the British navy).

September

1   (Thurs) After a period at Mrs Clarkson's, STC arrives at Allan Bank.

5   W goes with him to Keswick, to support STC when arrangements for separation are made.

6   Catharine W is born.

7	W and STC return (with his daughter Sara; Hartley and Derwent are soon afterwards placed in the Revd John Dawes's school at Ambleside, but are at Allan Bank on Saturdays and Sundays).

19	W, STC, and Sara H are on tour, in the Duddon valley.

22	They leave Eskdale for Wastdale.

27	Reflecting on the failure to recognise authors of genius in their day, W thinks the proposal to extend authors' copyright from fourteen to twenty-eight years after their death is insufficient.

29	He thanks Samuel Rogers for raising £31 8s. for the Green fund, and comments on Crabbe, whose pictures are nearly all 'mere matters of fact', with little poetic quality.

October

2	(Sun) Catharine is baptized, Catherine Clarkson acting as godmother by proxy.

19	W meets Southey, Spedding, and William Calvert at Greta Hall, to organize the sending of a protest to the King against the Convention of Cintra; (the project is abandoned when Lord Lonsdale refuses his support).

November	De Quincey comes to Grasmere, and is such a favourite with W's children that he stays at Allan Bank. During the second half of the month W is busy setting down his thoughts on the Convention of Cintra (a subject he frequently discusses with STC). He writes to friends, hoping they will obtain subscribers for STC's proposed weekly *The Friend*. They are having continual trouble with smoky rooms, wet cellars, and workmen about the house. With fifteen members of the household (including Hartley, Derwent, and servants) there is much work to be done; they have land, and keep a cow, two pigs, and poultry; they bake all their bread, and mangle or iron all their washing.

December	Continual cleaning necessitated by smoke doubles the housework.

27 December	A first instalment of *Concerning . . . the Convention of Cintra* appears in *The Courier* (Daniel Stuart's paper).

1809

10 February   Tom Hutchinson has at last obtained a farm, to be shared with John Monkhouse, at Hindwell, Radnorshire (sixteen miles from Hereford); Mary M and Joanna H will accompany them.

March   De Quincey is in London to superintend the proofs, and W's revisions, of the pamphlet protesting against the Convention of Cintra, and supporting the Spanish struggle for independence against Bonapartist imperialism. Dove Cottage has been rented by W another six years, for De Q. STC has been absent, professedly with the intention of having the first number of *The Friend* published on 1 April.

April
1   (Sat) At Appleby, with STC and Mr Brown, the Penrith printer, W and Southey stand as first and second securities at the signing and sealing of papers, for the publication of *The Friend*, with Mr Wilkin, Distributor of Stamps. On his way home, W sleeps at Sockbridge, RW's inherited estate.
29   John Wilson calls at Allan Bank (and stays until the following afternoon; he hears W read *The White Doe* and 'Christabel').

May
1   (Mon) De Q is still in London supervising W's pamphlet. W has begun the revision of *The White Doe*, and proposes to write of public affairs in *The Courier* for financial reasons. STC intends another visit to Penrith (from Keswick) to launch his weekly.
5   In a letter to STC, who is ill at Keswick, W urges him always to be *beforehand* with his work, reverts to his fear of being prosecuted for libel in his pamphlet, and drafts his first plan of arranging his poems according to subjects and classes.
23   He receives some unstitched copies of his pamphlet from De Q.
c. 30   After considerable delay, partly from W's habit of sending alterations, mainly because De Q had annoyed the printers, the Convention of Cintra pamphlet is published. W tells Poole that he has no confidence in STC's 'moral constitution', and hopes *The Friend* will not appear. STC cannot keep it going; he has been three weeks at Penrith, and nothing has been heard of him since his arrival.

June
1   (Thurs) The first number of *The Friend* appears.
13   After being absent the greater part of four months, STC
     returns to Allan Bank, a week with Thomas Wilkinson and
     without spirits having restored him. TW was 'the Father' of
     The Friend, D thinks (*L*2, 356).
c. 22 W joins Wilson's fishing-party, which, with ten servants,
     and tents and baggage borne by ponies, crosses over to
     Wastwater for a week.

July   Many visitors at Allan Bank, including Southey and some of
his friends, and Mr Clarkson and his son Tom, with the latter's
tutor, the Revd Samuel Tillbrooke of Peterhouse, Cambridge.
George Hutchinson is there for the whole month, and more. While
at Kendal for twelve days, D buys kitchen furniture and other
articles for De Q's cottage. W, who has too much company to write,
is depressed by the defeat of Austria at Wagram. He and Wilson are
thinking of a tour in Ireland. Late in the month STC sends off the
material for the third and fourth numbers of *The Friend*.

August (late)   To prevent smoky rooms in the winter, Mr Crump is
having all the chimneys raised; the house is full of workmen (and
they will be there two months).

September
13   (Wed) W and MW return, after a few days with Wilson.
18   Sara H has been busy transcribing for both *The Friend* and W;
     she has written out his first version of *Guide to the Lakes*, to
     serve as an anonymous introduction to Joseph Wilkinson's
     drawings of the Lake District (published 1810). De Q has
     been at Grasmere, briefly at DC, then at Allan Bank; now that
     he has a servant, he will soon live at DC, where he has a
     huge collection of books.

December
14   (Thurs) W's 'Reply to Mathetes', a response to Wilson's essay
     on the moral problems of adolescence, appears in *The Friend*
     (where it is completed on 4 Jan 1810).
(Just before Christmas) As the workmen have left, and the
extension with its large bow window overlooking the crags and
wood behind Allan Bank has been completed in W's study, D (in

the absence of MW, who has been at Kendal a few days) arranges his books, which have been stowed in heaps in the lodging-rooms, and ensures that the house is restored to order.

25 Although Christmas Day was to have been spent with De Q, he, STC, and the Ws have been persuaded to spend it with Wilson, in his very comfortable cottage at Elleray, where MW joins them.

27 Return to Grasmere.

1810

January

2 (Tues) The Ws and their children, with Lloyd's children, are at DC, where De Q gives a firework display.

9 D hopes that RW, who has been at Stockbridge, and shown his usual reluctance to visit them, will come in the summer; she asks for a statement on their financial position, on which nothing has been heard since Lord Lonsdale paid his cousin's debts. They intend to economize, give up tea-drinking, and find a house where coal is cheaper; it must be near a grammar school, for they can't afford to send the boys to boarding-schools.

February

22 (Thurs) The first part of W's 'Essay upon Epitaphs' appears in *The Friend*; two others have been completed. From October he has contributed to this publication sonnets on Tyrolean resistance to Napoleon, translations of Chiabrera's epitaphs, and 'Reply to Mathetes'.

28 STC, who 'either does a great deal or nothing at all' (*L2*, 391) has been composing with a rapidity which is 'truly astonishing'; he dictates to Sara H (whom he still loves), and rarely revises, sometimes completing a whole number of *The Friend* in two days. John Monkhouse, who arrived about two weeks earlier, suffering from the kick of his horse, is still receiving surgical attention.

March

15 (Thurs) *The Friend* ceases publication. About this time, or

earlier, Sara H leaves (probably with John M) to stay at
Hindwell; she has failed where Wilkinson succeeded.
23 D tells RW, from whom there has been no reply, that she and
W looked at a suitable house the previous week, at Bouth, six
miles from Ulverston on the Kendal road.

April
7 (Sat) Catharine is very ill at breakfast time, after eating
quantities of raw carrot (which Johnny and 'Sissy' – his sister
Dorothy – had cut up for 'bullets'); she is convulsed for seven
hours.
12 STC continues to talk as if *The Friend* were still being
published.

May
c. 2 (Wed) STC leaves Allan Bank, for Keswick.
10 D is relieved to know that they are not leaving Grasmere;
they are to move into the parsonage in a year's time, when
the house has been made more comfortable for them. They
will miss the views ('sweeter than paradise itself') from all
sides of Allan Bank (*L2*, 406). The first part of the portfolio
edition of Wilkinson's *Select Views* has appeared, and W
writes scathingly of them to Lady Beaumont.
12 Birth of William Wordsworth.
c. 20 W, who has added considerably to *The Excursion* since
February, and needs a change, goes to stay with RW at
Sockbridge.

7 July   After a three-day journey from Kendal via Manchester,
Ashbourne (from which they walked with John Wilson's friend
Alexander Blair to Dovedale in the evening), and Derby, W and D
walk to Coleorton Hall, where they are the Beaumonts' guests,
arriving at 10 p.m.

August
6 (Mon) W leaves for Hindwell, Sir George accompanying him
part of the way; they visit the Leasowes, the estate of
Shenstone (author of *The Schoolmistress*; died 1763) at
Halesowen.
7 From Hagley they return to Birmingham, and see Otway's
Venice Preserved in the afternoon.

8   W returns part of the way with Sir George, then visits Mr
    Blair's.
9   CW, who is with the Lloyds and has heard of W's visit, calls
    and dines at Blair's; W sups with CW and Priscilla at the
    Lloyds'.
10 W leaves at 3 a.m. by coach for Worcester and Leominster.
    With two others he takes a chaise for fourteen miles, sleeping
    at Presteigne, five miles from Hindwell.
11 With a guide to carry his luggage, he arrives there at 11 a.m.
    D, after leaving Coleorton on the evening of the 10th to stay
    with the Clarksons at Bury St Edmunds, is met by Mr
    Clarkson at Cambridge.
12 At Cambridge she is impelled by W's recollections in *The
    Prelude* to see Newton's statue (iii, 46–63) and the ash-tree (vi,
    66–94). Finding herself alone with the guide on the roof of
    King's College Chapel, she panics. She and Clarkson reach
    Bury in the evening.
19 W plans to make a short tour of the Wye in the coming week,
    from Radnor to Hay-on-Wye, thence to Builth (on which road
    he met Peter Bell's original), on to Rhayader, and over to
    Radnor.

September   He returns to Allan Bank. A day and a half of his
holiday have been spent with Sir Uvedale Price, an enthusiastic
landscape gardener, at his Foxley estate in Hertfordshire.

23 September   Montagu and his third wife (his former hostess and
housekeeper, whom W cannot bear) arrive. (They stay about a
month. M's son Algernon has been at the Ambleside school with the
Coleridge boys since the spring. At Keswick they persuade STC to
live with them in London; W thinks it expedient to tell Montagu
what to anticipate.)

October
c. 14   (Sun) W writes to D (at Binfield, after much sight-seeing
        in London with H. C. Robinson) that Catharine is dangerously
        ill.
18   STC leaves Grasmere, with the Montagus, for London.
19   D returns to London, where she is exhausted and persuaded
     to stay two days by the Lambs (who are kindness itself; she

has to wait another day for a seat on the coach before returning by Manchester).

26   W, MW, and D, with their young maid Sarah Youdell, take Catharine and William for a change of air to Hacket in Little Langdale, where Sarah's parents live. (Sissy and Thomas have already been there two weeks.)

27   He reads the 'Morning Hymn' from Book v of *Paradise Lost* as they sit in the morning sunshine; D had never felt Milton's power more. He returns to Grasmere in the evening, D accompanying him part of the way; returning, she is lost, and has to be escorted to Hacket after being up to the knees in mud in a tract of peat-moss. (For Hacket and the Youdells, see *Ex* v, 670–837.)

November
8   Scarlet fever and wintry winds around Allan Bank make the Ws move to Wilson's warm house at Elleray. (Wilson is engaged, and away much of the time with Miss Jane Penny, daughter of a wealthy Liverpool merchant).

December
18   (Tues) They return to Allan Bank, which is still cold and uncomfortable; Catharine, who had been like a skeleton when D was recalled, is now healthy again, although lame.

25   A large party, including three servants of Mr Wilson, gathers for Christmas dinner with the children in the kitchen.

28   The Ws dine with De Quincey.

30   In recent weeks W has written several political sonnets; he has more faith in popular Spanish and Portuguese patriotism than in Wellington.

1811

10 February   The children have not thrown off the whooping-cough completely, and W is suffering from trachoma. MW's uncle Henry has died, leaving properties worth more than £50,000; (she and Joanna inherit an estate which lets for £100 p.a., D writes).

27 March   W writes to Wrangham. He has not heard from STC since he went to London in October, and he thinks there should be no further concessions to Catholics; (the Catholic Emancipation Act was not passed until 1829).

28 March   He writes at immense length to Captain Pasley, whose essay *The Military Policy and Institutions of the British Empire* he has just read twice, some parts three or four times. Both think it foolish to make peace with France until she is defeated, but W disagrees with P's assessment of French strength and wealth, insisting that the critical factor is the national *mind*; the liberation of peoples depends more on their feelings than on military conquest. England requires a new martial policy and something more difficult to achieve, a new education, 'a higher tone of moral feeling', and 'more of the grandeur of the imaginative faculties' (*L2*, 481; cf. 'September 1802. Near Dover').

12 May   D tells Mrs Clarkson that they are now regular church-goers for the sake of their children, including Hartley and Derwent C, and occasionally Algernon Montagu; they are friendly with the curate William Johnson. By this time W has learned from Mrs C how 'cruelly injured' STC feels, after hearing from Montagu what W had predicted (M's indiscretion being provoked very early by STC's intemperance). W has resumed work on *The Excursion*. (At some time in 1811, probably in the spring, before leaving Allan Bank, W writes 'Characteristics of a Child Three Years Old' – on Catharine; cf. the Jan–Feb 1813 note.)

11 June   Not wishing to keep the Crumps out of their home, the Ws have removed to the parsonage, though there has been no time to make the intended improvements.

16 June   Three disadvantages are soon evident: it faces east, and the sun is lost too early; it is too exposed to public view; it stands in a wet field, which is unsuitable as a playing-ground for the children. The workmen are with them, as at Allan Bank.

July (end)   Shortly after Sissy's departure for Miss Weir's school at Appleby, W and M leave with Catharine and Thomas, and the maid Fanny, to stay at the seaside near Bootle. (For the first part of their journey – past the old dog of the dead Grasmere parson who was noted for his drunkenness and for turning hay in November moonlight, past Loughrigg Tarn, and below Hacket, from an eminent point in front of which greetings are waved by Betty Youdell, and along Yewdale, which recalls the days when W plundered ravens' nests – see W's 'Epistle' to Beaumont, 'Far from our home by Grasmere's quiet Lake'.)

4 August   D and Sarah Youdell take John and Willy to Hacket (returning on the 8th).

September   The Bootle party return to Grasmere after almost six weeks' absence. From Duddon Bridge the children are driven by Fanny to her sister's in Yewdale, where they are rejoined the next day by W and M, who have walked up the Duddon valley to Seathwaite, then over Walna Scar Pass. Arrangements are made for W to meet Sara H at Warrington towards the end of the month, on her way back after a long absence at Hindwell.

October   Dr Andrew Bell arrives with Southey, and is taken to the school, where he instructs the master (William Johnson, the curate) and W in his method. (W teaches regularly about this time, as do, later in the year, both MW and Sara H.)

3 November   D informs RW that, as he seems determined not to visit them, she and MW hope to stay with him a few days at Stockbridge. Sara H is back, after a few days with the Luffs at Patterdale, and her brother Henry is with them.

20 November   In a letter to Lady Beaumont, enclosing a copy of his sonnet 'To the Poet, John Dyer', W speaks highly of *The Fleece* (1757) and thinks Dyer may be superior in imagination and purity of style to any poet since Milton. (During the month W writes inscriptions in verse for the grounds and gardens at Coleorton.)

December (late)   He is working on *The Excursion*, and on a new arrangement of his poems.

1812

6 February   W requests the help of Lord Lonsdale, if he finds any office at his disposal. He explains why his poetry has not been profitable – one reason being his inability to associate with any class

or group of writers, for fear of sacrificing independence of judgment
– and states that he chose to be a poet after being denied the
profession for which he was most inclined and perhaps best
qualified (the Army; writing to Wrangham a few weeks later, he
says that his returns from poetry have been less than £140).

18 February   On his way from London to Keswick, STC, after
collecting his boys from school, passes through Grasmere without
calling on the Ws, as they wished.

26 March   He makes no effort to call, after receiving four letters in
three days from the Ws, but leaves for London via Penrith.

April
c. 12   (Sun) W, anxious for reconciliation with STC, sets off for
London. (MW and Tommy travel with him as far as Chester,
on their way to Hindwell. W visits the Lloyds at Birmingham,
and his cousin William Cookson at Oxford. He stays several
days with William's father, Canon of Windsor.)
27   He leaves Windsor and reaches Grosvenor Place (the
Beaumonts') in the evening.
28   To CW's, only to find that he is in the country. He looks at
Wilkie's pictures in Westminster Hall, seeks out Montagu,
with whom he dines and spends the evening, and is struck
by the sumptuousness of his apartments.

May
2   (Sat) He has discovered (from STC's letter to Richard Sharp,
24 Apr) that STC has described him as his bitterest
calumniator, had much trouble finding Lamb in order to
settle 'the business' with Montagu, and (the previous evening,
with a note of admittance from Sharp, who keeps him well
supplied with franks) attended the House of Commons,
where he heard Perceval.
8   Lamb's attempts at mediation having failed, with STC refusing
to meet Montagu, W asks Robinson (HCR) to see STC, which
he does without delay; STC promises to have a statement
ready for W on Sunday. W visits Washington Allston's
studio, and is delighted with his picture of Cupid and Psyche.
(Next morning he describes it in a letter to Mary, saying that
his pleasure would have been greater could he reconcile

himself to the sharp contrast between the white naked figures and their background.) At a party he meets Sir Humphry Davy and the lady he has recently married; he thinks her plain and affected.

10   Josiah Wedgwood, whom W met at the House of Commons, calls and offers to act as mediator with STC, whom he has not seen for seven years. HCR calls on STC and takes his statement to W. The facts bear out W's denials.

11   HCR calls on W, who draws up denials and explanations for STC. Impressed by his integrity and delicacy, HCR prefers 'the *coolness* of such a man to the heat of C'. He does not find STC at home on his first visit, but calls again after an early dinner, and finds the Lambs there. HCR has just heard the news of Perceval's assassination about an hour and a half earlier. STC is shocked and speaks warmly in P's favour; later he tells HCR in a half-whisper that W's letter is perfectly satisfactory, and that he had answered it immediately.

12   W breakfasts with Dr Bell and William Johnson, now head of one of the new 'Central' schools in London, by the persuasion of Bell, who had been impressed by his work at Grasmere.

13   W breakfasts with the poet Bowles. An exchange of letters has effected a reconciliation between him and STC, STC accepting W's account of what happened between him and Montagu.

17   He dines at the Beaumonts' with STC, Wilkie, and Allston. The Bs are so alarmed by the violence and rioting of Nottinghamshire Luddites that they may not go back to Coleorton in the summer.

22   Dines with STC and the Morgans (STC's hosts). Late in the evening he arrives at the Lambs', where he reads *The Waggoner*; had there been time, he would have read *Peter Bell* in preference.

23   W reports that he has now breakfasted twice with Davy and his wife. Davy is an expert angler; his wife must be rich or extravagant, for they live most stylishly in Berkeley Square. W leaves the Beaumonts' by carriage for STC's lecture (no doubt with Lady B, who had bought a large number of tickets for her friends, to help STC).

25   Dines with the Bs at Lord Mulgrave's, where he has an interesting talk with the American painter Benjamin West. Afterwards at Lady Crewe's he meets the Princess Regent.

26 Dining with the Bs at Rogers', he observes Lady Caroline
    Price coquetting with her old paramour, and Sir Uvedale
    Price overgorging himself and falling asleep immediately after
    dinner.
27 At the Bs' he meets Mr Lister, who would be pleased to show
    him a glen, unknown to travellers, near Malham and Gordale.
28 In Greenwich Park with Sir George and Rogers, he is sadly
    reminded of JW by the sight of three returning East Indiamen.
29 After attending STC's lecture, he dines and spends the
    evening with the Morgans.
30 Calls at STC's and walks with him to Hampstead, where he
    dines with the poet and dramatist Joanna Baillie.

June
4 (Thurs) Catharine W, after being seized with convulsions
   most of the night, dies soon after 5 a.m. She had been in
   good health, and had run upstairs in glee the previous
   evening, knowing she was to sleep in her mother's bed.
   Writing to Mary (at Hindwell), W refers to an affecting letter
   he has sent her from Annette and Caroline; he has given his
   reply to Tom Monkhouse, one of whose merchant friends
   will ensure it reaches France.
6 Mary's letter confirms that Annette has written on the need
   for W to make a settlement on Caroline.
8 W leaves London before the arrival of D's letter, to visit CW
   (rector since 1808) at Bocking in Essex. He has met many
   people in London, spoken highly of Burns, and found far
   more poetry in Blake than in Scott and Byron, whose first
   two cantos of *Childe Harold* have been creating excitement in
   the capital.
10 D's letter on C's death (cf. W's sonnet 'Surprised by joy')
   reaches him at Bocking. Instead of proceeding to the Clarksons
   at Bury as arranged, he will leave for Wales on the morrow,
   hoping to be in time to break the grievous news to Mary.
14 Reaches Hindwell, to find M disconsolate. He has stayed a
   day in London, thinking it better that she should have his
   arrival to look forward to after hearing of their loss from Tom
   Hutchinson (to whom he knew Sara H had written; her letter
   had been delayed in the hope that W would arrive in time to
   break the news, as he would have been had he received D's
   letter in London on the 8th).

July   W and M return to Grasmere after outings in Wales which eventually he persuaded her would provide some relief. Two days later D leaves for a holiday of more than two weeks by Ullswater, first with Captain W and his wife, now at Eusemere, then with the Marshalls, and her 'aunt' Rawson, at Watermillock. One day, back at Grasmere, she and W climb Fairfield; she is giddy above Dove Crag, and would have fallen (perished, she thought) had he not grasped her in time. Another day they have tea at Robert Newton's lodging-house with two clergymen, Samuel Tillbrooke and C. J. Blomfield, the future Bishop of London. These two and Richard Sharp, who is very entertaining, walk with the Ws (except Mary, who cannot bear to think of her time there with Catharine) one afternoon to Hacket, and have tea with Betty Youdell; Tillbrooke's flute-playing there is the subject of W's sonnet 'The fairest, brightest, hues of ether fade'. Thomas looks ill, and Dorothy (Sissy) is wayward and difficult.

August
8   (Sat) W, MW, and D go to Greta Hall with the educationist Dr Bell, taking Dorothy, who will be happy with her companions Edith Southey and Sara Coleridge.
10   W is with Richard Sharp and Samuel Rogers at Low Wood; they watch wrestling at Ambleside.
16   Of their visitors, Rogers and Sharp are the most frequent. Mary Monkhouse has been a guest since the end of July, and has gone with Sara H to spend a fortnight with Miss Weir at Appleby.

September   W and D have a walking-tour, including three days in Borrowdale, and call wet and dirty at Greta Hall on their way home. Dr Bell stays two weeks with the Ws, and D revises his work on the 'Madras System' of teaching.

10 October   Tom Hutchinson and Joanna have been staying with the Ws; with Sara H and Mary Monkhouse they go off to Wigton; Mary's brother Tom goes to Penrith, where they will all stay until the races are over, then return to Grasmere.

November
2   (Mon) Wedding of Tom H and Mary M at Grasmere; W and John Wilson are signatories.

17 W, MW, and Dorothy return after a period at Greta Hall, during which W visits Lord Lonsdale, who promises to do all he can for him.

December

1 (Tues) Thomas, the most sweet-tempered of the W children, dies of pneumonia after measles. W writes to De Q at Liverpool, asking him to come as soon as possible. D is away; she has been staying at Watermillock.

2 D, having heard news of Tom's illness, sets out for Keswick on her return journey, and is met by W at Threlkeld. They are about to send for a chaise when told that a man is about to set off for Grasmere with a cart. In this D lies as she is conveyed to 'the house of mourning' (*L*3, 71). MW, worn and thin, receives her with fortitude.

17 W writes to Lord Lonsdale, telling him of his loss, and asking for time to consider his proposal of an annual gift of £100 until some other means of support can be found for him. Lord L had seen Lord Liverpool and Mr Long of the Treasury to no avail. The letter is from Ambleside, to which the Ws have moved with their three surviving children. William has measles, and they know they must be near a doctor 'to guard against the worst' (*L*3, 55).

27 W and MW are left with William, D and Sara having returned with John and Dorothy on the 24th. W writes, accepting Lord L's gift.

1813

January

2 (Sat) W and MW return with William from Ambleside. They are determined to leave Grasmere, as so much around them, including the churchyard where Thomas played and walked to school, continually recalls their lost ones.

5 W has heard, after applying to rent Rydal Mount (recently bought from the Norths by Lady Fleming, who lives with her mother Lady Diana Fleming at Rydal Hall), that Mr Jackson will come in a day or two to discuss terms. The two ladies have formed a good impression of W from his active interest in the adoption of Dr Bell's plan at Grasmere school. The

Norths are leaving in February, but have a right to the house until May Day; they are not likely to oblige Lady Fleming, and are unfriendly to the Ws, Mrs North having been offensive to D when she deputized for MW on the management committee for the Green orphans.

January–February　W works on *The Excursion*, adding a portion, notably a transfer from his own experience, on the loss of his two children, to the Solitary (cf. iii, 622ff.). This passage included 'Characteristics of a Child Three Years Old' in the past tense, and the lines which were published separately as 'Maternal Grief'. The Ws are disappointed that STC has not fulfilled his repeated promise to visit them after the death of Thomas; he has ignored their letters.

March
6　(Sat) W indicates that he is ready to accept the Distributorship of Stamps for Westmorland and the Penrith district of Cumberland, for which Lord Lonsdale is recommending him.
14　He agrees to pay Mr Wilkin, the retiring Distributor, a pension of £100 p.a.

April
1　(Thurs) By this date W has received £100 of the £300 lent to Montagu as an annuity investment in 1795.
6　His appointment being confirmed, W goes to receive instructions from Mr Wilkin at Appleby. Rydal Mount has been empty more than three weeks, but remains locked until loads of wine have been removed from the cellars.
19　W has learned that Lord Lonsdale and Sir George Beaumont have agreed to act as sureties for him as Distributor of Stamps.

May
1　(Sat) Removal to RMt.
c. 12　W goes to comfort his 'cousin' Mary Peake (near Cockermouth); she is the daughter of his cousin Richard of Branthwaite and Whitehaven, and her husband had been killed by the cannon-ball which injured her fifteen-year-old brother John on his frigate the *Peacock*.
17　W leaves RMt for Appleby to assume his duties as Distributor of Stamps.

30 He has been busy during the last six weeks visiting his Sub-distributors in various towns.

August
 2 (Mon) With MW he is at Whitehaven, to pay his respects to Lord Lonsdale, and fulfil an invitation to visit Mr Blakeney, secretary and treasurer of the harbour trustees.
17 Daniel Stuart and his bride spend a day with the Ws when RMt is full of company.
31 Sara H leaves for Stockton-on-Tees.

11 September W and others of his family have been to local sales, buying lots of furniture and fittings for RMt. Tom Monkhouse has sent some best quality carpets, a Turkey for the dining-room and a Brussels for W's study, from London. They have had many visitors; D has entertained her Grasmere friends, all keen to enter RMt. W has dined with the Bishop of Llandaff; his son and John Wilson have dined with the Ws. Mrs Peake and her young sister Dorothy (who is to stay until the following summer and be taught with Dora, as Dorothy or 'Sissy' is now called) are expected today. John now attends school at Ambleside with the Coleridge boys. W has left for Penrith, where he has to attend to Stamp business; he will be absent eight or nine days, calling at Lowther and having to take action with his Sub-distributor at Kirkby Stephen. His main office is at Ambleside; when free, his clerk John Carter is to help at RMt, particularly in the garden.

4 October D (staying with her friend Mrs Cookson at Kendal) writes of Hartley Coleridge's increasing oddities; he needs the discipline of another school before he goes to college, but she does not expect STC to take action. MW is glad that D and Sara have been spared the 'punishment' of Mr Blakeney, who has been 'glued' to the Ws from morning to night. At Lowther Castle W has met *'heaps of fine folks'* (*L3*, 125), including the Duchess of Richmond (who will be hostess at the Brussels ball on the eve of Waterloo).

10 October D has heard of company at RMt, including Dr Parry the Stamp Office inspector, whom the Ws had taken to dine at De Q's, where they met John Wilson and his wife Jane.

October (late) Montagu sends his son Basil, who has been mentally and physically ill, to Ambleside, hoping he will benefit from W's influence.

November   Robert Southey takes the oath as Poet Laureate.

December (early)   By this time Sara H is back at RMt.

1814

January   Basil, who had been very ill while on a visit to Miss Barker, a neighbour of the Southeys at Keswick, has remained under her care.

19 January   D goes to assist her friend Miss Barker.

February
9   (Wed) RW marries his servant Jane Westmorland.
21   W, suffering again from trachoma, employs an amanuensis. (During D's absence, great alterations are being made to *The Excursion*, a fair copy of which is being made for the printer.)

April
16   (Sat) Montagu has £200, the remainder of the capital sum borrowed from W, ready, D thinks fit to apprise Mr Addison, in the absence of his partner RW. (This sum is paid on 17 May, a final settlement of M's debts to W taking place on 27 Dec 1817.)
24   D is still with Miss Barker, her main business being to keep the peace between her and the 'Fricker' sisters next door. A month has passed since she returned after a week at RMt. Basil is not eager to leave a place where he has lived 'Scot Free', but she must find him lodgings again in Ambleside when she returns home, as she would have done yesterday but for the weather. She has yet to see the proof-sheets of *The Excursion*. Dora now goes to school; W has recovered from the influenza he suffered in the winter, but MW is thinner than ever, and will be all the better when Mary Dawson, their old cook (who has been employed by De Q) comes to RMt. D exults in the defeat of Napoleon, but thinks it absurd that he

should be allowed a large income on Elba; what can he do with it except intrigue for power?

28   Knowing that STC is at Bristol, W requests Tom Poole to see him about the future of Hartley; he needs another type of school. A fund should be raised for his university education; Lady Beaumont has already offered £30 p.a. W's income from his Distributorship has proved to be £100 less than he was led to expect. He refers to his 'great Predecessor' Milton with reference to *The Excursion*, that portion of *The Recluse* which he is preparing for publication.

4 June He seeks Lord Lonsdale's permission to dedicate *The Excursion*, and *The Recluse*, to him.

July

18   (Mon) Just before setting off on his tour in Scotland, mainly for Mary's health, he informs Lord L that he has asked Mr Longman to forward his Lordship a copy of *The Excursion*; (the dedicatory poem is dated 29 July). He, MW, and Sara H travel in the 'car' used in 1803; John (aged eleven, destined to spend a few weeks with the Malcolms in Eskdale for the benefit of his education, since he is so backward) accompanies them on a black pony.

19–31   Their tour may be indicated by the places where they stay overnight: Keswick, Carlisle (thence to Brampton, Naworth, where they join the party celebrating the wedding of a Stamp Distributor, and Lanercost Priory), Burnfoot in Eskdale (two nights with the distinguished Malcolm family), Moffat, Douglas Mill, next morning to Lanark, with a view of Robert Owen mill-workers in their 'gay clothes' by the river (as it was Sunday, the Falls of Clyde had to be seen the next morning), then to Glasgow, after seeing the hanging gardens of Baroncleugh and the pictures at Hamilton House. They stay one night in Glasgow, where they shop and admire the cathedral; then two nights with Mr Robert Grahame, just outside Glasgow. After a night at an inn on Gare Loch, they cross to Roseneath Castle, then travel north by Loch Long to Arrochar, and down to Luss, where they stay two nights. Next morning (Sunday) they cross Loch Lomond on their way to Drymen and Aberfoyle.

August

1–3   (Mon–Wed) At Callander they stay two nights, visiting the Trossachs, where they are drenched; then via Lochearnhead to Killin. About this time *The Excursion* is published.

4–25   They make their way on a long tour to Glencoe, along the Great Glen (where W is most impressed by the Foyers waterfall by Loch Ness) to Inverness and Beauly, then south via Blair Atholl to Edinburgh.

26–30   Here they dine with John Wilson's mother and meet 'all the wits' (*SHL*, 79) in town, including the young writer R. P. Gillies, with whom W walks and talks on contemporary poets, chiefly Hogg and Byron.

31   To Traquair, where they meet 'the Ettrick Shepherd' James Hogg and Dr Anderson, editor of *Works of the British Poets*, familiar to W from his brother John's volumes.

September

1   (Thurs) With Hogg they travel over to St Mary's Loch and Hogg's father's cottage, then down the Vale of Yarrow past Newark Tower to Selkirk (cf. 'Yarrow Visited').

2   They breakfast with Mrs Scott at Abbotsford, and with her visit Melrose Abbey; after lunch with Lord Buchan at Dryburgh Abbey, they drive on to Kelso, where they stay the night.

9   They reach Rydal with John, after spending two days at Burnfoot, and possibly a day or two at Greta Hall (see 17th).

16   D and Sara H set off for Hindwell, which they reach on the 27th, after staying at Kendal, Liverpool (with Mr Crump), Chester (with a cousin), and Shrewsbury. About this time James Hogg is a visitor at RMt; observing with others a meteor, he describes its path as a triumphal arch in honour of the meeting of poets. De Quincey, the story goes, hears W ask who are the poets, and Hogg later takes revenge, to his subsequent regret, by writing a 'further portion' of *The Recluse* in parody.

17   W writes to Dr Anderson, suggesting additional volumes to his 'British Poets', to represent a large number of excluded poets, a list of whom he sends, drawn up with Southey 'a few days ago'.

27   The Marshalls and three of their visitors have tea at RMt, and

MW is embarrassed that they are staying the night (one only) at Ambleside and not with her.

29 After a few days at Lowther Castle, W leaves for RMt, probably calling at the Marshalls' on the way.

October

13 (Thurs) W has called at Sockbridge and found RW absent; he is exasperated by his brother's silence on his financial position, and would like to know what is due to him, in case RW dies. He and MW dine at Rydal Hall.

14 They go by Troutbeck Chapel to Elleray, where they dine with Wilson.

23 Blakeney calls at tea-time and stays late; fortunately he sleeps at the inn (but he dines with them next day).

26 W and MW call on De Q, who is ill. ('Laodamia' is written during Oct.)

November

4 (Fri) W is at Lowther Castle. A few days earlier the Duke of Devonshire had been there, and expressed a desire to see him, after reading *The Excursion* during his Irish tour.

12 W writes to Gillies; (see the sonnet 'From the dark chambers of dejection freed', which W says had been written in Edinburgh). (During the winter he is busy writing the preface to the 1815 edition of his poems and the 'Essay, Supplementary to the Preface'; see 14 Feb 1815. He and MW have been proof-reading the poems.)

December

c. 4 (Sun) William's illness, which is much more alarming after W has written, makes him urge D to return from Hindwell and relieve MW, who is exhausted with tending and amusing her boy.

15 D has returned, two weeks sooner than had been intended.

31 W informs the Clarksons that he is anxious about the sale of *The Excursion*, and hopes that it can be promoted among Quakers by *The Philanthropist*, partly to repay the cost of his Scottish tour, still more in order that a cheap edition (the present one costing 2 guineas) can be published to put it within reach of poorer readers. He has read Jeffrey's review, and counters it with the views of eminent people such as the

Duke of Devonshire; Charles Lamb has called it 'the best of
Books'. W and D hope to attend Caroline Vallon's wedding
next April.

1815

January   W is annoyed on hearing from Lamb that the latter's
review of *The Excursion* in *The Quarterly* has been drastically cut and
altered by the editor William Gifford.

February
 1   (Wed) He thanks Sir George Beaumont for allowing him to
dedicate the forthcoming edition of his poems to him.
 c. 5   A letter from W to De Q suggests that the latter, in London,
is helping to see W's poems through the press.
 14   W's letter to Gillies suggests that the 1815 preface and
supplementary essay have been completed recently; see 18
Feb.
 17   W and M take William on a visit to Mrs Knott; W reads the
story of the Grasmere knight, based on one of her ancestors,
and the welcome result is that she orders a copy of *The
Excursion* (cf. vii, 923ff.).
 18   W intends to plan the first part of *The Recluse* completely
before starting its composition; (*The Excursion*, as its 1814
preface indicates, is the second part, the first and third to
'consist chiefly of meditations in the Author's own person').
W and D are correcting proofs. D's letter shows that the 1815
preface has been completed very recently, after the
supplementary essay. Late in the evening W is reading *The
Faerie Queene* (cf. 20 Apr).
 26   Two proof-sheets of *The White Doe of Rylstone* arrive.

March
 13   (Mon) W asks Poole to send the £10 he promised to help
Hartley Coleridge, who is entered at Merton College, Oxford,
where, with a Postmastership of £50 and other bequests, he
should manage. If further money is required, W and Southey
will advance it. He has fears for Hartley, and in the presence
of Southey, and with his support, has advised him not to
neglect his studies, but aim at independence. Hearing news

of Bonaparte's escape from Elba, W hurries to Ambleside to consult the newspapers.

16 This news makes W and D give up planning for the present to attend Caroline Vallon's wedding. W believes that if Bonaparte were a man of genuine talent, he would do noble work in unifying Italy and giving it independence.

27–9 Visit of Colonel Pasley, at a time when events in France give them plenty to discuss.

April

3 (Mon) W sets off with MW for a few days at Kendal, officially to appoint a new Sub-distributor.

8 Writing to Sara H at Hindwell, D refers to John's laziness and the indiscipline in Mr Dawes's school; William is spoilt by his father. (For some time W has been revising classical literature in order to give J the necessary coaching for university entrance; hence poems such as 'Laodamia', 'Ode to Lycoris', 'Dion'.) Early copies of *Poems by William Wordsworth* in two volumes (published later in the month, and excluding *The Excursion*) have been sent out. This edition includes a dedication to Beaumont, an engraving of his 'Peele Castle' picture as frontispiece, the preface, and 'Essay Supplementary to the Preface'. The poems are arranged in classes, as adumbrated at the end of 1811.

20 The dedication of *The White Doe of Rylstone* in Spenserian stanzas to MW is completed.

May

2 (Tues) W and MW set off for London, hoping that Sara H will travel to Tom Monkhouse's, and that they will meet both of them. They are taking Hartley to Oxford. W wishes to see Lord Lonsdale, and explain why his great love of RMt and its surroundings makes him unable to accept the more lucrative position of Collector of Customs at Whitehaven which his Lordship has offered him.

7 HCR meets them at the Lambs' (and again on the 9th), and accompanies them to their lodgings near Cavendish Square.

22 W writes to STC, requesting him not to publish his poem 'To William Wordsworth' (cf. 7 Jan 1807); its commendation would be prejudicial to both of them. Lady Beaumont having revealed the views of STC on *The Excursion*, in his letter of 3

April, W asks him to explain his *comparative* censure. (He probably finds STC's answer of 30 May not very illuminating.)

23 W breakfasts with Benjamin Haydon, who passes two 'delightful' hours with him. (W's known wish not to attend parties where Hazlitt is present makes a vengeful critic of a political – Bonapartist – opponent.) Among others with whom he breakfasts during May are Walter Scott, HCR, and Wilberforce.

27 W calls on Godwin.

June

1 (Thurs) W, MW, and Sara H breakfast at HCR's, then visit St Paul's.

2 *The White Doe of Rylstone* is published, quarto edition, with an engraving of a picture by Beaumont, at 1 guinea.

12 Haydon makes a plaster cast of W's face, and notes that he bears the operation like a philosopher. They call on Leigh Hunt.

15 HCR calls on W at his lodgings. They discuss Hazlitt's attack on him in *The Examiner*; W calls on Leigh Hunt (the editor), who disclaims the article (on Milton's *Comus*).

18 HCR breakfasts at Wordsworth's (he is out); he stays chatting with the ladies until W returns. John Scott, editor of *The Champion*, and Haydon stay a considerable time.

19 W, MW, and Sara H leave London to stay with the Clarksons at Bury St Edmunds. (Here they most probably read details of Napoleon's defeat at Waterloo on 18 June.)

29 W and MW travel to CW's at Bocking, intending to begin their journey home via Cambridge and Coleorton on 1 July.

August (early)   The Beaumonts spend nine days at Rydal before taking rooms at Keswick. Dora now attends Miss Fletcher's school, and learns Latin at home. John is to become a boarder with his headmaster Mr Dawes.

12 September   W writes to Benjamin Haydon from Lowther Castle.

October

7 (Sat) CW's wife Priscilla dies unexpectedly after delivering a still-born girl.

12 Her brother, Charles Lloyd, is taken to Birmingham for

treatment, after being mentally deranged eleven weeks. W accompanies him and his wife to Manchester, where he sees them into the Birmingham Mail. D is at Brathay looking after their eight children.

November

24 (Fri) Writing from Kendal, Sara H says that De Quincey has at last gone to Edinburgh with Wilson, who was in the Lake District about a fortnight. W and MW were all night with him at Elleray; De Q was often tipsy. He doses himself with opium, and drinks like a fish. 'We believe', she writes, he will marry Peggy Simpson after all.

28 W writes to Mrs Clarkson, after hearing from her of the death of his friend Captain Luff, who had emigrated with his wife to Mauritius.

December

8 (Fri) D and W walk via Kirkstone to Patterdale, where they sleep.

9 He goes to Sockbridge, to make arrangements for a final settlement with RW; D, to Penrith.

15 They return, after staying at Lowther Castle and Sockbridge, and meeting Mrs Peake, her uncle Captain W, RW, his wife (whom D likes), and their son; on the way back they sleep at Hallsteads, the Marshalls' new home on Skelly Neb near Watermillock.

21 W sends Haydon three sonnets, the first written on receiving his last letter (in Oct), the second the next day, and the third the day after (his letter suggests he has been too busy to write any poetry since he left London): 'High is our calling, Friend!', 'How clear, how keen, how marvellously bright' (suggested by the view of Langdale Pikes), and 'While not a leaf seems faded'.

26 W and MW, after travelling to Keswick on Christmas Day, reach Lowther Castle via Penrith. (MW intends to stay with Miss Weir at Appleby, while W visits Sockbridge to ensure that all the W accounts are settled, and surety given for their properties, with RW. Otherwise, if RW dies, no settlement can be reached until his son's coming of age.) They do not expect to be back until the New Year. John has improved

under the supervision of Mr Dawes. Reports on Charles Lloyd are not favourable; Mrs Lloyd is preparing to leave Brathay, her boys to stay with Dawes.

1816

January
c. 11 (Thurs) W returns from Sockbridge, his accounts having been settled.
18 On this day of thanksgiving for the defeat of Napoleon, W writes the first stanza of 'Ode' ('Hail, orient Conqueror of gloomy Night') in front of RMt before church-time. He writes interestingly to Wrangham on *The White Doe of Rylstone*.
29 W sends three sonnets on Waterloo to John Scott, editor of *The Champion*. (During the month he finishes *A Letter to a Friend of Robert Burns*.)

22 February W acknowledges the receipt of J. Scott's *Paris Revisited*; he agrees with his estimate of Napoleon, but not with that of Wellington, who, he thinks, lacks magnanimity.

25 March W congratulates CW on his appointment to the rectorate of St Mary's, Lambeth, and also of Sundridge, Kent. RW is very ill. C. Lloyd is lodged in the Retreat at York, where he ought to have been sooner; one or two of his boys dine at RMt each Sunday. W objects to the ordination of a 'rank Methodist', W. Carus Wilson (original of Brocklehurst in *Jane Eyre*).

April
4 (Thurs) The Ws have received a letter from Jean-Baptiste and Caroline (Vallon) Baudouin; (their postponed marriage took place on 28 Feb). They have secured Ivy Cottage, on the main road below RMt, for Tillbrooke in the summer.
27 Godwin stays the night at RMt (and leaves with bitter feelings about W's political views).

May
Early in the month the Thanksgiving 'Ode' and related pieces, with recent sonnets, are published in such a form that they can in

future be bound with his collected *Poems. A Letter to a Friend of Robert Burns* appears about the same time.

11 (Sat) W is relieved that RW has executed his will. (RW has been in the Montagus' care, and W has written to Montagu and CW urging them to ensure that RW does all that is necessary on behalf of D and himself.) Montagu has some 'little affairs' to settle with him, W reminds him (*L3*, 311).

19 RW dies at CW's; (he is buried in Lambeth Church).

June (probably)   A letter to Mr Addison, formerly RW's partner, illustrates how much of W's time has been taken up as one of the trustees of RW's affairs.

June (mid)   MW goes with her brother John to stay with him at Stockton-on-Tees.

July (early)   W and Sara H spend three days viewing Mr Marshall's estates and manor at Scale Hill, with visits to Loweswater, Crummock, and Buttermere.

8 July   W leaves to join MW, intending to return with her via Bolton Abbey and caves in Yorkshire.

2 August   W sends advice to HCR on the best way of seeing the Lake District on his way north.

September
 5 (Thurs) HCR arrives in the morning; at RMt again in the evening, he meets Mr Tillbrooke.

13 In the course of a long excursion, in poor weather, during which W and Thomas Hutton (a Penrith solicitor, trustee with W and CW of RW's estate) attend auctions of the latter's land at or near Cockermouth and Ravenglass, W takes HCR from Cockermouth to Ennerdale, and over Cold Fell (where he tells HCR the circumstances leading to his father's death) to Calder Abbey.

23 For HCR he writes a request to the Revd W. Carr that he show HCR places of interest around Bolton Abbey.

24 From Ambleside HCR calls on W, who accompanies him over Nab Scar on his way to De Quincey's for dinner; afterwards De Q brings him back to RMt, where HCR has tea with the

Ws and Sara H, and 'four hours of conversation as varied and delightful' as he ever enjoyed. He takes his leave of the Ws that evening.

October
4   (Fri) W returns to RMt, after spending some time with the Beaumonts at Keswick.
5   He asks Hutton to let him know if MW can help RW's widow at Sockbridge while her son is ill.
21 He writes to Hutton from Lord Lonsdale's, at Whitehaven.
28 The Beaumonts leave RMt for Coleorton.

November
25 (Mon) As there has been much business with sales of RW's land to settle his affairs, Hutton has expressed a wish to resign his trusteeship. W recommends him to ask Thomas Wilkinson to undertake the office.
28 He informs Keats's friend John Hamilton Reynolds that his poem (submitted for W's criticism) would be better if it were shorter, asking him to accept copies of his Thanksgiving 'Ode' and *Letter* on Burns (for which he sends an order to Longman), and to remind his publishers to send copies of both (ten and a hundred respectively, as requested on 31 Oct) to an Edinburgh bookseller.

December   Correspondence with Hutton on sales continues, and W recommends Captain W of Penrith for the trusteeship. (He has not written much poetry during 1816.)

1817

January   After hearing that Hall, his Kirkby Lonsdale Sub-distributor, has been arrested for debt, and discovering that he cannot pay him £300, W procures a Bill of Sale and raises the money from Hall's effects. He is afraid that if Hall is declared a bankrupt he may have to find £100 himself to pay what is due to the Stamp Office.

20 January   W acknowledges the honour done to him by Haydon in wishing to include his head in the picture of Christ's entry into

Jerusalem. H has sent him a copy of the sonnet 'Great spirits now on earth are sojourning', in which Keats pays high tribute to W, who would like to visit London in the spring but dreads the expense. (Until RW's affairs are settled, he will have little to spare, and the education of his children grows more costly.)

February   Much of W's time is taken up in consultations with Thomas Hutton on RW's affairs.

15 February   D returns, after being with the Rawsons at Halifax since October, the last fortnight with Mrs Cookson at Kendal. De Q marries Margaret Simpson.

2 March   Writing to Catherine Clarkson (who has been living more than a year at Playford Hall, with its farm of 400–500 acres, near Ipswich), D is as usual very informative about the children: Willy, still treated by his father as if he were a baby, now rides to school on an ass; John is greatly improved; Dora is becoming fond of the piano, but takes no pride in Latin. W and D are most anxious about the settlement of RW's affairs; if there is a Chancery suit, D is certain she will inherit nothing from her father's property. The Kirkby Lonsdale stamp debt has been settled without loss to W.

5 April   W receives acknowledgment of the £35 he has sent the Baudouins; (he makes an annual payment, usually £30), until 1834, when HCR arranges a final settlement of £400 on Caroline).

May   W writes 'Ode to Lycoris'. He has a strong desire to accompany Southey on the Continent, but RW's affairs detain him.

23 June   With MW, W climbs Helvellyn for the second time in three weeks, the first with D after a few days with the Marshalls at Hallsteads. In two or three weeks he will be on a visit near Calder Abbey (HCR's favourite), he informs HCR, who had been disappointed with Furness Abbey after leaving RMt.

August   W sits for his picture by Richard Carruthers, while Sara and Joanna H are enjoying themselves with friends on Windermere. (During the summer W writes 'Composed upon an Evening of Extraordinary Splendour and Beauty'.)

19 September He tells Gillies that he has skimmed parts of STC's recently published *Biographia Literaria*. In a few days he intends to leave for at least a fortnight, first with Lord Lonsdale at Lowther Castle, then with the Marshalls at Hallsteads.

13 October The Ws return to RMt. D and MW have spent two days with Captain W and his wife (m. 16 Sep 1816) at Eusemere, while W was at Yanwath with Wilkinson. Southey has returned from France, where he saw Caroline (the image of John W), her mother, husband, and daughter Dorothée. W has written a few short poems, and intends to work hard on *The Recluse* in the winter.

November (late) W and MW travel to London with Sara H, his main objective to discuss the settlement of RW's affairs with CW, the third trustee. The mail being full, W travels on the outside of the coach, and finds Lord Lonsdale's boots a protection from the cold night air.

December
They stay with CW at Lambeth and Sundridge, with Tom Monkhouse in Queen Street, and in lodgings (48 Mortimer Street).

2 (Tues) As he sits for Haydon, W reads aloud from Milton, in addition to 'Tintern Abbey' and 'The Happy Warrior'; (H began the inclusion of W's head in his 'Christ's Entry' on 22 Dec).

27 W is at Lamb's when HCR arrives; later he dines at Monkhouse's, where he meets Tillbrooke and STC. HCR observes that he is not cordially responsive to the latter. (When she hears of this Mrs Clarkson attributes it to being in the company of several people; W, however, was still dissatisfied with his treatment in *Biographia Literaria*.)

28 At Haydon's W meets Keats. Lamb, excited by drink, makes fun of Mr Kingston, Comptroller of Stamps, who had come to meet W.

30 W and STC attend a large dinner-party at the Lambs'; HCR notices that while STC philosophizes in a rambling way to his audience, W spends most of the time in conversation with Thomas Noon Talfourd.

1818

January

3 (Sat) Keats calls on W, and is surprised to find him in a stiff collar before calling on Mr Kingston. In the evening Mr Carruthers brings his almost completed portrait of W for inspection.

4 Haydon, the young painter Nash, STC's nephew John, and Mr Alsager (one of Lamb's friends, and a visitor to RMt the previous summer) are the Ws' dinner-guests; Charles and Mary Lamb and their friend Thomas Manning are expected in the evening.

5 Keats dines with the Ws in Mortimer Street. (Perhaps it is on this occasion that he finds MW beautiful and Sara H enchanting; cf. his letter to Haydon of 23 Mar 1818.)

6 The Ws and Sara H dine at Samuel Rogers'.

15 Haydon does a chalk-drawing of W's head for MW. She and W set off to visit the Cooksons at Windsor.

19 One of the last things W does before leaving London is to visit Lord Lowther, the elder of the two sons of Lord Lonsdale who are contesting the Westmorland seats; Lord Lowther's opponent is the formidable Henry Brougham. The Ws leave for Coleorton (where they will stay for a few days on their way home; Lady Beaumont likes MW to read to her). Sara H has already gone to the Clarksons at Playford Hall.

26 W remains at Kendal, waiting for the parcel of Stamp Office accounts, sent on from his office, to be found by the Kendal coach proprietor. His interests are primarily political, however; he spends most of his time assessing the position for Lord Lonsdale after the adoption of Brougham as parliamentary candidate. The 1818 Westmorland election, on which he has been in regular correspondence with Lord Lonsdale since he left Rydal in November, has become his major preoccupation. So fearful is he of the effect of demagogy on the uneducated populace, after the example of the French Revolution, that he is to remain a staunch Tory, devoting far more time and thought towards ensuring a steady, enlightened advance to democracy than to any other issue.

31 W and MW reach RMt about 9 p.m.

February

2   (Mon) After receiving an inquiry about his accounts from the Stamp Office, W sends Mr Kingston an explanation of the delay.

14   He has written two addresses to the freeholders (the only people allowed to vote at the time); part of the first appears in *The Kendal Chronicle*.

24   HCR hears part of Hazlitt's lecture on W; it is so contemptuous of his *Letter to a Friend of Robert Burns* that HCR loses his temper.

28   Part of the second address is issued as a broadsheet. (W's correspondence for several weeks is monopolized by electioneering business, communicated to Lord Lonsdale.)

March

7   (Sat) *The Carlisle Patriot* includes a reprint of the broadsheet.

23   Brougham's processional entry and speech at Kendal. D has come with Henry Hutchinson, and has a view from the window opposite that from which B addresses a huge crowd (not a gathering of freeholders). She makes a report for W (which he sends the next day to Lord Lonsdale); B, she writes, 'looked ready to lead a gang of Robespierrists set to pull down Lowther Castle and tear up the very trees that adorn it' (*L3*, 444). B, recognising that W has been his chief publicity antagonist, makes much of it allusively, though his remarks are lost on the crowd.

6 April   Revised and enlarged during March, W's two addresses are published as a pamphlet, for general circulation if the Lowthers do not object. Dora is now at Miss Dowling's school (Miss D having taken over Miss Fletcher's).

2 May   Should no one better qualified by found, W is ready, he informs Lord Lonsdale, to explain the proposed Bill on the administration of all public charities, when the new (pro-Lowther) newspaper appears. (Brougham had started investigations of abuses in the administration of educational charities.)

27 June   John Keats and Charles Brown, on their way to Scotland, call at RMt and find none of the Ws at home. (At Bowness they had heard that W was canvassing there a few days earlier. He is now at

Appleby for the polling-period. The two Lowthers were returned, but B promised to continue the fight, which he did unsuccessfully in 1820 and 1826.)

July The first editor of the new paper, *The Westmorland Gazette*, having proved unsatisfactory very quickly, De Quincey, most probably on W's recommendation, takes his place.

August
Early in the month W is prepared to purchase property which can be divided for sale into twelve freeholds to counteract the spread of the Brougham faction. (This Ivy How estate in Little Langdale – Iving Howe near Hacket – is subsequently bought and divided into eight lots, sold to relatives and friends, including CW, Hutchinsons, Tom and John Monkhouse, and Mr Gee, tenant of Tillbrooke's Ivy Cottage at Rydal.) Later in the month Lord Lowther spends three days at RMt.
23   (Sun) The Beaumonts, after two or three days at RMt, are at Keswick, and W, now with Calvert at Keswick, intends, weather permitting, to go fishing with Sir George at Wastdale on the 25th and 26th. D is left to make arrangements for the accommodation of William Wilberforce and his family at Rydal.
25   Following an advance party of seven servants with quantities of luggage, the Wilberforces arrive.

September
17   They have tea at RMt. The Revd John Fleming of Rayrigg, W's school-friend, is there with his son. Thomas Monkhouse is on holiday with the Ws. Dora, boarding with Miss Dowling, is homesick.

October
3   (Sat) After some time with the Marshalls at Hallsteads, the Beaumonts leave RMt with D for Keswick.
5   D leaves for Miss Barker's (now in Borrowdale). William Collins, R.A., after painting Sara Coleridge as 'The Highland Girl' at Keswick, and being a guest at RMt with the Beaumonts, leaves for the south.
6   The Beaumonts and the Wilberforces dine at Miss Barker's. W is otherwise engaged: he advises Lord Lowther on the

question of counteracting charges made by political opponents, with a reference to the controversy started by Brougham's pamphlet on the administration of charities at St Bees School, of which Lord Lonsdale is a benefactor.

7   As they are free and the weather is propitious, Miss Barker and D are taken to Seathwaite, where they set out with a guide to climb Esk Hause, then Scafell. (D's description of the climb and views is included in W's *Guide to the Lakes*.)

15 Wilberforce (a man of sweeter temper never lived, D wrote) leaves Rydal; (Mrs W and some of her family remain for more than another week).

November

15 (Sun) W buys the Ivy How estate.

28 Still keyed-up politically as a result of local agitations and the continued purchase of land to increase Broughamite freeholders, W believes that 'the feudal Power yet surviving in England is eminently serviceable in counteracting the popular propensities to reform which would unavoidably lead to revolution' (*L*3, 508). (Even so, in the latter part of the month, he has written more than half of the Duddon sonnets. On 12 Sep Haydon had written to him, 'I hope these abominable politics will no longer interfere with your poetry.')

December

1   (Tues) W falls asleep from sheer exhaustion; in addition to twenty-one Duddon sonnets, he has completed three from memories stirred by *Views of Caves near Ingleton, Gordale Scar, and Malham Cove in Yorkshire*, the work of the artist William Westall, who stays at RMt about this time.

One diversion from W's obsession with politics is his effort, later this month, to find a place for John at Charterhouse, the only *public* school W would consider, because it has adopted Dr Bell's system, which helps the slow learner. Shirts, and arrangements for J's journey, are made in confident expectation (but the application is unsuccessful on the grounds that he is above the entrance age of fourteen). John is most reluctant to go.

18 MW reports great improvements at Ivy Cottage, under the superintendence of Mr Gee.

1819

(During the winter of 1818–19 W revises 'Composed upon an Evening of Extraordinary Splendour and Beauty', 41–9, probably, as he admits in an undated letter to the painter, under the influence of Allston's 'Jacob's Dream'.)

7 January   A grand ball takes place at RMt.

12 January   D writes: Dr Bell called unexpectedly, and was detained for the ball. Mrs Coleridge is a guest, and those two sweet girls, her Sara and Edith Southey, create much merriment and piano-jingling with Dora. Mr Johnson from the Central School in London is expected on Saturday, when Mrs C leaves, 'but for two days only'. John is to stay at home a while and be taught solely by W, who has written nothing but 'some beautiful sonnets' recently.

(W sent copies of the three occasioned by Westall's 'views' to the artist, who, given W's permission 'to make what use of them he thought proper', sent them promptly to *Blackwood's Magazine*, where they appeared, to W's annoyance. Since its editor, his former friend Wilson, had appeared critical of *A Letter to a Friend of Robert Burns*, W had refused to take *Blackwood's*, though Wilson still admired his poetry.)

21 April   W declines to subscribe to a monument to Burns. His works are his best monument, and efforts would be better spent improving copyright, so that authors' children are not neglected. About this time Sara H returns, with Mary (Monkhouse) Hutchinson and her three children, to RMt.

c. 22 April   *Peter Bell*, dedicated to the Poet Laureate Robert Southey, is published. (As a result of J. H. Reynolds' 'antenatal' skit entitled 'Peter Bell, A Lyrical Ballad', the first edition is soon sold out. Incited by an abusive review in *The Literary Gazette*, the ladies at RMt persuade W to publish *The Waggoner* without delay.)

May (late)   *The Waggoner* is published, appropriately dedicated to Charles Lamb.

5 July   W attends the dinner at Ambleside celebrating the anniversary of Lord Lowther's election.

1 August   D writes: Mrs Luff has returned, and is looking for a cottage. W is at Lowther Castle; he has done nothing lately except a few sonnets, 'but these are exquisitely beautiful'. (Some of them may be for *The River Duddon*.) Tom and Mary H left a fortnight ago for Stockton.

2 September   W, Tom Monkhouse, Sara H, and John W fish at Coniston.

5 September   D writes: Sara has gone to church (Grasmere) on her pony with Tom M; the rest of the family on foot, with Lord Lowther (who arrived for dinner on Friday). Mr Gee is to dine with them that afternoon, and perhaps De Q, of whom little has been seen. Miss Barker is now living at Boulogne. Their only 'remarkable' visitors this summer have been William Howley, Bishop of London (the next Archbishop of Canterbury) and his lady.

September (later)   W writes the poem 'September, 1819' and its sequel 'Upon the Same Occasion'. He suffers from trachoma, as he had done earlier in the year. His pro-Lowther political vigilance continues unabated.

c. 20 October   T. Monkhouse takes Willy to London, where he will be under the care of the Revd W. Johnson, head of the Central School, until he is old enough for Charterhouse; he will spend Christmas at Sundridge.

November   De Q, who has neglected his responsibilities, is asked to resign the editorship of *The Westmorland Gazette*. W begins preparing a third volume of his miscellaneous poems for the press; 'he says he will never trouble himself with anything more but the *Recluse*' (*SHL*, 165).

21 December   W writes the sonnet 'Lady! I rifled a Parnassian Cave', to be sent with a selection of poems by Anne, Lady Winchilsea (1661–1720) and others, transcribed by Sara H, as a Christmas present to Lord Lonsdale's daughter Lady Mary Lowther (married to Lord Frederick Bentinck in 1820).

December (late)   The Christmas minstrels (and fond thoughts of Willy with CW at Sundridge) inspire the stanzas addressed to CW which ultimately become the dedication to *The River Duddon*.

1820

16 January   W is still unable to read or write by candlelight; he has received the chalk drawing of him made by Haydon in January 1818. He asks the latter how Keats is, 'a youth of promise too great for the sorry company he keeps' (*L3*, 578). (Later in the month, perhaps, writing to HCR, he expresses the view that Byron's *Don Juan*, the first two cantos of which were published in July 1819, will 'do more harm to the English character' than any other contemporary publication.)

February (early)   A majory preoccupation with W is the necessity of having both Lowther brothers stand for the new election. His family is disgusted that Brougham should send the advertisement of his candidature to *The Times* when the King is dying; it appears on the day of his death.

April   *The River Duddon* is published with other poems, including a shortened version of 'Vaudracour and Julia', and *A Topographical Description of the Country of the Lakes*. D goes to London, where, having lost most of her teeth, she has seven of her remaining eight extracted and a new set made. She stays at Lambeth (which she reaches late at night on the 14th). Her principal purpose is to supervise the proofs of a complete edition of W's poems in four volumes, excluding *The Excursion*; this edition appears at the beginning of September. (A second, relatively cheap, edition of *The Excursion* also appeared in 1820.)

April (late)   W's refusal to lend Benjamin Haydon money (he has made it a rule never to lend a *friend* any money which he cannot afford *to lose*) upsets Haydon, who indulges his abuse of W with Hazlitt, ready to add fuel to the flames.

5 May   W supports John Wilson's application for the Chair of Moral Philosophy at the University of Edinburgh. About this time the two Lowthers win the Westmorland seats again.

May (later)   The election over, his poems under way, his children all at boarding-schools or away from home – John now at Sedbergh – and their financial position more secure than before, the Ws can prepare for a foreign tour, which, though with no settled plan, they had hankered after since the end of the Napoleonic war. In drawing up their itinerary, they owe much to Richard Sharp.

22 May   W and MW set off for London. (They stay with Robert Jones at Souldern, and at Oxford: cf. 'A Parsonage in Oxfordshire' and the two sonnets 'Oxford, May 30, 1820'.)

June
2   (Fri) HCR finds W and MW at the Lambs'.
11   He breakfasts with them at Tom Monkhouse's, and discovers that W is ready to omit a number of passages in *Peter Bell* which have incurred censure.
23   D writes to Dora: W's eyes are a little better; he will see a physician again to see if travel will be injurious to them. He has heard that Maryport, Cockermouth, and Workington have been added to the area for which he is responsible as Stamp Distributor. CW, who has been ill, is staying with the Hoares at Hampstead; (if his health does not improve, D will give up the tour and stay with him at Sundridge).
24   HCR takes D to the exhibition of historic portraits at the British Gallery.

July
At the beginning of the month, or earlier, W sits to Francis Chantrey for the bust which Sir G. Beaumont has commissioned.
8   (Sat) The Ws attend the marriage of T. Monkhouse and Jane Horrocks of Preston.
10   They leave Lambeth for Dover, where they join Tom, his wife, her sister, and a maid, who are to accompany them. (Except for one sheet, which had not been received and was left for CW, all the proof-reading had been completed, MW probably being able to give D more assistance than W could.)
11   Walk to Dover Castle before breakfast; reach Calais at 1.30 p.m.
13   To Bruges, after travelling via Dunkirk.
14   After an early morning tour of the city, they leave Bruges with regret, by packet-boat to Ghent.
17   After sight-seeing in Ghent, and spending Sunday in Brussels, they leave for Waterloo, where they are guided over the battlefield by Lacoste, who had been Southey's escort there.
20   After visiting Namur, Liège, and Aix-la-Chapelle (Aachen),

where the cathedral supplies little Carlovingian romance, they reach Cologne, their centre for two days.

25 They arrive at Frankfurt, after following the Rhine valley via Coblenz and Bingen, and visiting Wiesbaden; (they travel to Darmstadt the next evening).

27 They follow the Neckar to Heidelberg, where they meet HCR's friend Mr Pickford and his family. (The next afternoon they leave for Karlsruhe. MW thought Heidelberg a delightful place, and wished she could return to it.)

29 At Rastatt the Monkhouses and D proceed to Baden-Baden, while W and MW go directly towards Schaffhausen.

August

1 (Tues) From Schaffhausen the whole party visits the Falls of the Rhine after dinner. Mrs Monkhouse is ill; D discovers she has lost her journal. (The next morning, before they leave for Zurich, it is brought by their guide, after being found by the path in the wood where they had sat above the cataract.)

5 After travelling from Zurich via Lenzburg and Herzogenbuchsee (where the Ws, having no room-accommodation for the night, are harried by fleas in their *voitures*, and, except for W, who is at last deep in sleep, witness a heavy and vividly memorable thunderstorm), they reach Berne.

7 From Berne to Thun, where in private grounds they see by chance an inscription to Aloys Reding, leader of the Swiss resistance against Bonaparte; (cf. 'Memorial, Near the Outlet of the Lake of Thun').

11 After visiting the Lake of Brienz during their stay at Interlaken, and climbing the Wengenalp from Lauterbrunnen to Grindelwald, they reach Meiringen (where they stay two nights).

14 A journey of two days, over the Brünig Pass past the Lungern and Sarnen lakes to Stans brings them to Engelberg with its yellow mountain, the Hill of Angels; they visit the abbey in the evening.

15 Via Stans, with Mount Pilatus looking stately ahead of them, to Lucerne.

16 They are joined by HCR. As Jane Monkhouse is unequal to long strenuous climbs, arrangements have been made for

her, Miss Horrocks, and their maid to travel to Geneva, where the rest of the party will meet them.

17   Sarnen, famous for its ancient open-air council (see W's 'Desultory Stanzas', added to his *Memorials of a Tour on the Continent, 1820*, at HCR's suggestion), lives up to its tradition for W when it upholds his complaint, supported by HCR, against a dishonest carman, and the cloaks and coats that have been withheld are restored that evening.

18   HCR introduces them to Mr and Mrs Grey, who congratulate them on the appointment of CW to the Mastership of Trinity College, Cambridge. D and MW, with the others, climb Rigi after being rowed to Küssnacht on a hot day. They stay at an inn on the top; during a thunderstorm that evening the lake is like a gulf of darkness 'except when blazed upon by the lightning'.

19   After breakfast, their youthful companions, a Scot and an American whom HCR had met on his way to Lucerne, leave them; (three days later the American, Mr Goddard, is drowned in a storm on Lake Zurich – cf. W's 'Elegiac Stanzas' in his *Memorials*). W, D, MW, Monkhouse, and HCR descend to the Chapel of Our Lady of the Snow, and walk on to Seewen (the next day to Brunnen).

21   From Brunnen, as they are rowed to the head of Lake Uri, they see the Chapel of William Tell; they walk to Altdorf, where they stay at an inn opposite the painted tower of Tell.

26   After proceeding up the Reuss valley, via Amsteg and Andermatt, crossing the St Gotthard Pass, and descending via Airolo and Bellinzona, they reach Locarno on Lake Maggiore.

27   By boat to Luino, which they reach at noon, after which they walk to Ponte Tresa, hiring a porter for their luggage. On Lake Lugano they coast the bare precipices of San Salvador, and reach Lugano at 8 p.m.

28   They climb San Salvador, from which they view 'enchanting scenes', including the Simplon mountains, Mont Blanc, the Monte Rosa like a bright pyramid high in the sky, the serpentine Po, and the towers of Milan. After descending, they have breakfast; then by boat to Porlezza and by cart to Menaggio on Lake Como.

September

1   (Fr) After four days on and around the lake (Cadenabbia their main centre), a visit to Pliny's villa, and one night at Como, they leave for Milan.

2   The climb to the cathedral roof, where D remains alone while the rest ascend the 'giddy central spire'. Afterwards, without respite, they visit the Brera to see 'the Emperor's Exhibition of pictures'.

3   After arriving too late to see a great military Mass in the Place d'Armes, where Napoleon used to review his troops, they see Leonardo da Vinci's mural of the Last Supper.

5   On their fourth day in Milan, Tom M and HCR decide to keep to the original plan, and start for Baveno, where the Ws will meet them after returning to Lake Como with two new companions (see *c.* 10 Jan 1826), who are on their way to Cadenabbia. The Ws regret not having seen Gravedona and the woods where W was lost thirty years earlier.

6   A long outing by boat on a dull wet day takes them as far as Colico near Fort Fuentes opposite Gravedona, where there is no time to call.

7   The Ws meet the Italian itinerant of *Memorials* as they leave Cadenabbia for Menaggio; they and their companions cross Lake Lugano on the afternoon of the eclipse.

8   From Lugano to Luino and across Lake Maggiore to Baveno, where Tom M and HCR have much to tell of their adventures.

10 At Domo d'Ossola the Ws decide to cross the Simplon Pass on foot, Tom and HCR and the luggage to go by the diligence. After seeing the Spittal where Jones and W had passed 'an awful night', they follow a road that makes the Gondo Gorge route easy. W is deeply moved when he catches sight of the track he and Jones had followed.

11 They cross the Simplon and meet HCR and Monkhouse on the road to Brig.

22 Following W's 1790 route in reverse, except for a memorable walk 'over the heights of the Gemmi' on the 13th (see 'Echo, upon the Gemmi'), the party has visited Chamonix and the Mer de Glace, the Castle of Chillon, and Lausanne, before reaching Geneva, where they find Jane, her sister, and the maidservant in good health.

25 They leave Geneva, where HCR had to listen to T. S. Mulock on the atheism and mystical nonsense of W's poetry; 'Muley

Moloch', W called him later, after the heroic character in *The Spectator*, paper 349. At Ferney the gentlemen of the party, unlike the ladies, are not disposed to enter Voltaire's house. They cross the Jura range and reach Morez.

28   They leave Dijon.

30   Having followed the Paris road via Sens, they reach Fontainebleau, where they explore the Palace and gardens.

October

1   (Sun) To their lodgings in Rue Charlot, the street in which the Baudouins live with Annette Vallon. W and D visit them.

The main purpose of W and D in Paris is to see Annette, Caroline, and her children. During their stay W is disappointed to find that the Temple, where Louis XVI and his family were imprisoned, and the meeting-place of the Jacobins, have disappeared. They visit Versailles. W meets Thomas Moore, the statesman George Canning, and Helen Maria Williams, whom he had hoped to meet in 1791. The statues and pictures of the Louvre move him far less than 'the wonders of the creation' in the Jardin des Plantes, with its live animals and its Museum of Natural History (*L3*, 642).

27   After arranging for their carriage to be sold there, the Ws leave Paris, their friends having departed earlier for England, HCR on the 9th, and the Monkhouses about a week later.

28   Reach Boulogne late, and stay at a comfortless inn, D being without Miss Barker's address.

November

7   (Tues) After ten days with Miss Barker at Boulogne, and a fruitless and dangerous attempt to sail in boisterous weather, they cross to Dover, where they stay the night.

8   They reach London very late, and do not find lodgings until the next morning. (For a full account of their tour, see D's *Journal of a Tour on the Continent, 1820*.)

18   HCR dines at Monkhouse's with the Ws, the Lambs, and John Kenyon. He notes an increase in W's mildness and tolerance, which 'must very much conciliate all who know him'.

20   He accompanies the Ws to the British Museum, for a hurried survey of antiquities, including the Elgin Marbles.

c. 23   At the end of two weeks in London, where W continues to sit for Chantrey, and there are meetings with Haydon, Samuel Rogers, and STC at Highgate, the Ws leave for Trinity Lodge, Cambridge.

December

6 (Wed) They depart for Coleorton, where they will stay with the Beaumonts. (D, satisfied that Derwent Coleridge is happy at St John's, has already gone to spend Christmas with her friend Catherine Clarkson at Playford Hall; Willy is to come from London to stay with them, and she intends to return to RMt in the New Year before John returns to Sedbergh.)

c. 12 On his way back from Scotland, Haydon is disappointed not to find W at RMt.

20 Leaving Coleorton, the Ws expect to be home on the 23rd. (A sonnet – or three – on King's College Chapel, written at Cambridge, and talks with Beaumont, arising from his proposed new church, prove to be the inception of *Ecclesiastical Sonnets*, 1822; cf. III, xliii–v and xxxix in this series.)

1821

9 January W and MW attend the funeral at Millom of his cousin John Myers (his contemporary at St John's College, Cambridge), and return by the Duddon, W's favourite river.

January (later) He has been on business at Appleby, and has to travel several miles in the Carlisle direction, with beautiful views of the Eden valley and river often in view, when suddenly, near Glassonby, he sees for the first time the ancient circle of Long Meg and her daughters (cf. W's note on his sonnet 'A weight of awe . . .').

February

5 (Mon) W thanks John Kenyon for sending him an elegant pair of eyeshades.

7 He has been obliged to displace someone recommended by Viscount Lowther for the Sub-distributorship at Appleby. On his way there, Mr Gee had accompanied him as far as Lowther, where they had been hospitably entertained by the rector Dr Satterthwaite.

18 De Quincey is still living at Blakeney's house Fox Ghyll, and MW wonders whether Tom Monkhouse would be interested in it if De Q gives it up in the summer.

March

16 (Fri) W returns from the sale of John Myers' furniture, cattle, etc.

27 He is very busy, D writes (doing historical research as he composes his long chronological series *Ecclesiastical Sonnets*), 'though he has not looked at the Recluse or the poem on his own life; and this disturbs us'. How different from Southey, whose will does govern his labours, she reflects. Willy is at Charterhouse. Mary has almost finished her journal of their European tour; D is making slower progress, having difficulty in communicating the effect of varied Swiss scenery on her feelings.

23 May Sara H, who had left Rydal early in February (before D's return from Cambridge) to stay with her brother John at Stockton-on-Tees, and has spent some time with her cousin at Harrogate, comes back sooner than originally planned, to see Willy before his return to Charterhouse, from which he had been removed by Mr Johnson at the end of March because of an outbreak of scarlet fever.

3 June W is still working on *Ecclesiastical Sonnets*, and D, on her journal of their continental tour.

23 July As a result of overworking in the spring, W is suffering from his old eye-complaint. With Edward Quillinan, who had come to Rydal in the spring, and lives by the Rothay river (after which his second daughter is to be named), he has discussed the possibility of touring in Ireland.

August

23 (Thurs) W requests Sir Walter Scott to receive HCR, who is touring in Scotland.

24 John Kenyon and his brother, who are staying at Ambleside, join the Ws and the Robinsons of York on Grasmere island; (Mrs R, W's cousin, is the widow of Admiral Hugh Robinson, d. 1802).

25 D has finished her journal. Mrs RW, who is very lame, and

her son, who speaks a Cumbrian dialect which D finds most barbarous, have stayed five weeks at RMt. Mr Quillinan and his wife, a daughter of Sir Egerton Brydges, are most amiable.

September

3 (Mon) W writes to Walter Savage Landor, thanking him for a present of his Latin poems, and showing familiarity with a number of Latin poems by English writers. (Landor admires W's poetry, and they continue to correspond, though they do not meet until 1832.)

12 W's old friend James Losh calls, and, being of opposite persuasions, they both keep off politics.

October

Early this month, after four days at Ambleside and RMt, on his way from Scotland, HCR is given a letter by W, asking Chantrey to make a cast of his bust for HCR.

16 (Tues) W thanks Lord and Lady Lonsdale for their efforts to help him financially by having William placed on the Charterhouse 'foundation'. (For this W has enlisted Viscount Lowther's aid since the early summer; Willy's withdrawal from the school in 1822 nullifies all these exertions.)

24 W leaves with MW for a week at Keswick after spending 'three weeks of labour in poetry' (*L4*, 89). His eyes have improved, but he cannot read by candlelight.

November

3 (Sat) Mrs Quillinan having been taken for mental treatment at Lancaster, consequent on the birth of her daughter Rotha in September, W sets out with her anxious husband for a Yorkshire tour of a week or so. (They visit John at Sedbergh, caves, Wensleydale, Middleham Castle, Jervaulx Abbey, Ripon, Fountains Abbey, Knaresborough, and York.)

24 W has turned from his sonnets to the writing of poems commemorative of his 1820 tour. (Initially a few were intended as companion pieces for D's journal, but this design was outgrown.)

December

4 (Tues) W writes to James Losh, arguing his political

consistency (an important statement), and giving reasons for his aversion to further concessions to the Catholics.

26   A ball at Miss Dowling's, in honour of Dora and Miss Harden, who are leaving school; Miss W and Mr H lead off, followed by Miss H and W. (The ball lasts until four o'clock the next morning.)

28   The 1820 tour has continued to be the subject of W's versifying.

1822

January   As Willy has made no progress at Charterhouse, W has decided to remove him in three months and send him to another school. Poems for *Memorials of a Tour on the Continent, 1820*, including 'To Enterprise', have been given priority; by the end of the month they have been sent to London for publication by Longman.

February
Ecclesiastical Sonnets follow. (Both publications are out in a few weeks.) W's trachoma has been aggravated by pressure of work.

20   He writes to Charles Lloyd at Kensington: he has not read his book on Pope's character, and reproves him for the misrepresentation which Hazlitt had seized to contrast the early democratic W with the friend of Lord Lowther (in *The London Magazine*, Nov 1821; cf. MW on the subject in Mary E. Burton's edition of her letters, Oxford, 1958, pp. 83–4).

March   Mrs Quillinan has recovered, and is reunited with Edward at Rydal; they move into Ivy cottage (the Gees having moved to Keswick).

April
13   (Sat) HCR reads extracts from W's *Memorials* to the Flaxmans.

16   *A Description of the Scenery of the Lakes*, with additions, including a contrast between Lake District scenery and that of Switzerland, is in the press, the first separate edition of this work. (It was published in a revised and enlarged form in 1823; the final text of *Guide to the Lakes* appeared in 1835. An 1842 edition included three geological letters from Professor Adam Sedgwick; they were increased to five in the 1853 edition.)

19 W writes to Viscount Lowther, asking if he knows anyone who needs a land agent: Tom H has lost most of his £14,000 while at Hindwell, where he has made large improvements, while the owner refused to lower the rent or relinquish the lease. (About this time Tom Monkhouse arrives with his family, after renting a house at Rydal for the spring.)

May

 3 (Fri) W complains to Lady Fleming about the hardships endured at RMt from the leaking roof, and urges the advantage of raising the walls, as her agent had recommended, when re-roofing.
25 Death of Mrs Quillinan. She had been severely burned, after her clothes had accidentally caught fire. Thinking she had recovered, her husband had gone to London on business, leaving her in the care of D, who nurses her to the end. MW is with W at Lowther (see next entry).
27 The Clarksons, after several entreaties, come to the Lake District again, and arrive at RMt while W is still at Lowther rectory with his friend Dr Satterthwaite, after sustaining a wound in the head when thrown from his horse as he was attemping to remount on his way to Haweswater with Tom Monkhouse.

June

 4 (Tues) W, MW, and Dora return from Lowther.
11 The Clarksons leave for Scotland.
12 W acknowledges the gift of Allan Cunningham's book of poems. Mr C (Chantrey's manager and secretary) must tell Mr Chantrey that Mrs W and her family like the bust of W more and more as it becomes familiar; Chantrey had sent MW a cast as a present in February). W's view is that it is of little value as a likeness but praiseworthy as a work of art. Edward Quillinan leaves Rydal with his children for Kent (where he leaves them in July to tour the Continent).
27 Willy returns from Charterhouse looking very ill; (eventually he is sent to Mr Dawes's school, where he is taught by Hartley Coleridge).

18 July   Hope in William's recovery has returned in the last three days, much to his father's relief.

6 August D writes: Willy has now recovered; the inflammation never wholly leaves W's eyes; CW and his three boys are delighted with Ivy Cottage, where they are staying; Dora returns with aunt Joanna from Coniston tomorrow; Robert Jones is to spend three weeks at RMt. Among their visitors have been Southey and Colonel Lowther. John, instead of going to college, is to return to Sedbergh for a year; he is one of a company of ten 'mountaineers' who are to row on Windermere against ten 'Cantabs', their challengers, now living at Ambleside.

September
Another visitor this summer is David Laing, an Edinburgh antiquary and bookseller.
10 (Tues) MW's brother John and his two sons arrive and lodge three nights at Ivy Cottage.
12 Sara H reports that Willy is a good boy, and quite attentive to his tutor John Carter.
13 She returns with her brother John and his two sons, taking Dora, and her harp, to Stockton. D and Joanna set off for Scotland (intending an absence of two weeks, which is prolonged to seven, mainly owing to Joanna's treatment for lumbago at Edinburgh). W accompanies them over Kirkstone, on his way to Lowther.
16 From Lowther Castle he writes to Samuel Rogers on his offer to promote the publication of D's *Recollections of a Tour made in Scotland*; she would like to raise money for another visit to Switzerland and Italy.

3 October W consults Richard Sharp on the advisability of selling his certificate for £2000 in French funds, which he had bought in February 1820 after consulting Lord Lowther. (Sharp's reply gives him more confidence in them, but W instructs that the certificate be left with him, to sell or not to sell, as he thinks fit.)

November
3 (Sun) Willy is ill again, and parental anxiety for his life is renewed.
12 Despite Sharp's reluctance to accept responsibility, W would like him to make the same decision for his French investment as Sharp does over his own.
13 D writes to Mary Laing, to express thanks to **her and her**

family for their many kindnesses to her and Joanna in Edinburgh; for W, who cannot write by candlelight, she writes a note to Mary's brother David. Willy's illness preys so much on his mind that he cannot read Sir Walter Scott's *The Bride of Lammermoor*.

19 D informs Quillinan, who is with his children at Lee Priory near Wingham, Kent, that Mr Blakeney has died, and his house Fox Ghyll, where De Q is 'shut up as usual', will be up for sale. Hartley Coleridge, the oddest creature imaginable, no taller than De Q, and with a raven-black beard, is now teaching at Mr Dawes's school.

December
Early this month W and D prepare a new edition of 'his little Book on the Lakes' (*L4*, 178).

18 (Wed) W writes to John Keble, Fellow of Oriel, on the admission of John, who will be twenty next June, to Oxford University, his mathematics not being equal, W fears, to the Cambridge curriculum.

19 Sara H returns from Stockton with Dora, whose health is much improved.

21 W has just composed (D writes) a poem (revised in Jan) on the foundation of the church at Rydal which Lady Fleming has decided to build.

1823

February
17 (Mon) W thanks Keble for helpful advice, and thinks that Augustus Hare of New College, whom he had met in the summer, might be interested in John's admission to Oxford.

18 W and MW leave Rydal for Coleorton (with Sara H, who is travelling directly to London) and a tour in the Netherlands.

March
5 (Wed) W writes the second of his two letters to John Keble from Coleorton Hall. The choice for John is between Exeter College and New College; W, hearing that the latter is for Winchester men, wishes he had not considered it.

c. 21 After being reassured by a letter from Hare, and meeting

John at Birmingham, the Ws are at Oxford, where J matriculates for New College. W probably meets Keble, as he had hoped.

c. 22   At Tom Monkhouse's, in Gloucester Place, he and MW rejoin Sara H, from whom they had parted at Derby on their way to the Beaumonts'.

April
1   (Tues) W and MW dine at Samuel Rogers', where they meet Sharp, Hallam (the historian), Cary (translator of Dante), and Thomas Moore.
2   At Beaumont's they see his recently acquired Michelangelo fragment, a sculpture of the Holy Family in haut and bas relief.
4   At Monkhouse's W gives a dinner for STC, Rogers, Moore, the Lambs, and HCR. ('I dined in Parnassus', Lamb wrote the next day: 'half the Poetry of England constellated and clustered in Gloster Place'; STC 'in his finest vein of talk, had all the talk . . . .')
5   W and STC attend Charles Aders' musical party in Euston Square, W silent, with his face covered; some think he is asleep.
8   W, MW, and Sara H leave London to stay with Quillinan at Lee Priory, his brother-in-law's neo-Gothic home.

16 May   After delaying their tour some two or three weeks because of W's trachoma, his 'vernal enemy', he and MW leave for Dover. (Their intended route is: Ostend–Ghent–Antwerp–Breda–Utrecht–Amsterdam via Haarlem, the Hague, and Leiden to Rotterdam, then Antwerp, returning either directly to Ostend via Ghent or by Mechlin, Brussels, Lille, and Ypres to Calais.)

June
11   (Wed) Return to England. (W's eye-trouble, and his aversion to society on that account had been a crippling factor, MW wrote.)
17   They reach London, where they stay with Lamb's friend Talfourd.
c. 23   After a short stay at Cambridge, they reach Harrogate, where Dora has been staying for the sake of her health.

July

14 (Mon) Mary Laing leaves RMt, after staying with D from Thursday evening.

15 After leaving Harrogate at 6 a.m. the previous day, and spending two hours at Bolton Abbey, W and MW reach home at 1.45 a.m., rousing D by throwing gravel up to her window. The doctor has advised Dora to stay a fortnight longer at Harrogate.

16 After dinner W goes to Ulverston via Hawkshead on Distributorship business (returning the next day along Coniston Water).

31 August D writes: Dora has been acting as a temporary teacher at Miss Dowling's; William is back at school (with Mr Dawes), where Hartley Coleridge 'does wonders'. T. Monkhouse (who is expected for the Penrith races) is negotiating for Fox Ghyll. Mr Tillbrooke has 'been with us for a few days', and talks of coming to Ivy Cottage when Quillinan's lease expires. The opium-eater De Quincey must have given up opium; he has returned from London looking 'quite well'. RMt had a large party last Sunday. Edith Southey has spent a week with them, and Sara Coleridge talks of riding over with Mary, William Calvert's daughter and Dora's school-friend, when Dora is free.

October

9 (Thurs) John departs, to begin his studies at Oxford.

21 Writing to a young unknown correspondent who wishes to be a poet, W says that it was not until his twenty-eighth year that he 'could compose verses which were not in point of workmanship very deficient and faulty' (*L4*, 224).

About this time, after reading the first volume of Southey's *History of the Peninsular War*, he informs the author that, in dealing with the Convention of Cintra, he has 'tickled with a feather' where he should have 'branded with a red-hot iron'. The people of Spain and Portugal had been the first to show the only way by which oppressive tyranny could be overthrown.

November

Early in the month W is at Lowther Castle.

9   (Sun) Back at RMt (see next entry), he has just completed a
    translation of Book I of the *Aeneid*.
12 D tells Mrs Clarkson that W, MW, and Dora had enjoyed the
    races and ball at Penrith – the first public ball to which Dora
    had been taken. Willy had accompanied her to Hallsteads,
    where she had met her cousin Mrs Rawson (formerly
    Elizabeth Threlkeld); he attended the Penrith races one day.
    D had visited Mrs RW at Penrith, and breakfasted with Dr
    Satterthwaite at Lowther, where W joined her from Lowther
    Castle. Proceeding to Haweswater in Lord Lonsdale's gig,
    they had then walked over the fell to Kentmere, across to
    Troutbeck, and on to Low Wood and home, which they
    reached towards 10 p.m. D was not a bit tired the next day.
    She reminds Catherine that the first time she saw Haweswater
    was from her home, when she went with the Clarksons from
    Eusemere to Mardale.

December
Early this month W has made much progress in translating Book II
of the *Aeneid*.
20 (Sat) Dora goes with Jane Dowling to join Sara H and Edith
    Southey at the Monkhouses' until the New year; afterwards
    Edith is to accompany her to Hendon, where she will stay
    (most probably with the Lockiers, friends of the Gees) until
    she can see London in the spring.
26 As the only Byron he has is a copy of *Lara*, given by Samuel
    Rogers, W cannot help Henry Taylor (dramatist and poet of
    the future) by quoting passages indicating where Byron is
    indebted to him (W); he refers to the third book of *Childe
    Harold* and his 'blank verse poem on the river Wye', and says
    that Mrs W had been disgusted with the plagiarisms from
    STC in one of Lord Byron's narrative poems.

1824

January
21 (Wed) To Walter Savage Landor W writes: 'in poetry it is the
    imaginative only, viz., that which is conversant [with] or
    turns upon infinity, that powerfully affects me'. In response
    to L's offer of a beautiful copy of Dante, he says that much

the *grandest* book on his shelves is Dante in the Parma folio of 1795, a gift from John Kenyon.

24 W conveys to James Montgomery, poet and editor of *The Sheffield Iris*, his regret that, after waiting to fall 'into a track that would have led to something', he has been unable to contribute to his publication on behalf of boy chimney-sweepers.

February

1 (Sun) He requests Allan Cunningham to ensure that the two casts of his Chantrey bust are sent off, one to Augustus Hare (John's tutor at New College), the other to STC's nephew Edward.

5 W replies to comments by Lord Lonsdale on his translation of the first two books of the *Aeneid*. Had he taken the liberty enjoyed by Dryden, especially in using his own images, he could have translated nine books with the labour that three had cost him.

17 W and D are at Coleorton. (Their visit had been postponed four weeks, and D's letter of 23 Mar does not suggest they kept to their original plan of staying *en route* with the Horrocks at Preston and the Crumps at Liverpool.)

March

19 (Fri) After a month with the Beaumonts, and a visit to John at Oxford, W and D join Dora at the Monkhouses' (67 Gloucester Place), where they stay.

29 Thomas Monkhouse has been ill. The Ws are going with the Beaumonts to see David Wilkie's pictures. (On the 31st they visit Hendon.)

April

3 (Sat) STC 'and other Worthies' dine with the Ws at Gloucester Place. (It was on this occasion, it seems, that W gave STC his *Aeneid* translations. The comments he later received were quite discouraging; he was attempting the impossible, and something '*so* much below' his genius.)

16 D writes on a cold, wet, windy day (Good Friday): arrangements for Dora's visit to Wales (where Sara H is staying); visits made to the Diorama, the Mexican Curiosities, the Panorama of Pompeii, and with the Beaumonts to the

British Museum. Quillinan and Dora have persuaded W to visit Lee Priory, but he is despondent (he has a cold) and may change his mind.

17 On Monday W and D are to meet Mr Irving; they have heard him preach twice. They have seen the Lambs often; at the Beaumonts', Charles was charming. Mrs Luff has just arrived (she lives in Bruton Street, Berkeley Square); she wishes to return to the north.

23 The Ws leave for Lee Priory.

30 With happy memories of Lee, the nightingales, and Quillinan's two daughters Jemima and Rotha, they return to London; they dine with the Revd William Johnson and his wife at the rectory in Bread Street, and sleep at a coffee-house in St Paul's Churchyard (where *An Evening Walk* and *Descriptive Sketches* had been published).

May

1 (Sat) To Clapton, possibly to see CW and his friend the Revd H. H. Norris.

4 They leave for Trinity Lodge, Cambridge (where W hears the news of Byron's death at Missolonghi).

20 Plans are changed: instead of returning to London, with CW, to stay with the Monkhouses before travelling to Wales, Dora, not wishing to leave her father, begins her journey home with him.

June Soon after the first week of the month (if she kept to her plans) D begins her journey from Playford Hall to Rydal, with Mrs Luff and her three brightly coloured singing birds from Mauritius, via Cambridge, Coleorton, and Yorkshire (probably Leeds), at each of which they are to stay two nights, then Kendal (a one-night stay).

July Hartley Coleridge is staying at RMt, where Willy is continually ill. W takes him on a tour for his health, but they have to return on the fourth day, after calling at Cartmel, where it had been hoped that he and Mrs Luff (at RMt) would spend a fortnight at the spa. She hopes to purchase Fox Ghyll; the problem is when will De Quincey quit.

August

c. 25 (Wed) W, MW, and Dora leave for Wales.

27 By steamboat from Liverpool they sail close under Great
    Ormes Head to Bangor, where 'stupendous preparations' for
    Telford's suspension bridge over the Menai Strait are admired.
28 Caernarvon Castle is viewed with the Crumps of Liverpool;
    by boat in the evening over the lake to Llanberis.
29 Walk by the lake while Dora rests and sketches; on foot over
    Llanberis Pass to Capel Curig.
30 To the valley of the Conway, and down to Llanrwst, where
    by prearrangement they meet J. H. Hobart, Bishop of New
    York, who had already met W at Rydal.
31 At Llanrwst they are met by Robert Jones; they drive with
    him to the Conway Falls (and on subsequent days until they
    reach Devil's Bridge).

September
1   (Wed) To Glyn Mavyn (where Jones has a curacy, in addition
    to the one in Oxfordshire) and Corwen.
2   Down the Dee valley to Llangollen, where they call on the
    celebrated recluses, the two ladies of Llangollen.
3   W sends them the sonnet 'A Stream, to mingle with your
    favourite Dee'.
7   To Conway, where Dora is highly impressed by the castle,
    and on to Aber, after spending three days in the Vale of
    Clwyd with friends of Jones.
8   After walking up the Aber valley to the waterfall, they
    proceed via Bethesda to Capel Curig.
9   Down the valley of Nant Gwynant to Beddgelert, where they
    are surprised to meet Augustus Hare; the afternoon is spent
    in the Vale of Ffestiniog.
10 To Barmouth via the Dolgelly road.
11 After rowing up the estuary to Dolgelly, they proceed to Tal-
    y-llyn Lake under Cader Idris.
12 They attend a Welsh church service, then travel to
    Machynlleth.
13 To Aberystwyth, and up the Rheidol valley to Devil's Bridge.
14 They explore valleys and falls in the neighbourhood. W com-
    poses the sonnet 'To the Torrent at the Devil's Bridge' during
    a storm, while Dora attempts a sketch; the chasm reminds
    him of Viamala (through which the Rhine make its way high
    up in Switzerland), as he saw it with Jones in 1790 (cf.

Descriptive Sketches, 162–3). From Devil's Bridge Jones departs for home.

15 The Ws reach Hindwell, where they meet Sara H, and find Tom Monkhouse wasting away (with tuberculosis). Tom and Mary H are considering a move to Brinsop Court farm, six miles from Hereford.

27 W, MW writes, has been composing verses on Mrs Luff's birds ('The Contrast').

18 October   After about five weeks, mainly at Hindwell, including a period at Foxley with the Uvedale Prices, and another with the Beaumonts at the home of Mrs Fermor (Lady B's sister), Worcester (Mrs F is ill, and dies about the middle of December, leaving W £100 as a token of her regard for his poetry), the Ws leave for Coleorton. At Hindwell, where Tom M's illness could never be forgotten, W had been 'the life of our party – doing always his utmost to amuse and keep up our spirits – which he always does God bless him! when there is a real necessity for his exertions. He had enjoyed his tour in Wales very much' (*SHL*, 291).

November
13 (Sat) They reach RMt, after three weeks with the Beaumonts at Coleorton Hall.
16 W writes to Alaric Watts, editor of *The Leeds Intelligencer*, thanking him for the gift of his *Poetical Sketches*, a copy of which has arrived during his absence from home.
19 He thanks Thomas Brydges Barrett of Lee Priory for sending him two volumes of his father Sir Egerton Brydges' rare works.

December
11 (Sat) He thanks Landor for a copy of the first two volumes of *Imaginary Conversations*; of these dialogues, he prefers the classical.
13 D to HCR: 'My Brother has not yet looked at the Recluse; he seems to feel the task so weighty that he shrinks from beginning with it – yet knows that he has no time to loiter if another great work is to be accomplished by him.' He and Dora were with the Southeys at Keswick four days last week. John has just returned from Oxford; Willy's health is good, but he is not strong enough to be sent away to school. Sara H

has 'a melancholy office' helping to tend Tom Monkhouse at Torquay, to which he had gone with his wife and child two days before the Ws left Hindwell. (He seems to have spent those two days with his brother John at the Stow; cf. *SHL*, 290–1.)

(The most remarkable of W's poems in 1824, probably written towards the end of the year, are on MW: 'Let other bards of angels sing', 'How rich that forehead's calm expanse!', possibly 'What heavenly smiles!'. 'O dearer far than light and life are dear' has a moving biographical significance: when W and Mary left Tom M at Hindwell they feared they had seen him for the last time; W lacked the assurance that friends 'by death disjoined' would meet again, and hoped to find comfort in Mary's faith.)

1825

January
6 (Thurs) W writes to Charles Lloyd's father, a Birmingham banker, on investing £500 in one of the railway companies that are being formed.
21 He requests Rogers' advice on whether to ask better terms from Longman, or seek another publisher.

February
12 (Sat) The debate on the King's Speech makes W fear that the maintenance of Protestant ascendancy in Ireland is threatened. On this he writes at length to Lord Lonsdale.
13 D's letter of 14 November 1824 to HCR, requesting that he communicate with Mrs Blakeney on the sale of Fox Ghyll, must have produced the desired results quickly, for she now writes that Mrs Luff was in such haste to gain possession that she has had workmen there for three months. Unfortunately De Quincey is in London, and cannot be compelled to remove until October. Owing to Tom Monkhouse's illness D thinks it better to defer her holiday until the Hs have settled at Brinsop Court.
25 Further to 'Elegiac Stanzas' on Mrs Fermor, addressed to Sir G. Beaumont, W has written 'Inscription' (= 'Cenotaph') and 'A Flower Garden', which MW sends to Lady B; the second

poem is based on the latter's garden and that of Lady Caroline Price at Foxley.

26　Thomas Monkhouse dies at Clifton, which he has preferred to Torquay.

March

10　(Thurs) Southey has been staying at RMt since Monday.

23　Writing again to Rogers on the question of a new publisher, W gives the plan (to which he kept) for five volumes of his poems arranged according to subject, in addition to *The Excursion*. The death of Monkhouse and his eye-infection make him indisposed to visit London.

6 April　A letter to Jacob Fletcher, whose tragedies and manuscript of his tour in Scotland he has read, suggests that W had some interesting distinctions to draw between the sublime and the picturesque, as well as on Longinus's use of 'the sublime'; (he had written a fragment on 'The Sublime and the Beautiful').

May

2　(Mon) W receives a copy of the first volume of Maria Jane Jewsbury's *Phantasmagoria, or Sketches of Life and Literature*, which she has dedicated to him.

4　D writes: W's eyes are 'better than for years past'; Willy studies under John Carter; Mrs STC and Sara went home ten days ago, after a happy stay of three weeks and three days with the Ws.

23　Miss Jewsbury calls at RMt.

27　W congratulates Beaumont on the engagement of his cousin and heir to the daughter of William Howley, Bishop of London. He has never had a higher relish of nature than during the present spring. He is sure that 'the Religion of gratitude' cannot mislead; it leads to Hope, and Hope to Faith. 'I look abroad upon Nature, I think of the best part of our species, I lean upon my Friends, and I meditate upon the Scriptures, especially the Gospel of St John; and my creed rises up of itself with the ease of an exhalation, yet a Fabric of adamant.'

29　He and MW, D writes, have worked hard preparing *The Excursion* for a new edition, with considerable curtailment 'in *some* parts'. MW reports that Mrs Luff is spending her fortune on improvements at Fox Ghyll and on its furnishing.

June

11 (Sat) W congratulates Sir Robert Inglis on his protest against the third reading of the Roman Catholic Relief Bill.

13 In a letter to Sir Walter Scott on the question raised by D, whether they had seen Anna Seward at Lichfield (she had corresponded with Scott, and left him her poetry, which he had edited for publication in three volumes, 1810), W reveals that he is preparing Willy for admission to Oxford.

15 He tells Lord Lonsdale that the motivation for a non-denominational college in London is political; considers that the teaching of such subjects as literature, languages, law, political economy, and morals by lectures useless and absurd; and thinks there are too many doctors, and that children will become mean and unfeeling if parents are not able to pay for medical treatment.

2 July D tells HCR they are planning a whole winter in Italy and a whole summer in Switzerland and the Tyrol, hoping he will be one of their party. She thinks that, between them, they could write an original and profitable account of their travels.

July (early) W, MW, Dora, and Willy travel for a holiday at Kents Bank, Morecambe (not far from Cartmel), mainly for Dora's health. (Later they are joined by Maria Jewsbury, who writes to her friend Alaric Watts, now editor of *The Courier* in Manchester, wondering if their publishers, Hurst and Robinson, would be interested in W's plans for a new edition of his poems.)

August

5 (Fri) Sara H returns to RMt (see 7 Oct 1825), after an absence of more than two and a half years.

6 As John Murray has not replied for three months to his letter on the subject of publication, W informs him that he feels free to make arrangements elsewhere; (see 6 Jan 1827).

7 W leaves Kents Bank (where the others, including Mary Hutchinson, are engaged to stay until the 16th) for Lowther Castle.

13 He informs Mr Watts that he is unwilling to dispose of the

copyright of his works, but authorizes him to deal with Hurst and Robinson for a new edition of his poems in six volumes, including *The Excursion*.

20 W is a guest at Storrs Hall, Windermere, for the three days of festivities in honour of George Canning and Sir Walter Scott. Scott arrives from his tour in Ireland.

21 Dinner guests include his son-in-law J. G. Lockhart, Lockhart's *Blackwood* supporter Professor Wilson of Elleray, W, Lord and Lady Bentinck, Sir James Graham, besides prominent politicians and members of the legal profession.

22 A grand procession of boats on Windermere, followed by a regatta.

23 After breakfasting at RMt, Scott, Wilson, and Lockhart (whose smile haunted Dora like an evil thing), accompanied by W and Dora, visit Southey at Greta Hall. (The day of Canning's visit to RMt is uncertain.)

24 W and Dora conduct Scott and his party to Hallsteads, then to Lowther Castle.

September

5 W informs Watts that Hurst and Robinson's offer is declined. His publisher Longman has visited RMt, and will consider his terms with his partners. (W's terms are not accepted.)

October

7 W and Sara H leave with John W (he for Oxford, they for Coleorton Hall; they are to meet MW, and her sister-in-law Mrs Mary Hutchinson, also for Coleorton Hall, at Derby. Mrs H had been taken by Sara H to Harrogate for her health while renovations were taking place at Brinsop Court; she had then joined the Ws at Kents Bank; after a month at RMt she had been taken back by MW to Harrogate, where she recovered. Her husband Tom met her at the Beaumonts', and returned with her to Brinsop Court two days later.) The summer had set a record for visitors to RMt.

November

3 (Thurs) Hartley Coleridge has given up teaching, and writes for the press.

9 W, MW, and Sara H leave the Beaumonts'. W's eyes, one especially, have been inflamed throughout their stay; having

always found fresh air beneficial, he drives home alone in a pony-chaise, bought by Sara at Ashby-de-la-Zouch. MW and Sara travel by coach.

17 After three days with the Jewsburys at Manchester (two for W, who took a day longer to arrive), and calling on Mrs T. Monkhouse and her sister at Preston, W, MW, and Sara reach RMt.

23 W acknowledges the receipt of Sir W. Scott's bust, which he found on his return, and hopes that Cunningham has sent an equally fine one of him (W) to Sir Walter.

29 W's letter to Lord Lonsdale marks one of his attempts at this time to secure influence for the election of John to a Fellowship at Merton College, so that he can continue his studies; (before the end of the year W learns that J, as a member of the diocese of Chester, is ineligible).

December

9 (Fri) W has purchased Dora's Field (as it was later called) for the building of a new house should RMt be required for Lady Fleming's aunt.

23 When informed of this purchase, and of W's wish to remain at RMt, Lady Fleming had replied that her aunt would come in 1827. D wonders, in view of the building expense that may face them, whether Mr Marshall of Hallsteads would care to purchase W's Broad How estate at Patterdale.

31 The frost is sufficient for W and John to skate on the margin of Rydal Water.

1826

January

c. 10 (Tues) D learns from HCR that Mr Graham (one of their companions when she and W returned to Lake Como, and boated across Lake Lugano during the eclipse; cf. 5–7 Sep 1820) was not British but American, a convicted forger who had come to England, where, after serving as a gentleman's amanuensis, he had inherited a large sum of money, and become a law student in London. He had lost heavily at 'the gaming table' on the Continent. After editing *The Somerset Gazette*, he engaged in literary swindling (translating Goethe's

Memoirs from a French translation), which HCR exposed in *The Westminster Review*. He narrowly escaped the gallows by issuing a forged bill of exchange. (Soon after his return to America he was killed in a duel.)

17   In answer to one who has asked if he may propose to Dora, W advises, as he would anyone without prospect of professional advancement, that ladies with fortune are as easily won as those without, and are for the most part just as deserving.

19   In doubt about the future of Hurst and Robinson, W asks Watts (to whom he has already sent his first volume for a new edition of his poems) to suspend dealings on his behalf. (H and R were the London agents of Constable, Sir W. Scott's publisher, and it was already evident to those affected that these firms, and the publishing firm of Ballantyne, and Scott himself, were bankrupt.)

February
17   (Fri) D reaches Brinsop Court (where she remains for the greater part of the year).
20   Writing to D, on or before this date, HCR reports what Lamb has to say on the forthcoming edition and arrangement of W's poems: 'there is only one good order – And that is the order in which they were written – That is a history of the poet's mind.'

29 March   After a period at Brinsop Court, John W is spending the rest of his vacation at the Stow.

27 April   W discloses to HCR that he paid £300 for 'Dora's Field', and for this reason has held out for that sum for the republication of his poems. He is still waiting to hear further on this question from Alaric Watts.

May   W becomes busy helping the Lowthers a third time against Brougham for the forthcoming Westmorland election, in which the Catholic cause is to the fore. This is one reason why he cannot visit north Wales (he had thought of climbing Snowdon with D); another is the planning of the new house. Hartley Coleridge's conduct is a source of growing concern.

30 June   The Westmorland election ends, W having spent the latter part of the month at Appleby, observing developments and reporting to Lord Lonsdale. The result is another victory for the Lowther brothers.

25 July   W sends John Kenyon the poem 'Once I could hail (howe'er serene the sky)', part of which he has composed that morning. He acknowledges Basil Montagu's gift of the first four volumes of his edition of Bacon's works, which arrived during the election period; also, from the publisher, a copy of *Friendship's Offering*. He thinks the latter suitable for the sofa table; it serves the needs of the *fine* world, but he prefers something nearer common life.

August (early)   W, MW, and Dora are at Marston Moor (site of the Civil War battle, 1644), after visiting York.

23 August   Joanna and Henry Hutchinson have been six weeks at RMt, and have gone to the Isle of Man for the rest of the summer; (they stayed on for the winter). Local lodgings are full of 'Lakers'; (Mrs Luff at Fox Ghyll has the Farquhars; Sir Robert did not stay long, but Lady F and her son remained six weeks). W's eyes have been very bad since the election; he is now at Lowther.

September
10   (Sun) Sir George Beaumont, Samuel Rogers, and other visitors dine at RMt.
18   A huge picnic party in Easedale, but W is too busy 'among his verses' to join.
19   He is the guest of Southey at Greta Hall, where he meets Beaumont and Rogers again.
22   They visit Buttermere. (By this time W's eyes are much improved, as a result of the application of 'blue stone' or copper sulphate on the recommendation of a visitor, F. M. Reynolds, editor of *The Keepsake*, a Christmas annual.)
29   W joins Rogers and Beaumont at Patterdale (probably Hallsteads), and accompanies them to Lowther Castle, where, with Southey, they are to spend a few days. (Perhaps the first three discussed the poetic possibilities of a story connected with Lyulph's Tower; cf. W's 'The Somnambulist'.)

5 October   HCR reaches Ambleside after a tour in Ireland. (Dora's illness prevents a visit to RMt, but he spends two days with W, who shows him Dora's Field, Mr Tillbrooke's 'knacky' cottage (Ivy Cottage, 'the Rydal wife-trap'), and a beautiful spring, a description of which is to introduce a portion of *The Recluse*. Edward Moxon is another visitor, probably about this time.)

October (most probably the third week)   Thomas Poole stays briefly with the Ws on his way home from Edinburgh. To give him a change from Somerset, W takes him for a fell walk over Loughrigg to the Langdale Pikes and back via Grasmere.

4 November   Return of D after an absence of nearly ten months; she had left Brinsop Court early in September, stayed a week in Worcester, another week at Leamington, more than a month with the Beaumonts at Coleorton Hall, and two days in Liverpool.

December
   4   (Mon) W offers his poems again to John Murray, on the terms M proposed in 1825.
 c. 7   W writes to Edward Moxon, thanking him for the gift of his 'little volume' *The Prospect and other Poems*. He thinks he has unusual sensibility, and therefore advises him to seek independence by staying in business (he is with Longman's): he should not pursue the Muses but let them pursue him.
  18   John W takes his degree; his tutor has written expressing regret that illness in the summer has made it impossible for John to take the honours examination. Having received no reply from Murray, W proposes to write to Longman on the publication of his poems; he has composed some very good sonnets lately, D writes, but has not brought *The Recluse* 'from his hiding-place'.

1827

January
   6   (Sat) W and John are at Sedbergh, at the invitation of J's schoolmasters. The same terms for publication that Rogers made with Murray in the spring of 1825 have been accepted by Longman, viz. W to pay two-thirds of the costs and

receive two-thirds of the profit. (W's first volume to Longman's had been sent on the 2nd.)
12   W invites Rogers to support the election of J. Kenyon to the Athenaeum. (D has already written to HCR, one of its first members, to the same end. Their efforts are successful.)
15   W and MW are busy preparing further copy for the publishers. The agreement is for a five-volume edition, the fifth being *The Excursion*.
25   John Murray tells HCR that he has been 'shamefully inattentive' to W's proposal, and is ready to publish 'on his own terms'.
26   John, now preparing to take Orders, returns to Oxford for a brief period.

February
6   (Tues) Sir George Beaumont's picture of 'The Thorn' is sent by D for W, with B's approval, to Mary Laing for exhibition in Edinburgh.
7   Sir George dies suddenly; (he leaves W £100 and a life annuity of the same amount).

March
5   (Mon) Edith Southey leaves, after helping to nurse her friend Dora for two months. (A few days later W has completed reading the second volume of Southey's *History of the Peninsular War*. It has given him great pleasure, but he cannot agree on one point: Napoleon would not have remained master of Europe but for Wellington, for tyranny works its own destruction.)
c. 10   Rydal Water has been frozen over, and W has enjoyed skating on it with William.

12 April   W acknowledges receipt of the first two numbers of *The Amulet, A Christian and Literary Remembrancer*.

May
2   (Wed) He refuses to contribute to the above. If he could have made an exception to his general rule not to appear in periodicals, it must have been *The Literary Souvenir* (edited by Alaric Watts, to whom he is indebted).
10   Copies of the new edition of his poems arrive from Longman.

21 Discussing Canning's refusal to serve in an anti-Catholic Cabinet, W tells Watts that he has a high personal regard for Canning, and will always honour him for being one of the principal agents in keeping the British army in the Peninsula against Napoleon, when the Whigs were clamouring for its recall.

30 W takes Dora to recuperate at Harrogate, where they have Sara H and the Southeys for company.

June

16 (Sat) On returning home, W finds a copy of *The Desolation of Eyam and Other Poems* from William and Mary Howitt of Nottingham.

22 Accommodation is found at Bowness for CW's sons, who had all won university distinctions, John and Christopher at Trinity, Cambridge, and Charles at Christ Church, Oxford.

28 August Edward Quillinan has been at RMt a few days. Dora is to be taken south for the winter, first to Brinsop Court. Dr W's *distinguished* sons are at Bowness, reading with other students and their tutor. After only a short stay by Tillbrooke, C. J. Blomfield, Bishop of Chester, and his wife have been at Ivy Cottage three weeks; his sermons are appreciated in the neighbourhood.

September (early) In order to see her ailing aunt Elizabeth Monkhouse, MW goes to Brinsop Court with Dora much earlier than was expected. The next day, with John Monkhouse, whom they meet at Threlkeld, and two Americans, Harriet Douglas and her brother (whose main business is to seek out people of distinction, and get married), the Ws, Southeys, and the Bishop of Chester ascend Saddleback and dine by the tarn. Harriet is so bewitched with everything at RMt that she wishes to be one of the family. After her departure W writes her a letter of advice: not to make a hasty choice in marriage, too many being ready to take advantage of her fortune; to seek composure of mind and restraint in speech by reading, not for prattle but for contemplation; she needs to relax, to commune with her heart, and be still. After the departure of Monkhouse and the Southeys, one of Augustus Hare's brothers (probably Julius), 'the most learned Man in Europe and the most entertaining' (*SHL*, 352), arrives.

15 September William Rowan Hamilton, Professor of Astronomy at Trinity College, Dublin, calls with two friends; W gives him a letter of introduction to Southey. Their evening talk ends with a long midnight walk, with no companions but the stars and their 'burning thoughts and words'.

24 September W sends advice on Hamilton's verses, and on his sister's.

26 October He writes to MW and Dora from Lowther Castle, giving details of plans to meet the former at Lady Beaumont's, and referring to Mr Gee's death (in Somerset, of which county he had become Deputy Lieutenant).

November
2 (Fri) W and D take a morning walk on Loughrigg Fell. He delays his visit to Coleorton so that MW can meet Edward Quillinan in Herefordshire during the first or second week in November.
26 CW is expected in a few days at Coleorton Hall, where MW and W have been Lady B's guests since the 17th.
27 Writing to Rogers, W indicates what encouragement he gave when Sir George talked of bequeathing his pictures to the nation; he hopes Rogers will follow Lord Stafford's example of presenting a work of art to the British Gallery, so that in course of time a noble gallery will be produced; (here the National Gallery is adumbrated).
c. 30 As CW and his son Christopher have not been able to come, W and MW invite them to join them at Brinsop Court and with John Monkhouse, not far off on the Wye. W has supported a proposal for a statue to Wycliffe at Lutterworth. John W is looking for a curacy, has been offered Whitwick near Coleorton, but hopes for something better.

December (early) News of the death of Dr Satterthwaite makes W write to Lord Lonsdale, suggesting that a word with the new incumbent might open the way for John, who has been waiting nearly a year for an eligible place 'to be ordained to'.

11 December (Whether W and MW have kept to their plan of leaving Coleorton on the 8th – with two days to follow in

Birmingham, two at Worcester with Mrs Willes, Lady B's cousin, and a day at Malvern, should the ground be free from snow – is not certain.) Hearing in Birmingham that Alexander Blair is a candidate for the Professorship of English Literature at London University, W, who remembers discussing the principles of taste and the merits of various authors with him years earlier as they rambled by the Trent, writes, wishing him success; (cf. 7 July 1810).

1828

January

9   (Wed) From Brinsop Court W orders copies of his bust for Quillinan and Charles W of Christ Church, Oxford. He tells Cunningham that he will order busts for John and Christopher when they are as settled as their brother. Their father and Edith Southey have been with them at Brinsop for Christmas. W is leaving for two days at Foxley.

21 Notwithstanding her accident at Douglas before Christmas 1826, which makes walking difficult, Joanna enjoys better health than for years; the Isle of Man agrees equally with her brother Henry, and they do not think of leaving it, D writes.

25 On his return journey to Rydal, which began on the 22nd, W writes from the Liverpool home of John Bolton (owner of Storrs Hall, Windermere), telling Lord Lonsdale that John is to be ordained for Mr Merewether's curacy at Whitwick. He realises the difficulty a patron could have with an incumbent in nominating a curate (cf. the entry for early December 1827). He had stayed one night at Chester, where he visited the Bishop (Blomfield) and accidentally met his old friend Archdeacon Wrangham, now rector of Dodleston, Cheshire.

29 W returns to Rydal.

February (early)   F. M. Reynolds and the proprietor of *The Keepsake* call, and offer W 100 guineas for twelve pages of verse in their annual. From one to whom he is personally indebted, at a time when money is needed to pay John's dues at Oxford and buy his requirements, including furniture and books, for Whitwick, this offer is irresistible.

26 February   He refuses a similar request from Allan Cunningham for *The Anniversary*, explaining what has happened.

March (early)   W urges MW and Dora not to stay more than three weeks with Mrs Gee near Bristol, owing to her straitened circumstances; (she will soon move to Hendon, where she starts a school). He advises them to spend a month with CW at Cambridge, where he will meet them. He gives good news of John (ordained as a deacon by the Bishop of Lincoln at Cambridge on the 2nd), and some details of poems for *The Keepsake*. (Five were included: 'The Gleaner', based partly on his recollection of a girl at Tillington near Hereford; 'The Triad' – Edith Southey, Dora, Sara Coleridge; 'The Wishing-Gate' (Grasmere); 'A Gravestone upon the Floor in the Cloister of Worcester Cathedral'; 'A Tradition of Oker Hill in Darley Dale, Derbyshire'.)

April
3   (Thurs) Oliver and Boyd having declined to publish the selection of W's poems proposed by James Dyer of Edinburgh Academy, because W will not extend permission for any future edition, he informs the editor that he may, if he wishes, print as many copies as required for his school and for a few friends.
c. 10   MW and Dora, before leaving for Cambridge, have visited Bristol to see Joseph Cottle, his sisters, and younger members of the family.
17   W and John leave RMt, W for Cambridge, J for Whitwick, his father intending to stay two days with the vicar, Francis Merewether, rector of Coleorton. Rogers has been sending him proof-sheet copies seriatim of the second part of his poem *Italy*.

May
10   W, MW, and Dora leave Cambridge, where CW has been busy and his sons delightful, for Quillinan's London home, 12 Bryanston Street.

June
3   (Tues) MW is on her way to Whitwick, where she will be joined later by W and Dora, D writes. They have met Sir Walter Scott, and visited Hampton Court with him. With visits to theatres and galleries, meetings with Mrs Lockhart (Scott's daughter), HCR, the Lambs, Talfourd, Rogers,

Kenyon, Southey, and STC, the Ws have enjoyed a full
programme.

18   STC and W having suddenly agreed on a Rhineland tour
with Dora, W breakfasts with HCR and STC at Charles
Aders', where final plans are made, Aders providing passports
and letters of credit. W is delighted to undertake this tour for
Dora's sake, even more for the opportunity to renew
friendship with STC.

22   The three travellers set off early for Ostend. (About this time,
perhaps, D takes William for a holiday with Joanna and
Henry H on the Isle of Man.)

25   At Brussels they meet the novelist T. C. Grattan (who thought
W inelegant but unaffected and modest; he discovered that
W's inadequacy in French was due to his abhorrence of
Revolutionary excesses, which had made him shun the
language).

August

6   (Wed) They return to Bryanston Street, after a tour which
took them from Ostend to Ghent, Brussels, the field of
Waterloo, Namur, and Dinant; from Namur by barge to
Liège; then to Spa, Aix-la-Chapelle, and Cologne; to
Godesberg (where – from 3 to 11 July, according to Dora –
they stayed with Aders' wife – a singer: Mr and Mrs Aders
were well-known in London for their musical and cultural
parties); then up the Rhine to Bingen and back to Godesberg,
where they stay several days. (While at Mrs Aders', on their
outward or return journey, W and STC meet the poet and
critic Schlegel, and visit his home at Bonn, where he is
Professor of Literature.) Then by steam boat to Nijmegen; by
coach to Arnheim and Utrecht; by barge to Amsterdam,
Haarlem, Leiden, The Hague, Delft, and Rotterdam; by
steamer to Antwerp; to Ghent, and by barge to Ostend. (The
tour produced only two poems: 'Incident at Brugès' and 'A
Jewish Family'.)

7   W calls in Bishopsgate in the hope of congratulating Blomfield
on his appointment as Bishop of London.

9   He declines William Jerdan's invitation to write letters from
the Continent for publication in *The Literary Gazette*. (Jerdan
had been so struck by the shrewdness and pleasantry of W's

oral descriptions that he had written him a *carte blanche* offer
for his Rhineland tour the day before W left London.)
10 W visits Charles Lamb at Enfield.
27 After spending two weeks with MW and John at Whitwick,
he and Dora arrive home with MW.

October
7 (Tues) W declines Jerdan's renewed request, admitting his
idleness as an obstacle. He thinks that style has to be forced
to impress in periodicals; his model for recording tours would
be Thomas Gray's letters and journal.
    (Shortly after this he adverts in a letter to CW on the
problem of finding a career for William, who had, like himself,
wanted to join the Army. His parents withholding their
consent, William had thought of becoming a foreign merchant.
Now W wonders whether he could follow John and enter the
Church, a course William had always resisted; for this he
would need to return to Greek and Latin, which he had given
up, and the question is where to find a tutor.)
24 W returns, not always defensively, to criticisms made by
Barron Field in April 1828 on alterations W had made in his
poems (in deference, F thought, to Jeffrey's criticisms in *The
Edinburgh Review*). W's reply had been postponed, partly
because he had hoped to meet Field and his wife at RMt
when he returned from his Rhineland tour.
29 He thanks Alexander Dyce for a copy of his edition of *The
Poetical Works of William Collins*. Dyce had asked why W
thought additions and revisions in John Bell's edition
spurious, and W answers almost wholly with reference to
'On the Superstitions of the Highlands of Scotland'. He
makes Shakespeare's *Pericles* an exception to his general
statement that nothing should be admitted as the genuine
work of a deceased author without external evidence.

November
7 (Fri) D leaves to take charge of John's parsonage at Whitwick
(staying longer than she intended with Miss Jewsbury at
Manchester).
11 Sara H leaves for Brinsop Court. Joanna is at RMt for the
winter. W, in his letter to Quillinan, says he has written no
poetry for nine months. He is afraid that the pirated edition

of his poems (published by Galignani, Paris) will damage his sales at home.

c. 22   W concludes 'The Egyptian Maid', 'a kind of romance with as much magic in it as would serve for half a Dozen'. About this time he sends £42 to Q for wine; (Q's family wine-merchant business is in Oporto).

27   In consultation with CW, W is still endeavouring to find a school for RW's son John (who has been left 'to run wild' at Keswick). Fees are high at Sedbergh, and he will inquire at Hawkshead; he will have him at RMt for Christmas.

December

6   (Sat) W writes to thank Lord Lonsdale for offering the living of Moresby near Whitehaven to his son John, hoping that his engagement at Whitwick may be fulfilled. He is to be ordained priest at Cambridge about the 20th.

11   W writes to Hugh James Rose, at Trinity, Cambridge, and author of *State of the Protestant Religion in Germany* (1825), backing Shenstone's schoolmistress against the teaching of girls by the Madras system; the 'Bellites' talk about moral discipline, but neglect the imaginative feelings.

15   W thanks Huntly Gordon for finding a teacher at Bremen who will prepare William for the mercantile business.

19   He is rather sharp with Reynolds, editor of *The Keepsake*, chiefly for saying what would suit *him* best; he must take what comes, and be content. W has written over 700 lines in the last month, including 'The Egyptian Maid'.

24   'Christmas cheer is in progress in the Kitchen to treat the villagers as usual', MW writes.

26   D writes from Whitwick to Jane Marshall: Mr Merewether is sorry to lose John; she will remain there six months until John moves.

1829

January

Early this month W falls headlong from his horse, but suffers no serious injury.

12   (Mon) W tells Alexander Dyce that Thomson, Collins, and Dyer had more poetic imagination than their contemporaries,

unless Chatterton is included in their period. Pope stands alone, but unfortunately he turned his high gifts to the plain, not to the heights.

26   He thanks J. M. Calvert for informing him of his father William Calvert's death. W has just spent a week at Keswick with Southey. (His fall, and absence from home since his recovery, has made it impossible for him to assess the contents of *The Keepsake*, he informs the editor about this time; he is displeased that Reynolds has excluded four of his sonnets and expected further poetry from him to make up the stipulated pages.)

27   Writing to Robert Jones, acknowledging his letter of the previous May, which MW had found, and which contained the news that W had been made a member of the Cymmrodorion Society, W states that his son William is about to go to Germany, where he will learn French and German, and continue the study of Classics, in case he should need to attend an English university.

On John Wilson's article in *Blackwood's Magazine* (xxiv, 1828), which argues that W, believing in the God of Nature, cannot be a Christian, and illustrates the absence of revealed religion in the tale of Margaret (at the opening of *The Excursion*), W tells HCR that JW is a 'perverse Mortal', and calls attention to his mawkish Christianity in *The Trials of Margaret Lyndsay* (1823).

In a letter to Hugh James Rose at this time W writes on the danger of infant schools, the substitution of book-learning or tuition for genuine education and maternal affection, and the harm done by fostering emulation. Book attainments will be of little avail unless they are accompanied by moral education, and children will appreciate education, and make more of it, if they know that parents have to be self-denying towards that end. (Subsequently – L5, 55 – he explains that he is not against education, but afraid that it may raise too high expectations. There must be reforms in university education and in schools for children of the middle and upper classes if the right aims and standards are to prevail elsewhere – L5, 99.)

(He has recently written 'The Russian Fugitive', a tale in verse from Peter Henry Bruce's *Memoirs*.)

25 February   After being inducted at Moresby, John W returns to Whitwick with his brother William, who is to stay there until his German tutor arrives in London.

March

3   (Tues) W writes at great length to Blomfield, Bishop of London, on the perils of the Church of England, between the Church of Rome which tolerates no private judgment, and the Dissenters who are 'impatient of any thing else'. His anxieties arise from the Catholic Relief Bill (introduced on the 5th, and made law in April; it gave equality of civil rights to Catholics), and are exacerbated by the hold of the Catholic Church on the Irish.

13   He asks CW to convey to his friend the Chancellor of the Exchequer objections to a proposed reduction in the rates allowed to Stamp Distributors. RW's son ('Keswick John') is at RMt, on his way to Hawkshead Grammar School.

April

9   (Thurs) Afflicted with trachoma again, W is obliged to employ Dora as his amanuensis in writing to G. H. Gordon. D has been very ill at Whitwick; she is unable to stand, and can scarcely speak. MW had left the previous day to nurse her. The holiday in north Wales which W had been planning with Gordon and D is postponed.

26   Dora is still W's amanuensis. Mrs Coleridge and her daughter Sara are at RMt. Were D to die, W dictates in his letter to HCR, 'the Phasis of my Moon would be robbed of light to a degree that I have not the courage to think of'.

May

2   (Sat) William, who has been 'the tenderest nurse possible', is still at Whitwick, D writes to HCR.

10   He leaves to stay at Trinity Lodge, Cambridge, before proceeding to London (where he will be Edward Quillinan's guest), thence to Bremen with his tutor Mr Papendick. (After a rough and stormy voyage they reach Germany in the second week of June.)

13   MW returns home from Whitwick, after witnessing weavers' demonstrations in Macclesfield and Manchester against wage reductions.

14   With Gordon's visit to Wales in mind, W recalls how, when
     he was with Jones in Montgomeryshire (in 1793), an inebriated
     Welsh parson threatened him with a carving-knife.

18   He informs HCR, who has invested money for him and MW
     (before setting off for a long holiday on the Continent), that he
     has not opened a book for nine weeks.

Later this month his eyes have improved, and he makes a five-
day excursion, probably with Dora, the last part in the Duddon
valley. (Miss Jewsbury spends almost a month with the Ws in late
May and June.)

21 June   John preaches his final sermon at Whitwick. Two days
later he travels north with D on their way to Halifax, where she will
stay with her aged 'aunt' Mrs Rawson before returning to Rydal.
(About this time De Quincey returns to the Lake District, to live at
Nab Cottage.)

July

4   (Sat) W tells G. H. Gordon that the editor and proprietor of
     The Keepsake have broken their contract, and he has finished
     with them. John is at RMt, on his way to Moresby.

8   Mr Gould, an American merchant, arrives with his wife,
     sister of F. W. Goddard; (cf. 19 Aug 1820).

9   They breakfast at RMt. W writes a letter of introduction,
     requesting they be shown round Trinity College during their
     visit to Cambridge.

18   News arrives of the death of Lady Beaumont. D is still at
     Halifax.

24   W writes to W. R. Hamilton for advice on a tour of Ireland
     which he is planning, perhaps with Dora. It would suit him
     to travel by steamboat from Whitehaven to Dublin, starting
     from his son's home.

29   Professor Wilson has been some time at Elleray with an artist,
     preparing (it is rumoured) a work on the Lakes. W informs
     Basil Montagu that Hartley Coleridge has been staying with
     Wilson, where he has behaved well, except for a disappearance
     of a few days, 'arising from a cause which is one [we] can
     guess at'.

August
2   (Sun) Writing from Patterdale, he acknowledges the receipt of two volumes of miscellaneous works by Joseph Cottle (the fourth edition), which Southey had delivered the previous day.
4   After staying with John Marshall's eldest son William at Patterdale Hall, then at Hallsteads, W reaches Lowther Castle.
10 From Lord Lonsdale's he travels via Keswick to join MW and Dora at Moresby above Whitehaven. (John has been visiting his Cambridge cousin Christopher in the Isle of Man. Builders are making improvements at RMt.)
15 W informs Hamilton that his plans have changed: he will travel with Mr Marshall and his son James to Holyhead, and will accompany them on a tour of Ireland after staying with him and his sister.
29 W and the Marshalls reach Holyhead, after travelling via Wigan, Wrexham, Llangollen, Betws-y-Coed, Capel Curig, Bangor (scenes visited in 1824), and over the new Menai Bridge.

September
2   (Wed) After staying three days at the Observatory with the Hamiltons, and seeing the main centres of interest in Dublin, W travels south with the Marshalls over the Scalp Pass to Enniskerry, visiting Powerscourt; then via the Glen of the Downs to Newton Mount Kennedy.
3   Via Roundwood to Glendalough and Rathdrum. At Keswick Dora is Sara Coleridge's bridesmaid.
4   W's tour continues along the Vale of Avoca to Arklow and Wexford.
5   At Wexford, where it rains all day.
8   D arrives home from Halifax, where she has been ill.
9   W and the Marshalls are at Cork, after travelling to Waterford, Carrick-on-Suir, Shanbally Castle (near Clogheen), Lismore, and Fermoy. They drive along 'the waters' to Cobh.
16 The leave Killarney after five days in the region, during which W and James M sail in the Bay of Glengariff and climb Carrantuohill, the highest mountain in Ireland; they have seen the lakes and everything worth seeing. Late in the day they visit the ruins of the abbeys and castle at Adare.

17 At Limerick W wonders what D thinks of the new room at RMt.

22 The tourists reach Sligo in the dark, after visiting the Falls of Doonass (on the Shannon) and travelling via Nenagh, Athlone, and Goldsmith's 'Auburn' to Edgeworthstown, where they stay two days with the Edgeworths, including Maria (who is very lively) and Professor Hamilton.

24 At Enniskillen W reflects on the state of Ireland: the Romanists are entirely under the command of the priests, and ready to create trouble at their bidding. He is apprehensive about the Established Church of Ireland, after hearing stories of recent murder and physical injuries in sectarian brawls.

25 Along the western side of Lough Erne to Ballyshannon, and on to Donegal. W talks to Protestants who think the country is not safe for them to live in.

26 They reach Londonderry via Strabane. As Mr Marshall has visited the Giant's Causeway, W and James propose to walk there from Bushmills, look at Dunluce Castle (the subject of a poem by Edward Quillinan), and proceed to Fair Head promontory. They will rejoin Mr Marshall at Ballymena on the 29th, and return via Antrim and Belfast, embarking at Donaghadee for Portpatrick.

October

11 (Sun) W reaches home. Sara H is back from Brinsop Court. (Christopher W and his friend John Frere stay at RMt about this time, on their way from the Isle of Man to Cambridge; Frere appreciates W's readiness to talk informatively on most subjects, and to listen.)

16 W writes to Alexander Dyce, thanking him for a copy of his new edition of George Peele's works. He would like to recommend passages from the poetry of Anne, Countess of Winchilsea, should there be a new edition of Dyce's *Specimens of British Poetesses*.

19 Writing to Catherine Clarkson, D says that cold is her horror; she is driven out in the family phaeton by Dora and taken round the garden in a bath-chair. W's eyes have been worse since his return, but have responded to strong medical treatment.

18 November   D reports that W has made his social visits (to

Lowther Castle, Hallsteads, Levens Hall, and Storrs Hall), and intends to resume *The Recluse* before it is too late. Quillinan has stayed three weeks instead of the expected three days at RMt; Edith Southey is now Dora's companion. Willy's health has improved, and with 'horse-exercise, and not over-hard study' he goes on very satisfactorily; he seems to be happy with Mr Papendick and his family.

November (later) W takes two London visitors as far as Stonethwaite in Borrowdale, spending the evening at Southey's, where Dora is; they return by Lyulph's Tower and in a fierce storm over Kirkstone.

1830

January
5   (Tues) John is spending a week at RMt, before going to Oxford to take his M.A. degree. W's eyes are still troubling him, but he has enjoyed skating on Rydal Water.
9   'He is still the crack skater on Rydal Lake', and 'the hardiest and the youngest' are scarcely a match for him in climbing mountains, D writes to the Lambs. She and MW urge him to continue 'his great work', but his resolution fails, and D fears it always will. Joanna H has been staying with them; she will return with her brother Henry to the Isle of Man in the spring. (About this time Dora, walking with W between Town End and Grasmere village, spies a bird's nest filled with the snow, from the image of which he creates the sonnet 'Why art thou silent!' – dated 18 Jan 1830.)
Late this month W discovers that Southey's neighbour, the Revd Chauncey Hare Townshend, with whom he had been friendly some time, entertaining him at RMt, is the author of an attack on his poetry in *Blackwood's Magazine* (Sep–Dec 1829); he describes it as 'a miserable maggot crawled out of the dead carcass of the Edinburgh review' (*L5*, 200).

February
18 (Thurs) W is still corresponding with Quillinan on a large investment he thinks of making through Q's family. Hartley Coleridge is wandering about like a vagabond, and sleeping in barns.

24 W sends J. W. Croker, now editing Boswell's *Life of Johnson*, a copy of a statement made by Sir Joshua Reynolds to Sir George Beaumont as evidence of Boswell's care in ensuring the accuracy of his records.

5 March D informs Mrs Coleridge, who is with Derwent's family in Cornwall, that Hartley's debts have been paid, and accommodation found for him with the Flemings at Town End (Grasmere).

March (later) W enjoys two outings: one to Ulverston by Coniston Water and up the Duddon valley with John, who makes his way over Birker Moor to Moresby while W returns over Wrynose Pass; the other with Stamp officials, whom he escorts to Borrowdale and Ullswater. As another example of his vigour, D instances his superintendence of terrace-making in Dora's Field; this terrace commands beautiful views over Rydal Water and Windermere.

April
Early this month W's letter to Dora (at Moresby for the benefit of the sea-air) is conveyed by Joanna and Henry on their return to the Isle of Man; he urges her to take care of her health and of John's pronunciation in church (lest 'northernisms' creep in); she should enjoy herself, and not 'hang over' books, especially novels.
13 (Tues) 'Keswick John' is at RMt for the Easter holiday; (his mother had married John Lightfoot, a Keswick attorney. Writing to Dora about this time, W is clearly in favour of her marrying; he hopes she will not be laid upon the 'dusty shelf'. Hartley C has been found lying intoxicated and unwell on various roads.)

A few days later W thanks Alexander Dyce for copies of his four-volume edition of John Webster and his *Specimens of British Poetesses*: he adverts to the poems of Lady Winchilsea in some detail.
22 Writing to HCR in Rome, D reports that Dora's health is improving from the sea-air and riding with John. W hopes to take her to Cambridge; Dora would like to visit Rome. Every year they become poorer, interest rates being so low, but they are spared the depression of industrial areas; emigration is common from both manufacturing and agricultural communities.
c. 27 W informs Quillinan that, although £1000 has been

withdrawn by Joanna from the proposed investment, he is still willing to have £3000 invested in a Kent estate. The Douglases, including Harriet (whose two brothers he narrowly but fortunately missed in Ireland), have made a sudden call, H and her invalid sister staying one night.

Late in April, or early in May, W tells Dora he would like to stay three days at Whitehaven with the Revd William Jackson (who had married one of the Miss Crumps of Liverpool) and seven with her and John before bringing her home. Her mother, who has been very fit and active, is suffering from lumbago, and from rheumatism in the arm she sprained a few months before the birth of Catharine.

May
11   (Tues) W leaves for Moresby and Whitehaven. His plan is to be Dora's escort on foot as she rides home on a mountain tour.
21   She is taken ill as a result of walking too much in Whitehaven and dining out.
27   W returns with Dora; she is unable to ride her pony (which is brought back by John).

June
 2   (Wed) W is pleased to learn that Edward Moxon has become a publisher; he hopes there can be a cheaper edition of his works when the 1827 Longman edition is sold out.
 5   He writes to Rogers, hoping he can help to find John a richer living.
 7   After meeting at Workington Hall a descendant of one who had been misrepresented in *Peveril of the Peak*, W writes to Sir Walter Scott, telling him that this descendant is ready to give him the true facts before his next edition is published. (As a result of W's letter, this edition included a long appendix by John Christian.)
12   The reason for W's being at Workington Hall emerges in his letter to CW: John is engaged to Isabella, daughter of John Curwen of Workington Hall and 'The Island', Windermere. John W would like CW to officiate at his wedding.
16   The poet Mrs Hemans is expected. (On 31 July Sara H writes: 'For one *long* fortnight we had Mrs Hemans & one of her

boys'; though good-natured, she has been spoilt by adulation, and 'her affectation is perfectly unendurable'.)

22 RMt is 'quite full', D writes; they have Miss Bertha Southey, her brother Cuthbert, and MW's nephew Tom from Brinsop Court.

24 (probably) To avoid the repetition of a severe winter like the last in Bremen, and in accordance with W's advice, William begins his journey to Düsseldorf (whence he travels up the Rhine to Cologne and Godesberg – where the waters had been recommended – in search of a suitable centre. His health improves after several weeks at Neuwied, near Coblenz.)

July John W and Isabella Curwen are at RMt nearly three weeks. Towards the end of the month, and during the early part of August, Professor Hamilton and his sister are the Ws' guests.

30 July W informs Rogers that he has not written a verse for twelve months, except a few stanzas (added to 'On the Power of Sound') when he returned from Ireland.

6 August D informs CW that, disappointed though they are that he will not be with them as long as was expected, he must spend the full time taking the waters at Buxton for his rheumatism. John's wedding is to be on 11 October, the anniversary of Mrs Curwen's own marriage; her brother will conduct the wedding-service. Dora, with Isabella on Windermere Island (Belle Isle), is recovering. Professor Hamilton is with W and Lord Lowther at Appleby (where the Lowthers are returned unopposed).

September (early) W writes to Henry Nelson Coleridge (Sara's husband and cousin), telling him of the agreeable visit of his father, one of STC's elder brothers; W had directed him to Hartley, who now dines in respectable houses but does not visit RMt.

9 September Richard Sharp, his sister-in-law, and his adopted daughter Miss Kinnaird have been the W's guests. CW has been with them a fortnight, and will stay another week. John and Isabella are also with them. W and CW have dined with Professor Wilson at Calgarth Park (Mrs Watson's) and Storrs Hall.

October

1   (Fri) MW goes with Ann, her cook, to prepare John's new home.

19 The wedding having taken place as arranged – a great event for the people of Workington – W is with Lord and Lady Lonsdale and other nobility at Whitehaven Castle (the Lonsdales' residence); MW is still busy fitting up J's new home; and Dora, one of the three bridesmaids, is still at Workington Hall. W informs Rogers that three copies of his illustrated poem *Italy* have been received at RMt.

23 W, MW, and Dora return home.

November

1   (Mon) They leave for Coleorton and Cambridge, their servant James taking Dora's pony (which she wants for riding at Cambridge with her cousins) to Lancaster, whence it will be ridden by W.

    After being at Heidelberg more than five weeks, William decides, early this month, to settle there for the winter, and becomes a student in philosophy at the University for three months.

7   W reaches Coleorton Hall before MW and Dora (who had stayed on at Manchester). He had stayed with Samuel Horrocks at Preston before joining them at the Jewsburys' in Manchester. On the evening of the 5th (Guy Fawkes Day), the firing of explosives had made him dismount and walk most of the way from Ashford to Bakewell. Next morning, after a view of Haddon Hall, he turned out of his way, tethered his horse, and walked through the park to Chatsworth (cf. the sonnet 'Chatsworth! thy stately mansion').

8   D writes to Mrs STC, now at Hampstead with Sara and her grandson: all MW's work in preparing John's new home has been wasted, for it was judged too highly situated and exposed for Isabella's health. She and J had returned to Workington Hall after their honeymoon in Scotland; fortunately a suitable house has been found near Moresby Church. D reports Hartley's continued delinquencies; (his friends pay for his board through her).

16 The Ws leave Coleorton, W on Dora's pony, for Cambridge.

17 He reaches Cambridge. On the way, during a violent storm,

he composes 'Elegiac Musings' in memory of Sir George Beaumont.

25 They dine with H. J. Rose and his wife, now resident, at Trinity; (Rose was the 'select preacher' at Cambridge, an office of distinction which he held in subsequent years).

26 At a time of continuing political agitation and poverty, W has recently seen a redness in the sky indicative of arson in the country near Cambridge. He is in great request, and has heard of the poetic promise of Charles and Alfred Tennyson. Dora is busy studying German.

December

13 (Mon) Southey and his daughter Bertha have been with the Ws a few days at Trinity Lodge.

16 W and Southey attend chapel on Commemoration Day, and hear James Spedding (son of W's school-friend) deliver his prize declamation.

19 W is entertained by Spedding and some of his friends; (Tennyson and Arthur Hallam had left for Somersby the previous day). He talks on revolutions (of which there had been a number in Europe during the year), judging that demagogy in England makes it a more relevant subject than poetry.

22 The Ws leave to stay with CW at his Buxted living in Sussex after a few days in London. W and CW stay with Joshua Watson, the Anglican philanthropist, while MW and Dora are at Hampstead with Mrs Hoare.

23 W, CW, Joshua Watson, and Southey dine at Lambeth Palace with the present Lady Beaumont's parents, the Archbishop of Canterbury and Mrs Howley.

24 W visits STC at Highgate.

27 He meets Joanna Baillie at Hampstead.

1831

January

3 (Mon) W returns to Quillinan's in Bryanston Street from Fulham Palace, where he had stayed from the 1st at the invitation of the Bishop of London.

5 He writes to thank the novelist T. C. Grattan, whom he met

in Brussels in 1828, for a copy of his new novel *The Heiress of
Bruges*, which he has sent on to RMt. He expects to join MW
and Dora at Buxted on the morrow.

Late in January, or early in February, W is to meet John Kenyon
at Brighton. He has dined five times with Lord Liverpool and
twice with a prince. At Brighton he meets Harriet Douglas and
her brothers.

21 February   W is called to London, to discuss the inclusion of
Cumberland in his Distributorship area.

March (early)   In London, W spends much time in anti-Reform
discussions with friends and politicians.

March (later)   W has a series of sittings for the painter William
Boxall (ending possibly in early Apr).

April
1   (Fri) William has left Germany and joined his father in
    London; W has tried to secure his appointment as Sub-
    distributor of Stamps at Carlisle.
12 On good terms with Haydon again, W calls and admires his
    picture of Napoleon; H suggests he write a sonnet on it.
18 MW and Dora reach their friend Mrs Hoare's at Hampstead.
19 They join W at Bryanston Street. He has met Henry Taylor,
    Charles Lamb (with Moxon), and his old critic Jeffrey, whom
    he treated as if nothing untoward had happened between
    them. (Rotha Quillinan accompanies the Ws when they leave;
    she is to stay with them until the winter.)
25 They leave Cambridge for Rydal. (MW is so afflicted with
    lumbago and sciatica on the journey that she has to be left
    with Dora at Nottingham, in the care of William and Mary
    Howitt, while W returns to attend to Stamp business.)
28 He arrives home in the evening, bringing Rotha with him.

May
2   (Mon) William returns to RMt, after a fatiguing journey with
    Dora's pony.
10 MW and Dora are at home. W is depressed by the success of
    Reformers in the elections, and by responsibilities for his new

area of Cumberland, where he finds confusion and disorder in Stamp agency affairs.

22　MW sets off for Cheltenham, to look after Dr Bell and his sister, who are both ill and helpless. Dr Bell had hoped that D could go; MW stays until the beginning of July, after he had rallied.

June

c. 9　(Thurs) W sends a list of *errata* to Moxon for the forthcoming edition of a selection from his poetry by Joseph Hine, a Brixton teacher and literary enthusiast whose school W had visited with Quillinan near the end of February, when W was prevailed upon to read 'Composed upon Westminster Bridge', which had been the subject of the lesson; Q had never heard him read better. W received tumultuous applause, far outdone when he asked for a half-holiday.

11　W sends H the sonnet 'To B. R. Haydon, on Seeing his Picture of Napoleon Buonaparte on the Island of St. Helena'.

13　He is invited to have his portrait painted for his college, St John's, Cambridge. (On this he writes the next day to Samuel Rogers, asking him to recommend an artist.)

July (mid)　After he and William have stayed at Moresby, W prolongs his absence from home by making a tour in the mountains.

23 July　He sends Sir John Stoddart his recollections of Sir Humphry Davy, for the biography by Davy's brother John.

August

10　(Wed) W and William buy a new horse; as soon as it has been given a fair trial, it will be sent to bring home MW, who has benefited from the sea-air at Moresby. Perhaps it can be used for the visit to Abbotsford, which W, after hearing of Sir Walter Scott's partial recovery from his long illness, wishes to make with Dora. (Scott's message that he would welcome a visit by W before he – (Scott) – leaves for Naples, for his health during the winter, had been brought by Henry Taylor, who had recently stayed with Miss Fenwick at RMt, while J. S. Mill was a guest there.)

30　W suffers once again from inflammation of the eyes.

September

5   (Mon) Forty, old and young, take part in a ball at RMt. D has
    spent ten days on Belle Isle ('The Island', Windermere) with
    John and Isabella.
9   John and Isabella set off for a tour in north Wales.
13 After delaying their journey because of his eye-trouble, W
    sets off with Dora for Abbotsford; (aggravation of his trachoma
    detains them two days at Hallsteads).
16 'There's a man wi' a veil, and a lass drivin'', an urchin
    exclaims as they enter Carlisle (*L5*, 434).
19 They reach Abbotsford, and W is shocked by Sir Walter's
    condition.
20 They are joined by W's nephew Charles, winner of the
    Chancellor's Essay Prize at Oxford, who had been staying at
    RMt, and had travelled up from Newcastle as planned. With
    Scott they visit the Yarrow and Newark Castle (cf. 'Yarrow
    Revisited'); W notices the light on the Eildon Hills as they
    return (cf. 'On the Departure of Sir Walter Scott from
    Abbotsford, for Naples').
22 They leave, after Sir Walter has written verses in Dora's
    album, for her father's sake.

October

17 (Mon) They return to Rydal, after a tour which, without
    newspapers, has done much to rid W's mind of alarms over
    agitation for electoral reform. From Abbotsford, W and Dora
    had visited Roslin, Hawthornden, Edinburgh, Stirling, Loch
    Katrine, Killin, Dalmally, Oban, the Isle of Mull, Inverary,
    Loch Lomond, Glasgow, and the Falls of Clyde. W walked
    much of the way; he had never seen Scotland under a 'more
    poetic aspect' (*L5*, 447), but visits to Glencoe and Staffa were
    precluded by a week's rain at Bonawe, where they had to
    leave their horse and take a more experienced one.
23 Robert Jones arrives, to stay more than two weeks at RMt.
31 W sends the antiquary Joseph Hunter information about his
    ancestry.

6 November   His nephew John (who, like Christopher, had been
made a Fellow of Trinity in the Michaelmas Term of 1830) arrives
from Cambridge to stay for the winter; W benefits much from his

company, in walks and talks. (William is now his father's Sub-distributor at Carlisle.)

December

3   (Sat) W begins the revision of *The Prelude*. Early this month he acknowledges the receipt of a copy of the annual *Literary Souvenir* from Alaric Watts. It contains a complimentary sketch of him, and he forwards his sonnet on Scott's departure from Abbotsford for the next issue.

27   He writes to John Gardner, a London physician (as he does to others), hoping to secure his nephew John (RW's son) a career in medicine.

1832

January

6   (Fri) D has been very ill again, but has begun to recover.

26   W writes to John Hymers, a distant connection and Fellow of St John's, Cambridge (who had met William, and taught him some German, at Neuwied), on the portrait requested by the college. Quillinan had arranged for H. W. Pickersgill to do the work, and the artist had been expected at Rydal in October. He has now returned to England from Paris, and Q will see him when *he* returns from Paris.

W has received *The Works of William Hogarth* from John Kenyon, and *Poetical Sketches of the South of France* by Benjamin Bailey, one of Keats's friends.

Dr Arnold, Headmaster of Rugby School, who had rented Spring Cottage after visiting the Ws on 7 August, has become one of W's friends (despite their political differences) during his Christmas vacation at Rydal. (The Arnolds stayed six weeks with their eight children, and all, except Mrs Arnold, became 'complete mountaineers', according to MW – *L5*, 510).

February

10   (Fri) Edward Quillinan's delayed visit to RMt begins.

c. 20   John ('Keswick') W, with the agreement of his mother and of CW (the latter and W being his guardians) is indentured to John Gardner. As he has never been to London, W suggests he be taken by Q.

24   W continues to write long letters to Lord Lonsdale on the
       politics of the Reform Bill (finally passed in June) and his fear
       of repeated mob violence. D is still confined to her room, and
       W is still busy revising *The Prelude*.

March (mid)   Q leaves Rydal with Rotha and 'Keswick' John; CW's
son John returns to Cambridge. (To W the outbreak of cholera in the
country has been less of a scourge than the revolution threatened by
the Reform Bill; cf. *L*5, 451 and W's sonnet 'Upon the Late General
Fast. [21] March, 1832'.)

May
  5   (Sat) W informs Pickersgill that he cannot visit London for his
       portrait owing to the alarming state of D's health. She has
       had another relapse, ten days previously, he informs CW.
 19   Lord Lonsdale will present John W to the vicarage of Brigham
       on the Derwent about two miles from Cockermouth. It is a
       richer living than Moresby, but like it has no parsonage.
       (Hearing about this time that John Marshall has bought the
       Derwentwater Estate for his son John, W sends his
       congratulations, and urges him to obtain the conveyance
       stamp from William, for the latter's benefit.)

June   W and Dora stay more than two weeks (from about the 11th)
with John and Isabella at Moresby. W has been there a week when,
to his astonishment, Walter Savage Landor arrives, after travelling
by steamboat from Liverpool to Whitehaven; the two poets are the
guests for a day at the home of one of the passengers, by Wastwater,
where they talk mainly of literature. Landor proceeds with his
Welsh friend via Borrowdale to Southey's, then to RMt, which he
thinks better than anything he has seen in England. To this period
W's poem 'Devotional Incitements' probably belongs.

July
 10   (Tues) Visitors to RMt have included Dr Arnold and his
       family, who are staying at Brathay for six weeks, and Julius
       Hare with another Trinity Fellow, Tennyson's friend J. W.
       Blakesley.
 16   W requests J. Gardner to obtain a pair of bluish spectacles
       with side-gasses to protect him from glaring light and sudden

changes of wind. (The four-volume cheaper edition of W's works is published by Longman about this date.)

20 Despite the inflammation of his eyes, he climbs Helvellyn with Dr Arnold and Julius Hare, thinking sadly of his ascent with Scott and Humphry Davy in 1805.

22 Tomorrow, before Hare's departure, they mean to climb Fairfield.

September

12 (Wed) Pickersgill has spent ten days at RMt, completing a chalk-drawing of W's head, and doing the groundwork of the portrait for St John's.

19 W writes to Dr Arnold on the Fox How property (next to Mrs Luff's Fox Ghyll), the purchase of which he is negotiating for Dr Arnold, who wishes to build a house for family holidays.

24 He sends his condolences to J. G. Lockhart on the death of his father-in-law Sir Walter Scott, on the 21st, not many weeks after his return from Italy.

10 November From Hallsteads, where he is staying with MW and Dora after visiting Lowther Castle, W writes to his old friend Spedding of Mirehouse, Bassenthwaite, pointing out with reference to a family legacy that nothing is gained by paying duties in London, but that both he and William at Carlisle will benefit if they are paid to the latter.

December

7 (Fri) Another election drawing near, W hopes that CW, who has a share in Little Langdale property, will be able to come up for the election on the 18th and 19th. There will be quite a family party. (CW comes, and the two Lowther candidates for Westmorland are returned.)

22 The Arnolds are expected to arrive; they are to spend their Christmas vacation at Fox Ghyll.

28 W sends a testimonial to support Derwent Coleridge's application for the headmastership of Stamford Grammar School; (DC is unsuccessful).

1833

February

5   (Tues) W has heard from HCR that STC is unwell. He reports that D has been confined to her room for five weeks, and may not live much longer; Dora caught cold at the beginning of the winter, and has been very ill.

23 He tells Quillinan that a year has passed since he wrote 'any poetry but a few lines'; he has rarely read any verse until this last week, when he has begun to accustom his ear to other authors' blank verse, in the hope that they will put him 'in tune for my own'.

20 March   He thanks Alexander Dyce for his present of the works of James Shirley (a completion of William Gifford's edition).

April

1   (Mon) He is at Moresby, helping John to settle questions concerning the building of his parsonage at Brigham. He has dined with Dr Ainger, principal of the theological college at St Bees, and written a poem on the birth of his grand-daughter ('To ——': 'Like a shipwreck'd Sailor tost'). The murmuring of the waves below and the shrill liquid music of the skylarks above are 'as good a prelude for devotion as any Psalm' (*L*5, 600).

7   W composes 'On a High Part of the Coast of Cumberland' ('The Sun, that seemed so mildly to retire'), with thoughts of his sixty-third birthday.

c. 22 To Dyce, who is preparing *Specimens of English Sonnets*, W recommends the inclusion of Donne's 'Death, be not proud'. He writes on sonnet structure; instead of thinking of it architecturally, he has come to regard the sonnet as a sphere or dew-drop. (Dyce's selection was dedicated to W.)

May

(possibly this month) Involved in correspondence as a result of Stanley's bill for the apprenticeship of slaves before their complete emancipation, W elucidates his views. There are three parties in this question: the slave, the slave-owner, and Parliament, or rather the people whom Parliament represents. Intemperate feeling tends to pitch the blame on the slave-owner or planter, whereas the people are to blame for having sanctioned the system. He recoils from slavery of any kind as much as anyone.

During this month he enjoys Southey's draft of *The Doctor* (vols 1 and 2, published 1834), and makes recommendations.

14 (Tues) W thanks Moxon for a copy of his (M's) *Sonnets*.

17 He thanks Lamb for the copy of *The Last Essays of Elia* which Moxon has forwarded. MW, D, Sara H, Dora, and he are delighted with the collection; he thinks he enjoys 'Old China' and 'The Wedding' as much as any other of the essays.

18 The Ws are happy to know that HCR is coming; if D's health improves, W will accompany him on his Scottish tour.

June

14 (Fri) HCR arrives.

17 After three weeks' absence, MW and Dora have returned from Stockton-on-Tees, where John Hutchinson has been seriously ill. They have driven unaccompanied in their little open carriage.

20 HCR, who has walked and talked with W and Thomas Hamilton (WRH's brother, who has spent a year in America, and is now at Ivy Cottage, where he is writing about America), dines with them and Sir Thomas Pasley at RMt.

July

2 (Tues) Sara H takes her niece Mary H (who had been at RMt a long period, then at Miss Dowling's school) back to Brinsop Court.

12 W and his son John leave with HCR (who has been on a visit to Southey at Keswick) for Whitehaven and the Isle of Man; Isabella stays at RMt.

17 W writes to his family from Greenock, after touring the Isle of Man.

25 W and John return to RMt. They have visited Staffa and Iona (the principal objects of their journey) and explored the Burns country, leaving HCR at Inverary in the hope that he will see more of Scotland when the weather improves.

August

c. 5 (Mon) As Distributor of Stamps, W is required to testify at the Carlisle Assize Courts. (He takes MW with him, and they return along the Eden, afterwards staying two nights at

Lowther Castle and three at Hallsteads. This tour and the one in Scotland produce *Poems, Composed or Suggested During a Tour, in the Summer of 1833.*)

*c.*10   W writes belatedly, from Lowther Castle, to congratulate Edward Moxon on his marriage to Emma Isola, daughter of Agostino Isola, and Charles Lamb's adopted daughter (cf. Mar 1789).

28   Ralph W. Emerson calls on W at RMt.

Late in August, or early in September, Samuel Crosthwaite paints preliminary portraits of W and D; (Crosthwaite's is the only one of the latter that is known).

25 September   Writing to CW, W indicates that Isabella and her baby daughter had been at RMt six weeks, that Sara H is at Brinsop Court, that her brother John died three weeks ago, and that his brother Henry, who attended him at the end, is with them on his way back to the Isle of Man.

29 October   Telling Robert Jones of his losses in the last seven weeks, W refers to the death in Vienna of his 'young friend' Arthur Hallam, whom W met at Trinity, Cambridge. He shares his horror of hostility to the Church with Francis Merewether, and is particularly shocked by the criticism of William Howitt, who had befriended him and MW; he has made some late additions to *Ecclesiastical Sonnets*.

c.14 November   W receives from HCR a present of Chalmers' *Biographical Dictionary* (16 vols). He has had a visit from a Patterdale innkeeper who would like to purchase his Broad How property; (W sells it to him in 1834).

December

5   (Thurs) Harking back briefly to the Reform Bill, W writes 'If this great world of joy and pain'.

c. 8   He has suffered a great deal from inflammation of the eyes since August.

29   Christopher W, Fellow of Trinity, who has been travelling in Greece with Richard Monckton Milnes, arrives unexpectedly.

31   A letter from J. Kenyon asking whether he is displeased with him rouses W to send his overdue thanks for Kenyon's poem

A Rhymed Plea for Tolerance. Months earlier Moxon had sent him a copy with no hint of its authorship; MW had read it to W. When the inscribed copy came from the author, W had wished to read the whole for himself, but the state of his eyes had made that impossible, and MW had been too busy to re-read it to him. He has heard from William of admiration in Carlisle for the illustrated edition of Rogers' *Poems*, and his letter to Moxon indicates his hope of receiving a copy from the author.

1834

January
Early this month John W stays at RMt.
13 (Mon) Three copies of Rogers' illustrated *Poems* arrive.
14 Christopher W departs for Cambridge, where he is to lecture in Greek.
15 At Keswick, Dora is bridesmaid to Edith Southey, who marries Mr Warter; the Archbishop of Canterbury has presented him to a living in Sussex.

March (second half) W and MW are to Moresby; one day he and John walk along the cliffs from Whitehaven to St Bees, with views of the Scottish hills, the Isle of Man, Black Combe, and Scafell.

April
3 (Thurs) In a letter to HCR, W indicates his disapproval of the Cambridge petition (passed by a meeting chaired by Adam Sedgwick) that Dissenters should be allowed to take degrees. He is afraid that the influence of the Established Church will be steadily weakened.
c. 30 He thanks Mrs Hemans for a copy of her *National Lyrics and Songs for Music*; and recommends a simple dedication of her *Scenes and Hymns of Life* to him rather than the lengthy testimony of her admiration, of which she has sent him a copy.

May
14 (Wed) He thanks Adam Sedgwick, Professor of Geology at Cambridge, for a copy of his *Discourse on the Studies of the*

University, but disagrees with the petition he had sponsored. (Sedgwick had argued that religious tests obstructed the advance of Science. Not until the Test Act of 1871 were Dissenters allowed academic posts at Oxford and Cambridge.)

17   W writes to Mrs James Hook of Leamington, the widowed sister-in-law of Mrs Luff's friend Lady Farquhar (who had recently married the author Thomas Hamilton).

June

10   (Tues) W thanks Henry Taylor for a copy of his play *Philip van Artevelde*.

11   He tells Quillinan that they would like to have Rotha 'running wild at Rydal for a couple of months', but not during the next six weeks, as their nephews (Tom and George H of Brinsop Court, now at Sedbergh School, Tom in his last term, before going to St John's, Cambridge) will be with them for their summer holidays.

14   W thanks Allan Cunningham for sending busts of himself to his two nephews at Cambridge, and another to Isabella and John (now temporary rector at Workington; W had written a reminder of this order in January).

21   Sara H returns, from London, with 'Keswick' John. Leaving Brinsop in February, she had stayed with Mrs Hook at Leamington, at Rugby with the Arnolds, at Trinity Lodge, at Playford Hall (where she had read and acted as amanuensis to Thomas Clarkson, almost blind with cataract), and with Mrs Gee at Hendon. She had twice visited STC, and been shocked by his appearance.

July

5   (Sat) W thanks David Laing for sending a copy of his edition of William Dunbar's poems. He is still unable to read much.

17   He has decided to publish his recent poems (*Yarrow Revisited, and Other Poems*, 1835), and is sorry that his publishers are not disposed to allow Moxon to publish them. (Later it is agreed that the publication be shared by Longman and Moxon.)

24   Dora thanks HCR for the copy of Tombleson's *Views of the Rhine* which he sent in June. The Arnolds are all at Fox How, and delighted with their new holiday home. It is hoped that Mrs and Miss Hoare from Hampstead will occupy Mrs Luff's house in August. William is at RMt, as, for a week, is Thomas

Monkhouse's daughter Mary (now an orphan, on holiday at Preston); 'Keswick' John will be with them a short time, on his way back from Keswick to Mr Gardner.

27 W receives news from H. N. Coleridge of STC's death. (Next day MW takes the news to Hartley, who calls at Rydal, seeming, W thinks, to grieve that he had spent so little time with his father.)

August
5 (Tues) John has arrived from Workington to announce the birth of his son.
11 Samuel Rogers arrives. (He stays in the Lake District until about 6 Sep, and visits Hallsteads and Lowther Castle twice with W.)

September W's letter of thanks to Mrs Hemans for a copy of her *Scenes and Hymns of Life* is conveyed by the Revd R. P. Graves, son of Mrs H's Dublin doctor. (He had visited the Ws the previous summer, and seeks a living in the Lake District. The Ws had done their best for him at Ambleside, but it was not until the death of John Fleming in Jan 1835 that they were able to help. Graves succeeded Fleming at Bowness, and remained a friend of the Ws).

30 September W thanks Montagu for his biography of Bacon, this sixteenth volume completing the edition of Bacon he has received from his friend. (Near the end of the month Mrs Southey suffers a mental breakdown. She is taken to the Retreat at York, and Sara H takes charge of Greta Hall for several weeks.)

3 November From Keswick she reports that Dora is very ill. Mr Carr diagnoses inflammation of the spine, and Dora is subjected to bleeding and blistering. She has not recovered by the end of the year.

27 December The Arnolds, now in residence, are delighted with Fox How.

1835

January
1 (Thurs) W replies to Thomas Noon Talfourd; he has been shocked to hear that Charles Lamb died on 27 December.

c. 11 He writes to Moxon on the same subject. His forthcoming publication (*Yarrow Revisited, and Other Poems*) interests him little. He was in the midst of the French Revolution, and does not wish to see its like in England, though Radicals and Whigs are driving the nation rapidly to that point.

13 From Lowther Castle he writes to Lord Lonsdale at Cottesmore, Rutland, asking him to inform Sir Robert Peel, the new Prime Minister, that he is willing to resign his Distributorship if it can be transferred to his son William.

February
3 (Tues) He hears from Peel, who cannot grant him his wish, but would like to know how he can help him. (In his reply of the 5th, W takes up the copyright question, twenty-eight years being too short a period to benefit a writer's dependants.)

c. 7 MW acting as his amanuensis, W writes philosophically to Robert Montgomery (Macaulay's butt in 1830), thanking him for the gift of his poems. A writer must be his own severe critic; no one will give a hundredth of the careful scrutiny which 'an author of sense and genius' will have bestowed on his own work. 'Posterity will settle all accounts justly.'

17 W and MW leave Rydal for London, to secure the influence William needs for obtaining a better post.

March
3 (Tues) HCR breakfasts with them, walks with them to Pickersgill's, and chats while W's portrait for Dora is being painted; they dine with Rogers.

9 W has seen Mr Thornton, Deputy Chairman of the Board of Stamps and Taxes, the Home Secretary, and others; he has left a note with the Chancellor, and Southey will mention his case to the War Secretary.

Later in the month W attends to the more controversial parts of 'Postscript, 1835', especially on the Poor Law Amendment Act, and HCR gives him much assistance in copying and revising it on the 22nd and 23rd.

25 The Ws meet HCR and Julius Hare at the Zoological Gardens.
27 They leave for Cambridge, after staying with Henry Taylor and with his relative Miss Fenwick. They have consulted Dr Holland in the hope of finding a cure for Dora.
30 At Cambridge W has seen his old school friend R. H. Greenwood, now Senior Fellow at Trinity, and viewed his portrait by Pickersgill at St John's.

April
3 (Fri) Death of Robert Jones.
4 W dines with the Master and Fellows of St John's College. He and MW have met their nephew Tom H two or three times.
In the middle of the month they spend a week with Mrs Hoare at Hampstead, where they meet HCR and hear alarming news of Dora.
24 They reach RMt, where they find their two invalids no worse than they feared. They have travelled via Coventry, where W noticed its three spires gilded by the light of the setting sun, and by Birmingham and Manchester, staying a night at each of the last two places.
c. 27 W writes to HCR, who had been mediating a final settlement with the Baudouins of £400 for Caroline.

May
c. 14 (Thurs) He thanks Moxon for a copy of his second volume of *Sonnets*, which M had dedicated to him.
c. 18 Writing to her cousin Christopher at Cambridge from RMt, where she has been staying since the 13th, John's wife Isabella refers to Sara H's illness. A few days later(?) James Spedding brings Alfred Tennyson to RMt to see W.
31 Sara's 'lumbago' has proved to be rheumatic fever.

June
7 (Sun) D, it seems, has short time to live.
16 'Rydal Mount is at present a *Hospital*', MW writes to Miss Fenwick, their old cook Ann being the fourth patient.
24 Sara H dies, 'leaving upon her face as heavenly an expression in the peace and silence of death as ever human Creature had', W writes to HCR the next day (cf. the sonnet 'November, 1836'). Fortunately Mrs Thomas Hutchinson is at RMt to help and comfort MW. In bed that night W composes the last

seven lines of a poem on the bird of paradise which begins,
'Who rashly strove thy Image to portray?'.

30   Sara H is buried at Grasmere.

6 July As Dora has had another setback, she cannot be taken to
(Mrs Hook's at) Leamington as had been hoped, W informs HCR,
who had offered to help with such a journey. D suffers more in mind
than in body, W writes.

2 August He tells Moxon that he has been 'reprinting and
republishing' his little book on the Lakes. (The 1835 edition gives the
final text; cf. entry for 16 Apr 1822.)

September
  1   (Tues) George Ticknor and his wife, visitors at RMt in March
        1819, arrive and stay until the 3rd; (see 9 May 1838).
  22   W, Southey, Adam Sedgwick, and others are made honorary
        members of the Kendal Natural History and Scientific Society;
        W's recent edition of *Guide to the Lakes* had been published at
        Kendal.
  26   From Lowther Castle, where E. W. Wyon makes a medallion
        portrait of him, W writes to CW, sending congratulations to
        his nephew Charles on his appointment as Second Master at
        Winchester. Much of 'Keswick' John's Sockbridge estate will
        have to be sold for the settlement of debts (cf. 26 Dec 1815);
        he and William are going to stay at Brinsop before John goes
        on to London. Later in the month, while walking from
        Lyulph's Tower to Hallsteads, W composes 'Airey-Force
        Valley'.

November
  2   (Mon) After staying at Workington with Isabella and John
        (who has been on a fortnight's ramble in Ireland), W is at
        Whitehaven Castle; he intends to bathe in the warm sea-
        baths, hoping to cure the sprain in his wrist.
  20   He sends Moxon a copy of his 'Epitaph' for Charles Lamb
        (the first version of ll. 1–38, composed the previous day, of
        'Written after the Death of Charles Lamb'); for this the Italian
        poet Chiabrera has supplied the model. W's arm has been
        sprained three months, and he is still unable to write.
  30   W sends the editor of *The Newcastle Journal* the first draft of

'Extempore Effusion upon the Death of James Hogg'. According to his niece Elizabeth H from Brinsop Court (who lived with the W's almost the whole of the year), he asked her to write down the first seven stanzas half an hour after reading of Hogg's death in that paper. (The next day he sends stanzas 8, 9, and 11; the 10th was added in mid-December, on hearing of the death of Mrs Hemans.)

December

11 (Fri) Charles Lamb's epitaph having started the 'train of melancholy reflexion' which led to 'Extempore Effusion', W, coming across the manuscript of 'At the Grave of Burns' has written the main part of 'Thoughts, Suggested . . . near the Poet's Residence', a copy of which he sends to David Laing.
25 HCR arrives at the Ws' invitation, taking lodgings at Rydal. After dining with the Ws, he walks with W and Dr Arnold beyond Fox How. (He remains until 1 Feb, walks with W, and makes a practice of staying at RMt in the evenings, after dining early with the Ws, to whom he brings much happiness.)
27 He notices that W is more tolerant; so far they have had little political sparring.
30 W is dejected by Dora's worsening health. Walking with HCR, he invites Hartley C, already drunk, to dinner; so anxious is W when HC departs that HCR hurries after him and takes him to his lodgings beyond Grasmere, Hartley falling four times on the way.

1836

January

2 (Sat) HCR is allowed to see D, who repeats fragments of poetry continuously.
7 He accompanies W to Elleray, the residence of Lady Farquhar and Mr Hamilton; during their walk W speaks with great eloquence and felicity on the poetry of Milton.
12 W writes to his nephew John, congratulating him on his coming of age, and urges the necessity of making decisions on the spot with the trustees of his father's Sockbridge estate, in order to settle outstanding debts as soon as possible.

15 He congratulates his nephew Charles on his marriage.
18 He writes, asking Miss Fenwick if she will be a sponsor to his second grandson (b. 27 Dec and named after him).
26 He sends a similar request to Sir William Hamilton of the Observatory, Dublin (knighted in 1835).
29 W speaks highly of Ebenezer Elliott's *Corn Law Rhymes*.

February

8 (Mon) He congratulates his nephew Christopher on becoming Public Orator at the University of Cambridge. 'Keswick' John has come, to decide what parts of his estate are to be sold. CW had hoped his three sons would acquire Westmorland freehold and votes; is C interested?
c. 17 W thanks Samuel Rogers for two superb volumes of Thomas Gray.

March

7 (Mon) W, whose attention has been much devoted to Church affairs, including the building of a second church at Cockermouth, informs Francis Merewether of Coleorton that he is leaving home for at least ten days. He proposes to attend the christening of his grandchild at Workington (Southey being the third sponsor). Both D and Dora have improved in health.
17 He is back at RMt with his three grandchildren, having – before the christening – attended the Sockbridge auction at Penrith. There had not been sufficient competition for any sale.

April

13 (Wed) Deputizing for its founder, John Bolton of Storrs Hall, who is ill, W lays the foundation stone of a school at Bowness, and makes an important speech on the subject of education, which is published in *The Westmorland Gazette* three days later.
18 Christopher W leaves Cambridge to become Headmaster of Harrow School.
Late in the month W writes to 'Keswick' John at Keswick, suggesting they travel to London together.

May

11 (Wed) They reach London late (in the early hours of the morning); W stays with his Church correspondent and adviser Joshua Watson. He has many inquiries to make concerning business (a new edition of his works, his investments, his Distributorship, William's future), and many family friends and people of life interests to meet.

12 At the Colonial Office, he meets James Spedding, Henry Taylor, and James Stephen, who unsolicitedly offers him £50 for the church at Cockermouth, and undertakes to speak with Thomas Spring-Rice, Chancellor of the Exchequer, on W's Stamp Office worries. He visits the National Gallery.

13 He dines at Lord Lonsdale's. Nothing so far has given him more pleasure than Watson's interest in William's future.

14 He finds Christopher in high spirits at Harrow.

15 With his nephew John he calls on HCR, meets Landor, then visits Rogers, with whom they drive on to Miss Rogers', where they lunch. They see the eclipse and visit the Zoological Gardens.

?19 He discusses a new edition of his works with Moxon at John Kenyon's.

?20 Cold winds have affected his right eye, with the result at that he is distressed by glaring sunshine. He is busy from morning to night; so many people have been introduced to him, he cannot remember one in ten. He and HCR have talked of a trip on the Continent.

23 He breakfasts with Henry Taylor, and calls on Kenyon, Pickersgill (on the framing of a portrait, for Dora, for which he sat in Mar 1835), and others. The previous day he had breakfasted with Rogers, called on the artist Wilkin, and Lord Holland, and visited the Johnsons in the evening.

24 Among the people he has seen are George Crabbe, the poet's son, and the Quillinans; he sits with Edward in Hyde Park, where they talk for an hour and a half. He visits the Colonial Office, where Stephen gives him assurances from Spring-Rice. At Lord Lonsdale's, the previous evening, he drank inadvertently from a decanter of water at dinner; he hopes no one noticed, for, as Lady Chantrey said to him the same day, everything notables say or do is the talk of the town.

26 W enjoys the first performance, with Macready in the title

role, of Talfourd's play *Ion* at Covent Garden, and the supper-party which followed (where he meets Robert Browning).

27   He meets Elizabeth Barrett at John Kenyon's.

?29   He breakfasts with Dr Holland, and meets his father, another medical man, at Mrs Hoare's; with both he discusses Dora's health, and notes their recommendations.

30   He has breakfasted with Gladstone, and is going to Hampstead with Mrs Marshall, with whom he is staying.

June

1   (Wed) With Mr and Mrs Lockhart he visits Harrow School, where the speeches are enjoyed and Christopher acquits himself charmingly.

4   He breakfasts at the British Museum with H. F. Cary, translator of Dante. The previous day he had walked with three distinguished Fellows of Trinity, Whewell, Blakesley, and Julius Hare. Mr Marshall has brought W assurances from Spring-Rice that any changes to be made will not endanger his Stamp Office income.

5   W, his nephew John, and Moxon visit Quillinan at his Woolwich cottage; they meet the artist Frank Stone there.

6   W returns to the City by steamboat.

7   He is to dine with Gladstone, and thinks of revising three volumes of his poems for the new edition before he goes abroad.

13   With Henry Hallam (the historian, Arthur's father) and Rogers, he visits Windsor Castle and Eton.

15   He breakfasts with the Marquis of Northampton, with whom he had attended Dulwich Gallery in May.

20   He moves to Edward Moxon's, in Dover Street. He has had a meeting with John Constable.

25   He has found London life too tiring. He has twice called at Lambeth on William's behalf, without seeing the Archbishop. His discussion of the copyright question with notables at Sir Robert Inglis's makes him confident that he will be the means of improving it. He has met Mr Westall twice, and dined at Lord Liverpool's.

27   He breakfasts with Spring-Rice, and discusses copyright law with him. He has been arranging his poems for a six-volume edition, including *The Excursion*. He has decided not to go

abroad for a while, and HCR, though disappointed, has forgiven him.

?29 The Marshalls, to whom he owes so much while he has been in London, have left for Leeds and Hallsteads.

July

1 (Fri) After staying at Hampstead, where everyone is pleased with his new set of teeth, W returns to Moxon's.

5 He leaves for St Albans and Manchester, with the Revd Robert Graves of Bowness.

7 Arrives home in the afternoon.

11 He writes to HCR on the possibility of a tour to Italy in the autumn, and gives him advice on the tour in Wales he is about to begin.

Late this month Quillinan is at RMt. W is busy revising his poems for the new edition.

August

16 (Tues) Dr Arnold, W writes to HCR, has advised that the best time to visit Italy is from mid-March to mid-June. Other reasons for deferring the tour are that his nephew John's affairs remain unsettled, that he would like to superintend the printing of his poems, and that this son John, who would be free at the time, would like to accompany them.

20 W replies to Thomas Poole's letter of 13 August, in which Poole promised support for the new church at Cockermouth, mainly from Sir Peregrine Acland. Unfortunately Lord Egremont of Cockermouth Castle favours the enlargement of the old church, and has given £2000 to be disposed of as the inhabitants think best; they have decided to have a new market-place. Had Dora been able to travel, W adds, they would have visited Stowey and Alfoxden. (Poole died in Sep 1837.)

September (third week) W and MW spend three days with John's family in the new parsonage at Brigham.

28 September Before leaving the previous week, Quillinan had helped with proof-reading ; MW has now taken his place. W finds time to walk with Sir John Taylor Coleridge, who is staying with his family at Fox How, which the Arnolds have lent him for six weeks.

24 October W thanks James Stephen for assisting with the proof-reading; at RMt they have completed more than two volumes.

1 November MW informs HCR that 'Keswick' John has been fortunate in the sale of his lands.

19 December Proof-reading continues. (The first two volumes of W's poems are published in 1836; the remainder in 1837.)

1837

January
9 (Mon) Writing to Christopher at Harrow, W says that Dora can now walk two hours, as a result of repeated practice on one of their terraces. He asks him to thank CW for the copies of his *Christian Institutes* which John and he have received. He dislikes the 'maudlin expression' and 'air of decrepitude' of the engraving from the Pickersgill portrait which serves as a frontispiece to the new edition of his works.
15 He thanks Samuel Carter Hall for the elegant present of *The Book of Gems*, and is particularly pleased with what it says on the Westmorland poet Langhorne, his poem *The Country Justice* being the first, with perhaps the exception of Shenstone's *The Schoolmistress*, that 'fairly brought the Muse into the Company of common life'.
28 He tells Moxon that the value of his new edition, in the eyes of the judicious, lies in the revision which has cost him so much labour.

February
1 (Wed) Opposition being expressed to Lord Lonsdale's patronage (he had promised to endow the proposed new church at Cockermouth with £150 p.a., but wished the patronage to be vested with the Bishop), and continual indifference and hostility being engendered by local radicalism, W loses interest and proposes to return the contributions he has received.
17 He had intended to take Dora to Leamington on his way to London for his tour with HCR. She has been prostrate with influenza, and the tour may have to be postponed. After

spending much on his new house, John cannot afford to go. Tom Hutchinson has fallen from his horse; his spinal cord has been damaged, and he has lost the use of his arms and legs.

March

2   (Thurs) W proposes to leave with MW and Dora on Monday. His wife is to visit her brother Tom; he and Dora will stay with Dr Arnold until the Friday, as Mrs Hook finds she is not free to have Dora at Leamington until the 13th. He is to stay with Miss Fenwick in London.

12   He settles details of their tour with HCR; Moxon will go with them as far as Paris.

13   He breakfasts at Mr Watson's, where he sees CW (who is leaving for Cambridge), and meets Hugh Rose (lately appointed Principal of King's College, London) in the Strand, looking very ill. Tomorrow Rogers is to take W to Mrs Hoare's at Hampstead.

17   He has seen the Marshalls, and Mrs Coleridge and Sara. HCR and he have bought a carriage, and will embark at the Tower Stairs on the 19th.

18   He has heard for the first time, from Quillinan's letter to Dora, of Landor's attack on him in *A Satire for Satirists*, published at the end of 1836.

20   Dora leaves Rugby for Leamington Spa.

24   W writes a long letter from Paris to Miss Fenwick (who wishes to have £400 invested for her godson's education), to be read and forwarded to MW. From Calais they had encountered snow and chilly blasts. There had been severe frosts in Paris, where, after much sight-seeing, W and Moxon have been struck by the view of the city from Montmartre. He has found all the Baudouins well.

26   Just before leaving Paris for Lyon, he sees the Baudouins again, and writes to condole with Mrs Clarkson, on the death of her son Tom after an accident with his gig.

April

8   (Sat) From Toulon he writes to MW; he would have written from Lyon but for a horrid cold caught while crossing the Tarare mountain. He was pleased with Vaucluse and its

Petrarchan associations, but most of all with the drive between Marseilles and Toulon, and the Mediterranean views.

10   It snowed, hailed, and rained on their way to Nice, W writes to D (left in the charge of Joanna H); their fingers were frozen. The postilion showed them where Bonaparte landed from Elba.

12   W and HCR leave Nice for Genoa.

14   The poetry of Chiabrera, who had lived there, endears Savona to W (cf. 'Musings near Aquapendente', 198–250).

26   After proceeding from Genoa via Massa, Lucca, Pisa, Volterra, and Siena, they reach Rome. From the Pincian hill just after sunset W observes on the horizon the broad-topped pine which had been spared at Sir George Beaumont's request (cf. the sonnet 'The Pine of Monte Mario at Rome').

29   They are staying by the Piazza di Spagna. Nothing has impressed W more than the interior of St Peter's. They intend to examine the principal pictures in the Vatican on Monday.

May

6   (Sat) They visit the painter Mr Severn, the friend of Keats who was with him when he died in the house overlooking the Piazza di Spagna.

13   HCR enjoys his birthday with W at Hadrian's Villa, and at Tivoli and the Villa d'Este.

17   HCR's friend Miss Mackenzie, who had done so much to make W's stay in Rome happy, takes them to Albano; they see the lake, and (next day) tour the volcanic pool of Nemi ('Diana's Mirror').

23   They leave Rome and turn north. W is rather homesick and tired from attempting too much in a short time; they have decided not to visit Naples, as the quarantine has been renewed after more outbreaks of cholera.

29   (evening) They reach Florence after visits to the waterfall at Terni, to Assisi, Arezzo, and the great Tuscan sanctuaries at Laverna and Camaldoli; as HCR had seen it at leisure six years earlier, W had journeyed on horseback, after starting at 5 a.m. with a guide, to see the third at Vallombrosa.

June

4   (Sun) He hears from Dora, who is in London (after staying with Mrs Gee in Hendon, she will visit her friend Edith – Mrs

Warter – in Sussex); MW is back at RMt. He has read
Talfourd's speech in the House of Commons on the duration
of copyright (in which he paid eloquent tribute to W), and
been 'incessantly' employed visiting churches and galleries,
although much time has been lost through their being closed.

7   At Bologna W is uncomfortable owing to the *length* of the
    streets. He is never thoroughly happy, HCR observes, except
    in the country.

12 On an excursion from Milan they visit Lake Como, where
    they meet the Ticknors. W's recollections of two previous
    visits help to make this one of their happiest days.

13 In Milan, they ascend to the roof of the cathedral.

14 Beautiful scenery between Bergamo and Iseo, where W enjoys
    a solitary ramble by the lake, makes this one of the best days
    of the tour.

16 They reach Desenzano on Lake Garda; W has to be content
    with a view of Sirmione, the promontory at the end of the
    Sirmio peninsula where Catullus had a villa.

17 By steamer to Riva at the head of the lake.

22 Having journeyed via Verona, Vicenza, and Padua, they
    reach Venice.

30 W oversleeps, after composing (for the first time during their
    journey, HCR believed); he had been working on 'The
    Cuckoo at Laverna'.

July

5   (Wed) After less than six days at Venice, where it was
    extremely hot, and travelling through the Alps, they reach
    Salzburg. For poetical reasons W wishes he had visited Italy
    years earlier. Absence fills him with remorse for having been
    impatient with MW while correcting for the last edition of his
    poems.

17 After rambling among the Austrian lakes, they reach Munich,
    where he finds a letter from Mary, who has urged him not to
    hurry but see as much as possible. HCR's loitering, gossiping,
    and lateness in going to bed has tried his patience; he has
    been unable to read by candlelight, and cannot pass the time
    writing verse because of the effect on his nerves and stomach.

21 They leave for Heidelberg, where W hopes to locate William's
    lodgings.

August

7 (Mon) He reaches Mr Moxon's in Dover Street.

8 Mrs Hoare brings Dora from Hampstead to see W; he proposes to take her to Broadstairs for her health. He calls on Mr and Mrs Johnson, sees Miss Fenwick, dines with Rogers and Thomas Moore, and spends the rest of the evening with Dora.

10 The birth of another son, and the losses sustained by Isabella's father from the flooding of his Workington coalmines, add prospectively to John W's financial difficulties. His father undertakes to do his best to find him pupils.

18 After seeing numerous friends, including Miss Fenwick, Mrs Hoare, and Mrs Hook, staying at Rogers', and taking Dora to Sir Benjamin Brodie for medical advice, W and Dora embark at Gravesend for Chatham, where they stay with his cousin Mrs Proctor Smith.

23 Leaving Dora at Chatham, where he called on Dr Davy (Sir Humphry's brother), W had visited Canterbury Cathedral. He reaches Broadstairs, where he stays with the Moxons; they dine with Rogers and his sister, who are also on holiday there.

30 MW receives from W the picture of him painted by Severn (for Isabella).

September

1 (Fri) he leaves Broadstairs with the Moxons.

3 He is the guest of the Archbishop of Canterbury and Mrs Howley at Addington Park. (MW's letter of 14 Aug suggests he may be anxious to help his son John to a more remunerative living.)

4 Writing to Dora, MW speaks of Quaker visitors, and of Ann's remark, when they wished to see W's study, that she thought it 'out of doors'.

8 From Dover Street he leaves London with Dora and HCR, to visit Tom H at Brinsop Court.

21 Dora, who had been expected to stay in the south, accompanies W *en route* for Rydal via Liverpool, partly to see her mother and D, partly because W is suffering from eye-inflammation, which could have resulted to some extent from reading CW's *The Ecclesiastical Commission and the Universities* on his way to Brinsop.

November

4 (Sat) Hartley Coleridge and his sister Sara have tea at RMt; MW thinks her a 'silly prating forward thing', anxious to parade her opinions.

7 Francis Merewether, on holiday in the Lake District, principally to stay with John at Brigham and with the Ws, leaves RMt with his wife and daughter.

12 Dora is back in the south of England for the sake of her health, and is now with Miss Fenwick at Dover.

16 Mrs Southey, who has never recovered from her mental breakdown, dies. (Within the next few days W visits Keswick and spends three hours conversing with Southey.)

December (first two weeks) Edward Quillinan is at RMt. While he is replying to a letter from Dora in which she states that her affection for him is Platonic, MW asks if she may read Dora's letter. Q's embarrassed and ingenuous offer to read part of it prompts her reply that, if she can hear only a portion, she would rather hear none, of it.

15 December W writes to Talfourd on his new copright bill, and on the prospect of securing American copyright for English authors. (Dora spends the Christmas–New Year period with her uncle and cousins at Cambridge.)

1838

4 January In answer to Sir W. R. Hamilton, who had just been made President of the Royal Irish Academy, W says he has nothing suitable for inclusion in its *Transactions*. If he were younger, he would set out his views on the essentials of poetry.

8 January He expresses his regret that Scott had put worldly ambition before devotion to literature. (His comment is occasioned by the sixth volume of Lockhart's *Memoirs of the Life of Sir Walter Scott*: three volumes had reached him while he was on his 1837 tour, and he had expressed similar views when he was with Dr Davy at Chatham.)

21 February He informs Sir J. T. Coleridge that Hartley had been very regular for many months, and calls occasionally; he is instructive and agreeable, though given to contradiction and paradox. (After deputizing as a teacher at Sedbergh School a year earlier, H acted there as deputy for the headmaster who died in the spring of 1838.)

March
  5 (Mon) Moxon having agreed to publish his sonnets, W invites James Stephen to check at the proof-sheet printing stage again. He has recently written the sonnet 'Said Secrecy to Cowardice and Fraud' against the secret ballot.
 23 He writes to Gladstone, requesting his support for the second reading of Talfourd's bill, which is being opposed by booksellers.
 26 He tells HCR he has written at least forty letters of this kind.

April
c. 5 (Thurs) W writes to Dora in London, and hopes she will see Tintern Abbey on her way to Brinsop. He chooses to ignore the conclusion of her letter (in which she revealed her wish to marry Edward Quillinan).
  9 He writes a testimonial for his nephew John, Fellow of Trinity, in support of his unsuccessful application for the headship of King Edward's School, Birmingham.
 27 He thanks J. G. Lockhart for his biography of Scott, the last volume of which he has just received. He condoles with him on the loss of his wife; he saw her last when she took them in her carriage to Harrow, and remembers how delightfully she superintended MW and Sara H at Abbotsford in 1814.
     About the same time, the second reading of the Copyright Bill being carried on the 25th, W sends his congratulations to Talfourd, and asks in what way he can be of further assistance. (Soon afterwards he writes on the subject to Sir Robert Peel, whose support he had canvassed but who had abstained from voting.)

May
  4 (Fri) He can merely thank Richard Monckton Milnes for the present of his *Poems of Many Years*, so much of his time being devoted to the Copyright Bill (with his grandchildren's benefit in mind).

9   George Ticknor, Professor of Spanish at Harvard, and his
    wife call at RMt; (these friends of W had renewed their
    acquaintance three or four times during his recent continental
    tour with HCR). MW asks Ticknor to encourage W to finish
    The Recluse. W tells him what is completed (of the first part
    there are only fragments; the third is untouched) and, when
    asked why he does not finish it, answers that he is in the
    same position as Gray was with a similar subject: he has
    'undertaken something beyond his powers to accomplish'.

28 W acknowledges Julius Hare's gift of his new edition of
    Guesses at Truth, and the honour done by dedicating it to him.

June

17 (Sun) Dr Kennedy, head of Shrewsbury School (still
    remembered for his *Latin Primer*), calls on W.

24 W thanks Talfourd for his exertions, and agrees with his
    decision to withdraw the Copyright Bill, owing to mounting
    opposition, until the next session. (The next day he writes in
    similar vein to Gladstone.) Dora has returned. Writing to
    John Kenyon (probably about this time), W explains that,
    owing to his poor eyesight, MW's lack of voice, and numerous
    engagements, they have taken much time to read his *Poems,
    for the Most Part Occasional* (1838). The poem on Stonehenge
    reminds him of his unpublished verses on Salisbury Plain; he
    confesses that, although, overcome with heat and fatigue, he
    had taken his siesta there, he was not visited by the Muse in
    his slumbers (as his poem suggests).

July

4   (Wed) W is on his way to Durham. From near Carlisle, he
    tells Moxon that he is accompanied by Miss Fenwick;
    tomorrow they travel to Newcastle by train.

In the middle of the month, after two days in Newcastle, they
make various visits in Northumberland, where Isabella Fenwick
(IF) has relatives and friends. *The Sonnets of William Wordsworth* is
published by Moxon about this time.

21 He receives an honorary degree at the new University of
    Durham.

28 A day after returning home, W thanks Moxon for kindness to
    his son John, who has been in London, after recovering from
    typhus fever. He tells HCR how pleased he is that Thomas

Clarkson has remonstrated in a pamphlet against statements about himself in *The Life of William Wilberforce* by his sons. (HCR had written a preface and supplement to Clarkson's *Strictures*, but the controversy which ensued did not end until 1843, when the Wilberforces withdrew the offending passages, and made some amends in the new edition.)

30   W informs Sir Henry Bunbury, who had included W's letter to C. J. Fox (cf. 14 Jan 1801) in his *Correspondence of Sir Thomas Hanmer*, that, although he sees no reason to regret its appearance, he cannot approve of the practice of publishing letters without consent, and thinks it will tend to check the free communication of thought. He also states, as he has done more than once, his wish that his letters be destroyed (or never published).

August

1   (Wed) W thanks David Laing for sending him first and early editions of poetry.

17   He thanks Kenyon for a copy of Elizabeth Barrett's *The Seraphim, and Other Poems*, in which he finds gratifying 'power and knowledge'.

19   Crippled by a rheumatic attack, W lies on the sofa listening to Sir William Hamilton, on his way to the meeting of the British Association at Newcastle.

30   The Marquis of Northampton calls, on his way back from the Newcastle meeting.

October

6   (Sat) John Peace, the City Librarian of Bristol, a great admirer of W, has tea at RMt; (the next day, at church, MW thinks he worships W more than his Maker).

8   W, John W (son of CW), Dora, and four daughers of a friend of IF (who had rented a cottage at Ambleside for a year) set off on a three-day excursion to the Duddon valley. W has to protect his eyes with dark spectacles, and uses his faded green umbrella against the wind.

November

c. 3   (Sat) He declines the invitation to stand as candidate for the Lord Rectorship of the University of Glasgow.

16   He writes his recollections of John Thelwall at the request of

the latter's second wife, who seeks material for the 1796–1801 period; (the second volume of his life which she had in mind never appeared).

December

c. 5 (Wed) W tells HCR that he has written nine poems relating to their Italian tour (cf. *Memorials of a Tour in Italy, 1837*, published in 1842).

18 He congratulates his nephew Christopher on his recent marriage to John Frere's sister.

22 He rejoices that HCR is coming to see them after Christmas, and tells him that the Arnolds arrived at Fox How the previous evening.

1839

January

During his stay (until 2 Feb) HCR dines habitually with the Ws.

15 (Tues) The Ws visit IF at Ambleside (and stay for two or three days).

18 HCR calls at RMt and walks with W. They meet Dr Arnold and talk of Southey. W speaks of him with great affection, and says it is painful to see how dead he has become when away from his books; W would rather give up books than people.

February

Early this month he sends a copy of his sonnet 'The Pine of Monte Mario at Rome' to Mrs Howley, in memory of Sir G. Beaumont (cf. 27 May 1825), and his condolences on the death of Hugh Rose, who had been the Archbishop's chaplain. He informs Quillinan that he has not forfeited his friendship, and that he will be welcome at RMt. (IF, hoping to smooth matters for Dora, has invited Q to stay with her; he does so for a week, from the 11th.)

18 (Mon) W and others, including Dr Arnold, have sent petitions in support of Talfourd's bill, and he hopes that Southey (the Poet Laureate) will do the same. Q has left for Ireland; W has had no private conversation with him, but Q knows his views and feelings.

27 The second reading of Talfourd's Copyright Bill is carried.

March   W is busy revising *The Prelude* for the last time.

April
1   (Mon) W and MW, accompanied by William and IF and her niece, leave for a month at Bath, where they hope their rheumatic ailments will be cured; (he suffers from a sprained ankle when he leaves).

c. 10   W points out to Talfourd that, if he had published *The Prelude* when it was completed in 1805, the copyright would have expired had he died in the meantime. His heirs will benefit by the delay in publishing which its personal character has dictated.

13   After receiving from Dora, who is with D at Rydal, a long extract from a letter in which Q has urged her to marry him without delay, W reproves him for making such a proposal in the absence of her parents, and asks what are the prospects he hints at of settling anything on her, though he cannot do so at present.

17   John Peace eventually meets W, after calling when they were all out the previous evening. Perhaps the poet W. L. Bowles writes his 'memorial' in Dora's album on this day.

19   W replies to Thomas Spring-Rice, Chancellor of the Exchequer, who has invited him to London to discuss the possibility of transferring his Distributorship to William.

22   William arrives in London, ready to give Spring-Rice the information he requires.

29   After hearing from William of Spring-Rice's favourable reception of him, W leaves directly for London; (MW is to visit Brinsop Court on the way).

May
1   (Wed) He asks Dora and her Kendal friend Elizabeth Cookson not to work too hard copying up *The Prelude*, and says he plans to meet her mother in London, and hopes to call at Cambridge on the way home.

7   William's hope of the Distributorship is deferred indefinitely owing to the resignation of the Ministry. (MW's letter to Dora on engagements for this and subsequent days indicates the busy social programme followed by the Ws in London.)

16   From the Marshalls' (41 Upper Grosvenor Street) W writes a

letter of condolence to his nephew Charles on the loss of his wife in childbirth.

26 MW and W have spent some time with Christopher at Harrow, two days with Charles at Winchester, and two days at Salisbury with Canon Fisher and his wife Elizabeth (W's cousin, daughter of Canon W. Cookson).

31 The Ws and IF leave London for Cambridge.

June

Early this month, on his way to Oxford, where he is to receive an honorary degree, W returns to London, while the remainder of the party return home.

7 (Fri) He breakfasts with Henry Taylor, and has a long but not very satisfactory talk with Quillinan.

9 He breakfasts at Kenyon's, to meet the American constitutional lawyer Daniel Webster, and becomes more reconciled to the idea of Dora and Q's marriage. (He enjoyed the ballet and opera the previous evening.)

10 W leaves London for Oxford.

12 At the Commemoration W receives his degree to tremendous applause. Tributes to him are paid by both the Public Orator and John Keble, Professor of Poetry. The Arnolds and John Peace of Bristol attend the ceremony. Another to be honoured is Baron ('Chevalier') Bunsen, theologian and diplomat, whom W had met in Rome.

13 W is the chief guest at Magdalen (Frank Faber's breakfast-party) with Frederick Faber and John Keble.

15 W leaves Oxford (and spends a few hours with the Arnolds at Rugby on his way to Rydal).

22 The Arnolds and Bunsen have already called at RMt.

21 August W writes to Dr John Davy, trusting he will advise his nephew John, now a qualified doctor practising at Fort Pitt, Chatham. (J had been very ill in the autumn of 1838; towards the end of 1839 he secures an appointment in the Ionian Islands.)

21 October As he does not know Christopher's address, W writes to his wife Susanna at Harrow, asking if she will request him to send the inaccuracies he had noted in the text of *The Excursion*, of which Moxon would like a new edition; (it did not appear until 1841). M has just sent a copy of Christopher's *Greece*; Dora and he have

scarcely had time to do more than look over its engravings, after a
visit to Lowther Castle.

November
1   (Fri) M has published the first collected edition of Shelley's
    poetical works, and sent Dora a copy. W informs him that
    Margaret Gillies has completed his portrait. (A specialist in
    water-colour miniatures, she had come up from London at
    her own request, and was to stay several weeks at RMt,
    painting additionally MW, IF – both away at present – Dora,
    and others in the neighbourhood.) W has now completed his
    revisions for the new edition of his poetical works, but wishes
    the twelve sonnets which were late additions to *The Sonnets of
    William Wordsworth* to be included.
3   W's intention during the coming week is to stay with the
    Lonsdales at Whitehaven until Friday, pass the next two days
    at Brigham, and meet MW and IF on the following Monday
    or Tuesday, whichever they find more convenient, at Greta
    Hall, where much family disharmony had broken out soon
    after Southey's return with his second wife. Relations had
    improved, but S remains confused, and unable to settle to
    composition, even of a letter.
21 Writing to Mrs Coleridge, chiefly about how they have found
    the Southeys, and enclosing Hartley's bills, MW reveals that
    Quillinan has been at RMt since the 19th (he left on 3 Dec)
    and that Joanna H, who is with them, proposes to stay until
    the spring.

Mid-December(?)   W's letter to Thomas Powell indicates his love
of Chaucer, his inability to refuse a first edition of *Paradise Lost*
though he has one already (given by Rogers), and the presence of
Miss Gillies, who has completed an excellent likeness of MW, but
not succeeded yet with Dora's.

23 December   To Professor Henry Reed, who had edited the first
American edition of W's poetical works in 1837, and whose first
American edition of *Lyrical Ballads* he had received early in the
summer, W apologizes for his tardiness in replying, and sends a
sonnet ('Men of the Western World! in Fate's dark book') he has

recently written. He tells how, 'the other day', when he was looking over the manuscript of 'Thoughts' (suggested on the banks of the Nith, near the home of Burns) and came to the last stanza, he immediately added another ('But why to Him confine the prayer . . .?'), feeling himself on 'the brink of that vast ocean' on which he 'must sail so soon'.

1840

January

2 (Thurs) News arrives of the death of CW's eldest son John at Trinity, where CW had helped to nurse him during rather a long illness.

9 W thanks Mrs Gaskell for doing her best to secure for him the 1525 ambry of his Penistone ancestor. Mr Westall is at RMt, making sketches which may be used as illustrations in editions of W's poetry.

16 W explains to his friend Barron Field, who has been out of the country for a long period, why he is opposed to the publication of his *Memoirs of the Life and Poetry of William Wordsworth*. It is taken up too much with combating criticism of the past to be helpful, and it contains many errors which others have made about him.

27 He has now written eleven sonnets on the capital punishment question.

February

12 (Wed) Dora leaves for London with IF, travelling by rail from Preston. (She will stay with Mrs Hoare and Sara Coleridge; after a period in London, she and IF will proceed to Somerset.)

21 W tells Moxon that he has placed his Chaucer translations at Thomas Powell's disposal, for inclusion in a selection of Chaucer modernizations, in the hope that they will eventually help to 'place the treasures of one of the greatest of Poets within the reach of multitudes'. The penny post has 'let in an inundation' of complimentary letters, as a result of the sales of his new edition.

March

9 He informs Quillinan that though he has no objection to the publication of his Chaucer translations, he has yielded to the judgment of others, and sent only 'The Cuckoo and the Nightingale' (wrongly assumed to be Chaucer's at the time). John's new living at Plumbland will increase his income by £420 p.a.

16 He writes to HCR, grieved to hear from him that Miss Mackenzie, who meant so much to him at Rome, has died.

24 W obtains a house at Ambleside, available from May to September, for IF, and writes the first draft of 'The Cuckoo-Clock' (suggested by the present she had given him for his seventieth birthday, when the poem was completed).

25 He thanks Mrs Gaskell for having a sketch of his ancestor's ambry made for him.

14 April He asks Moxon to let him have any money which is due to him, so that he can help his son John. Dora is expected home in about a week.

Late April(?) He has received from C. H. Townshend a 'penitential recantation' of the only criticial strictures which had given him 'concern worth speaking of' (cf. Jan 1830).

23 May He informs Mrs Gaskell that, thanks to her interest, the owner of the ambry has presented it to him; (it arrives in June).

July The Queen Dowager and her sister appear in Rydal; W meets them at the lower waterfall and conducts them to the higher. He leads the Queen to the principal viewpoints of his 'little domain', with special emphasis on that from the summer-house which shows Rydal Water to advantage. Lord Howe draws her attention to his friend Sir George Beaumont's pictures; she shakes hands with MW, and asks to be introduced to Dora.

W visits the Southeys. The Poet Laureate does not recognise who he is until he is told, and W cannot hold his attention.

For seven days W, MW, Dora, IF and a niece of hers, with Quillinan and his elder daugher Jemima, are on tour: Keswick, Buttermere, Ennerdale, Calder Abbey, Wastdale, Eskdale, Duddon, Furness Abbey, and Coniston.

31 August   While climbing Helvellyn with Q, Dora riding the whole way to the summit, W composes a sonnet suggested by the etching he had received from Haydon of his picture of the Duke of Wellington on the field of Waterloo.

September
10   (Thurs) He sends Haydon a *third* revision (not the last) of lines in his recent sonnet. As he dictates his letter, he is sitting to Pickersgill, who is painting his portrait for Sir Robert Peel.
14   He is at Lowther Castle with his guest Samuel Rogers, and they are to visit the Duke of Buccleuch at Drumlanrig Castle, Dumfries.

October
16   (Fri) He has just returned home after a ten days' absence with MW.
28   She leaves Rydal to see her brother at Brinsop Court.

November
Early this month W writes to IF, who has been visiting friends in the north-east of England; he had accompanied her to Newcastle. He wishes she and MW were back at RMt.
14   (Sat) He has returned from Brigham, where his grandchildren are well; Isabella has been seriously debilitated with 'a kind of intermittent fever'. As he travelled home with John, three miles south of Keswick, they met the mail coach speeding downhill, and, though John drew close in by the wall on the left, their wheel was violently struck; they were driven through a gap in the wall, the shafts were broken, and their horse leapt back into the road, breaking the traces and galloping off without pause until it reached the turnpike at Grasmere.
24   Lord Howe has written, expressing Queen Adelaide's sincere trust that neither W nor his son has been injured; (they had been shaken, but suffered no serious injury). In his letter to IF reporting this, W refers to 'Lady Cadogan, as she calls herself, my dear ruin of a Sister'.

24 December   HCR arrives. (He finds W 'in full vigour of health and intellect', and MW 'as delightful as ever, being a model of goodness'. D has improved, but her mind is feeble, and she has no command over herself, though she speaks 'nothing absolutely insane or irrational'.)

1841

January
5   (Tues) HCR attends a dinner party at RMt with the Arnolds and James Spedding.
19 W has been reading Cowper's *The Task* aloud recently.
21 He reads 'The Norman Boy' to HCR, who thinks the poem will be popular.

February The copyright Bill was lost, W writes, because its pledged supporters were attracted from the House by dinner, after spending a long time on a vote of thanks to the Forces in Syria. He congratulates CW on his recovery after a severe accident.

March
4   (Thurs) He has been copying out manuscript poems from 1793 onwards, and may venture on another publication. John Carter has been checking the six volumes of poetry for another printing. Dora and IF travel for London, which they will leave at the beginning of April; (in the meantime Dora will be at Hendon with Mrs Gee, paying visits to her cousin at Harrow and to Mrs Hoare at Hampstead; IF will spend the first fortnight at Henry Taylor's).
    (Later this month) W has not yet had the courage to examine *The Borderers*; he has written more than a hundred lines of 'Musings near Aquapendente'. He sleeps badly from overwork, and hopes to improve from a holiday.
26 He tells HCR that Kate Southey has been at Rydal six weeks, three of them at RMt, and that he will do all he can to comfort the children of his 'afflicted Friend'.
31 W and MW leave for Brinsop Court (where, after a day at Birmingham, they stay ten days).

April
14 (Wed) They reach Bath, after travelling along the Wye to

Tintern Abbey (where they meet Dora and IF), sleeping at Chepstow, and crossing over to Bristol by steamer.

c. 20   HCR calls on the Ws at IF's, Bath.

May

11   (Tues) Dora and Quillinan are married at St James's, Bath; John W officiates, and William acts as best man.

14   After visiting Alfoxden and Nether Stowey – the object of W and MW's 'pilgrimage' – Dora and Q set off with William for the north, Wm for Carlisle, and the bridal couple for RMt, W, MW, and IF for Exeter and Plymouth (from which they make a delightful afternoon excursion to Mount Edgcumbe).

June (first week)   After visiting Racedown, the Ws had parted from IF at Charmouth (she to stay with her sister and brother-in-law in Somerset). They spend a few days with the Fishers at Salisbury, whence they enjoy short outings to Old Sarum and Wilton, proceeding via Southampton to Winchester, where they stay with their nephew Charles and are introduced to the city and cathedral.

June (later)   In London, where they meet many friends, they stay first with the Marshalls. W tires of society and the tediousness of 'Dabblers in Literature', but is pleased to receive acknowledgements of gratitude from members of the opposite sex and the young. He attends the launch of H.M.S. *Trafalgar* at Woolwich, with a vast crowd on land and water, visits Windsor, and goes with Rogers to Hampton Court, where they walk in the gardens on finding the Palace closed; he remembers his former visit here with Scott, Mrs Lockhart, and others. Bishop Blomfield and his family seem pleased to see him and MW; (W did not always approve of the bishop's liberalism).

July

7   (Wed) The Ws are at Harrow School, which Sir Robert Peel attends to hear the speeches; his son wins the prizes for Latin prose and verse. W is given a place of honour, and, in HCR's words, is 'quite reverenced'. He arranges to see Peel in Whitehall two days later on the copyright question.

10   From Harrow he goes to London to dine with HCR.

13   The Ws leave London for Coleorton with Emmeline, a young daughter of the Fishers at Salisbury, who is to stay with them

at RMt. She writes verses, and is considered a prodigy by W. (They spend eight days at Coleorton; one day, when staying with the Merewethers, they drive to a beautiful part of Charnwood Forest to see the monastery which is being built for Trappists; the interest taken in it by Lord Shrewsbury and 'other Romanist Grandees' makes W wonder rather apprehensively where it will all end.

22   The Ws reach Rydal, and find Mrs Mary H from Brinsop there with her daughter Sarah.

August
5   (Thurs) He informs IF that Emmie attaches too much importance to intellect and literature; she is a child of five years in knowledge of the world and practical sense, and such an imaginative creature of sensibility that he fears for her future.

10   Valentine Le Grice, STC's friend, visits W and tells several anecdotes of STC at Christ's Hospital, and many particulars of Lamb's boyhood.

30   W admires the fortitude, resolution, and cheerfulness of Mary H while she is afflicted by the rheumatic illness of her daughter. Emmie is sweet and affectionate; she is attached to Mrs H, and already beginning to acquire useful domestic habits. W has heard that the Wishing-Gate is destroyed, and has written the poem 'The Wishing-Gate Destroyed'.

4 September   He writes to John Peace, telling him that his visits to Alfoxden, Nether Stowey, and Coleorton were 'farewell visits for life'.

4 October   IF returns to RMt, as W had wished.

November
4   (Thurs) CW (who retired from Trinity in Oct) leaves, after a week at RMt.

8   W has revised his sonnets on capital punishment in the light of invited comments from Lockhart and Henry Taylor, who includes them in a long article on W's sonnets for the December *Quarterly Review*.

December

2   (Thurs) From Lowther Castle W writes to IF at RMt. He has
     seen his grandchildren at Brigham, and visited Plumbland
     with John. He has had difficulty with the prefatory poem for
     Poems Chiefly of Early and Late Years (including *The Borderers*
     and *Memorials of a Tour in Italy, 1837*, which is to appear in
     1842.

24   HCR brings Dora to RMt, expecting to take her back about
     the 16th or 17th of January.

26   After dinner W takes HCR with him to see his old servant
     Mary, an annual Christmas call.

1842

January

11   (Tues) HCR: 'The evening, as usual, at the Mount. We played
     whist' (a practice begun in Dec 1838).

17   W's inflammation of the eyes has returned as a result of
     imprudently walking in the cold wind. He thanks J. G.
     Lockhart for his article on copyright in *The Quarterly Review*.

18   HCR and Dora leave; William has been staying at RMt.

February

21   (Mon) Moxon has shown W's dedication of *Memorials of a
     Tour to Italy, 1837* to HCR; it is 'precisely what, and every
     thing' he could wish, HCR writes to MW.

23   W protests against the under-punctuation of a poem by John
     Peace, and asks him what he thinks of the person who wrote
     nineteen sonnets ('opened a battery of nineteen fourteen-
     pounders') against his capital punishment sonnets.

March

1   (Tues) writes to Quillinan, expressing complete confidence in
     his integrity, just before the latter has to face trial in the
     Brydges case. (Q had carelessly become involved in
     transactions which proved to be fraudulent, and had to pay
     his share in restitution and in legal costs. W's awareness of
     this involvement, and of Q's uncertain financial prospects
     had been one of the main reasons for his protracted
     disapproval of Dora's marriage.)

23   Had he foreseen the labour of correcting for his new volume
of poems, he would never have thought of it, W tells Moxon;
he detests publication and all that belongs to it. He insists
that four corrections he has overlooked on three consecutive
pages shall be made in ink. He does not want copies to be
sent to any reviewer or editor of magazines or journals.

April

7   (Thurs) He cannot let the morning of his birthday pass
without informing Dora that his heart is full of her and all
that concerns her; he is glad she likes *The Borderers*.
17   He informs Talfourd that he would be pleased to see him
when he is in the Lake District. One house likely to be free
then at Ambleside is now occupied by Dora, Q, and his two
daughters.
19   He thanks Mrs A. M. Woodward for a copy of *The Book of
Sonnets* which she has edited, and for dedicating it to him.

May

Early this month the Ws are in London; he wishes to surrender
his Distributorship to William, and use his influence while the
new copyright bill, introduced by Lord Mahon, is being debated.
(The passing of this bill leads to a considerable improvement, the
twenty-eight years being extended to forty-two, as the alternative
to life, whichever is the longer.) W has already discovered that
there is little hope of a pension, but is relieved that Dora,
recurrently ill, has been seen by Dr Ferguson, who has been sent
by Henry Taylor. He has been invited by the President of the
Royal Society, the Marquis of Northampton, to attend his soirées.
He dines at Rogers' with the Archbishop of Canterbury, the
Bishop of London, and Gladstone.

9   (Mon) W, MW, and William breakfast with HCR. W leaves a
letter on the Distributorship transfer at Lord Lonsdale's for
Sir Robert Peel's attention. Wm dines with Lord Lonsdale.
10   MW writes: 'Father or Willy . . . are fully occupied – running
after this or that influential person in the House of Lords –
then to the Stamp Off. and so on.' W spends the day with H.
Taylor.
12   HCR calls on the Ws, and discusses poems in W's latest
publication.

22 W attends church with Haydon, and has to be wakened; they call on Rogers.

28 From breakfast time with Lord Adare to dressing for dinner, W drives round with Rogers, calling on *Great* folks, MW writes. William deputizes for her at dinner with Lord Monteagle (Thomas Spring-Rice).

29 W breakfasts and attends church with Haydon. At Kenyon's dinner-party he is too tired to talk much against the loud conversation of the various groups.

31 He and Haydon dine at Talfourd's; as they walk home after an enjoyable evening, H thinks W 'rather low' because his last volume of poems has not been received with acclaim.

June

1 (Wed) The Ws go with Dora to Mrs Hoare's at Hampstead; they are joined for dinner first by HCR, then by Quillinan and William, then by CW, who is in good health and such excellent spirits that W is almost silenced. He had slept most of the way there, by the side of Lady Parry, after lively greetings with Professor Adam Sedgwick when they were about to set off.

13 W attends Miss Coutts's large *haut ton* party; any enjoyment he has in meeting friends is extinguished by the news of Dr Arnold's death the previous day.

14 He sits for Haydon, and they talk about their merry dinner with Lamb and Keats.

16 The Ws leave London. Peel has agreed to the transfer of the Distributorship, but Lord Lonsdale has been reluctant to press for the Government pension just yet.

28 From RMt W refers this question to Gladstone, explaining that he has forfeited half his income, over £400 p.a.

July

2 (Sat) HCR tells his brother that W is lonely, IF having left RMt for a time, and has invited his company. W and John Carter are busy transferring Stamp Office property and papers to Carlisle.

11 Not wishing to refer the pension question again to Lord Lonsdale, W leaves it to Gladstone to take appropriate action whenever a favourable opportunity occurs.

21 The Ws were sorry to find that he was in lodgings at

Ambleside, and not their guest, HCR writes; he does not mean to stay long.

28 It would have been an odd meeting if HCR had been with them, W comments on the visit of Wilberforce's sons the previous day (cf. 28 July 1838). F. W. Faber, who is writing, poetry very rapidly, has made several calls.

16 August   W's eye has improved, and he feels stronger. From 8.30 a.m. to 1 p.m. he waters transplanted hollies and works in the hayfield.

21 September   He tells a correspondent that he has heard little of 'the persecution which the Oxford Divines are undergoing'; he has no personal acquaintance with the Tractarians, except with Keble, as meek and humble-minded a Christian as may anywhere be found. He has just added four sonnets to his ecclesiastical series (III.xxvi–xxviii, xxxi).

October
13 (Thurs) W thanks Gladstone for exertions on his behalf.
17 Immediately on hearing that Sir Robert Peel has offered him a pension of £300 p.a. from the Civil List, W writes again to Gladstone. He sends the news to CW, adding that he and MW are just setting out to visit Colonel and Mrs Howard at Levens.
22 IF has returned to RMt, and the Ws expect soon to pay visits via Kirkstone to the Marshalls, and to William in Carlisle.
26 W thanks Elizabeth Barrett for her sonnet on Haydon's portrait of him.

November
 8 (Tues) He is at Brigham with John's family.
11 Dora and Q are at RMt.
16 'Miss Fenwick, who is now under our roof for the winter', W writes.

December
24 (Sat) W composes the sonnet 'Wansfell! this Household has a favoured lot'.
29 At Rydal HCR does not find W 'over-polemical'. W is a *high* churchman, but does not 'go all lengths' with the Oxford

School, though they claim him as their poet. Mr Faber, on the other hand, is a flaming zealot for the new doctrines, and does not conceal his predilection for Roman Catholicism.

1843

February

6 (Mon) The Ws are astonished to hear from Mrs Hutchinson of the engagement between William W and Mary Monkhouse (cf. 24 July 1834); she is just of age, and has 'a pretty good fortune', Quillinan estimates. All three will be coming to RMt from Brinsop shortly. Dora returned on Saturday, after spending ten days with the Marshalls at Hallsteads. She and Q are now in lodgings at Ambleside.

15 Southey has had an apoplectic seizure, Q reports.

March

9 (Thurs) IF refers to the *Notes* on which she has been working hard; she has been helped by Q. (These are the notes on W's poems, based on memories and points of view which she had persuaded him to talk about during the winter evenings when he was able to read little.)

21 Death of Robert Southey.

23 Though uninvited, W, accompanied by Q, attends his funeral.

April

1 (Sat) W declines the offer of the Poet Laureateship made by the Queen, on the grounds that he is too old to undertake the duties which pertain to the office. Q's answer to Landor's attack on W appears as an imaginary conversation in the April number of *Blackwood's Magazine*, and is read approvingly by HCR in the Athenaeum; it was prepared without W's knowledge.

4 Being assured by the Lord Chamberlain, the Earl De La Warr, who had recommended him, that the appointment is wholly honorary, W accepts the Poet Laureateship with great pleasure.

9 In a letter to HCR, Q alludes to William's broken engagement. W and MW have been staying with IF at Keswick, W driving to Rossthwaite in Borrowdale, which he has not seen for

some years; they return tomorrow. IF's main purpose at Keswick, from which she is expected to return on the 17th, is to persuade Kate Southey to seek reconciliation with her sister Edith (Mrs Warter).

20　A fête, organised by Dora and Q at IF's expense, is given to 120 or more children (all girls, for the boys are too boisterous) in Mr North's field, to celebrate the Poet Laureate's birthday (the 7th).

1 June　Thinking of IF's departure to London in about a fortnight, Q believes that 'neither the poet nor his wife, happy as they are in each other, is ever quite happy without her, that is for any prolonged absence from her'.

July
7　(Fri) For three weeks he and Dora have occupied Mr Curwen's residence on Belle Isle, Windermere; they have interchanged visits with W and MW more than once. Owing to his wife's illness, John W has left his two sons Willy and John at RMt, and they are coming on the 10th.

24　Q and his two daughters accompany W and MW back to Rydal. W should have been at Buckingham Palace for the Queen's Ball, to which he had been invited by the Lord Chamberlain at rather short notice. His apology had been that he had not received the invitation in time; to make his reply more convincing, he had headed it 'The Island, Windermere'. Joanna H, on a visit to her mentally unstable nephew at Elton near Stockton-on-Tees, has had a paralytic seizure.

August
2　(Wed) W informs IF that his nephew John (back from the Ionian Islands) has been examined by Dr Davy, whose report suggests a deterioration in his lungs.

17　He asks Moxon to send more copies of *The Excursion* when Christopher W calls on his way to Rydal. W has been handicapped for six weeks from inflammation of one of his eyelids. On Belle Isle, with the Quillinans, he and MW dine with Professor Wilson and his daughter; Q, who has heard that Wilson never recovered from the shock of his wife's death, thinks his cheerfulness 'rather assumed'.

18 Dora returns with her parents to RMt, on her way to Brigham, to look after the children while John takes Isabella to London for an examination by Dr Ferguson.

29 Q brings Dora back from Brigham. W meets them at Keswick; he has come to see his nephew John, who is with his mother and in a delicate state of health.

30 W and MW leave to visit Joanna H at Elton; they sleep at Hallsteads. If Joanna is well enough, they will spend a few weeks at Brinsop, while the Quillinans take care of D at RMt.

September
21 (Thurs) W writes to IF (MW has told him he must write to his 'Love'): they reached Brinsop Court the previous afternoon, having slept at Birmingham after leaving Stockton in the morning and spending six hours in York, visiting relatives and attending a service in the Minster. (Joanna died not long after the Ws had left Elton.)

27 HCR reaches Brinsop in the morning, and finds Tom H enjoying 'as good health as is possible, with the entire use of his lower limbs'.

28 The Ws visit Hereford with HCR; two elderly spinsters are proud 'to entertain the *great poet* at a dinner modestly called a luncheon', and the Dean spends more than two hours surveying the cathedral with them.

29 W and HCR are on a two-day visit to John Monkhouse, now almost blind, at the Stow, on the Wye, about twelve miles off.

October Back at RMt, W thanks the American writer R. H. Dana for news of the artist Allston's death, and sends him what information he can about him; their acquaintance was short, but W admired him and his paintings.

December
2 (Sat) He thanks John Taylor Coleridge for critical comments on the 'Inscription' verses he has written for Southey's memorial in Crosthwaite Church near Keswick.

9 W, MW, and IF have been 'charmed, affected, and instructed', Q reports, by Miss Harriet Martineau's *Life in a Sick Room*. Dora is with William at Carlisle, where Q will join her on Wednesday; after making a visit or two on the way back, one

to the Marshalls at Hallsteads, they will be home in time to greet HCR on or before Christmas Eve.

11   After reading his nephew Christopher's *Theophilus Anglicanus*, a book designed to instruct his Harrow pupils in Church principles, W writes the sonnet 'Enlightened Teacher, gladly from thy hand'.

20   W gives CW details of how a publisher, without permission, has included far more of his poems than was expected in an edition originally designed as a school-book, for his own scholars mainly, by Mr Gough, a teacher at St Bees when W gave his consent, and now headmaster of Carlisle Grammar School.

24   Having spent the day after his arrival with the Ws (he usually spent his Sundays with them), HCR returns to his lodgings, where he falls head foremost down the stairs in the dark.

25   He sends for W's servant James, who fetches the Ws. They summon the local doctor, and with him comes Dr Davy, who was with him by chance. Q calls, and W (several times), in the evening.

26   HCR is taken to RMt, where he is much more comfortable.

30   Hearing that Mrs Arnold from Fox How is below, he has James help him to dress, and surprises the ladies at tea.

1844

January

5   (Fri) W thanks Alexander Dyce for presenting him a copy of his edition of Skelton's works. He wishes he had seen them sooner, as Pope said when Hall's *Satires* were shown to him in his last years.

24   HCR leaves Rydal.

30   IF sets off to visit friends in Durham County, and stays the night at Hallsteads (where she remains until Feb because the Stainmore road is blocked with snow).

6 February   The Ws receive a china breakfast and tea set from HCR (who is accustomed to sending them gifts after his Christmas–New Year holidays at Rydal).

March

c. 15   (Fri) IF returns.

21 Writing to Gladstone, after receiving a copy of his essay 'Present Aspects of the Church', W refers to the Tractarians' mistakes and his dread of Romanism, which attracts 'the two extremes of our artificial society, the opulent and luxurious, never trained to vigorous thinking . . . and . . . the extreme poor'.

26 He tells an unknown correspondent that he receives books or manuscripts or requests for autographs 'at the rate of every day in a year'.

31 He writes to condole with Lady Frederick Bentinck on the death of her father Lord Lonsdale.

April

7   (Sun) IF informs HCR that they are organising a fête at Rydal Mount for all the village children (300 at least) and their neighbours on Tuesday next (in celebration of the poet's seventy-fourth birthday). MW tells him that Isabella, who has been in Madeira with John for a long period for the sake of her health, must, after a change of climate, spend the winter in a warm country. W has been working hard for some time, attempting to improve the versification of *The Excursion*.

12 He tells Moxon that since his departure they have not had many visitors; yesterday, two of Burns's sons and Lord and Lady Monteagle (Mrs Marshall's daughter); today, Professor Sedgwick.

May

4   (Sat) W and MW go to see their grandchildren at Brigham; their plan is to stay with William at Carlisle, and perhaps visit Newcastle.

15 Quillinan expects them to return on Saturday.

20 June W is at Flimby, on the Cumberland coast between Workington and Maryport, hoping that Dora will benefit from the sea-air. (He enjoys his solitary walks during his five days' visit, but is saddened that Q cannot regulate his temper in accordance with the demands his wife's indispositions too frequently make, and that he converses little with her, devoting his time to his papers and books.)

July

9   (Tues) MW and W are 'Darby and Joan-ing it' with their three grandsons at RMt; he tries himself working in the hayfield. Q is in Ireland; Dora and his daughters are still at Flimby, and IF is in the London area.

14   The tourist season has begun, and CW (who stayed for three weeks), Moxon, and Rogers are expected. So too is a friend of Professor Reed, Henry Inman, now in London, who is to paint W's portrait. Julius (Archdeacon) Hare will soon be at Mrs Arnold's; and Professor Hamilton, with Mr Graves at Bowness. Talfourd has taken a cottage by the Rothay river for ten weeks from the middle of August. Pending engagements have made it impossible for W to accept an invitation to the Burns celebrations. He and MW are reading Stanley's life of Dr Arnold.

21   By Ullswater, as he rides home from Lowther Castle, W thinks no country could be more beautiful. Q is at Flimby, but goes to Ireland again on Tuesday.

22 (or 29?)   Professor William Hamilton, Professor Archer Butler, Mr Graves, and Archdeacon Hare dine at RMt, where 'a rout of some thirty or forty' is expected in the evening. Yesterday, W writes, 'Mr Hare gave us . . . what Mrs Wordsworth called a magnificent Sermon'.

With these friends, on a bright late July day near Loughrigg Tarn, while they are admiring the splendour of the Langdale Pikes, W looks down and sees (he thinks) a dark star-shaped fossil, which proves to be the shadow cast by a daisy on a stone under an almost vertical sun; cf. the poem written early in August, 'So fair, so sweet, withal so sensitive'.

16 August   W receives from Elizabeth Barrett a copy of her collected poems.

September

23   (Mon) Quillinan is on Belle Isle, but Dora, who came to take care of D in her parents' absence, is too ill to leave RMt. John W and Isabella have been at Lucca three months. The Inman portrait of W ('the last and best', though the sitting lasted hardly four and a half hours, MW writes) is on its way to Philadelphia. IF is now in Somerset; W had been planning to build a cottage for her in Dora's Field, then in the Wishing-

Gate field at Grasmere, if an exchange of the two properties can be made with Lady Fleming. (Nothing comes of these plans, partly because IF cannot agree while Dora has no house.)

28 W returns after visits which take him with William to a friend near Kirkby Lonsdale, to Hornby Castle in the Vale of Lune, finally to the Howards at Levens (where MW joined him on the 25th).

October

4 (Fri) W is pleased to hear from CW that his son Christopher has been made a canon of Westminster, for his position at Harrow (where discipline was difficult) had been undermining his health, and he was not suited to it.

15 He asks Gladstone to give attention to the plan for extending the railway from Kendal to Windermere.

16 His sonnet 'On the Projected Kendal and Windermere Railway' (dated 12 Oct 1844) appears in *The Morning Post.*

Later this month and early in November the Ws are away about four weeks: two weeks at Leamington, timed to coincide with IF's visit there, followed by visits to Cambridge and to H. W. Faber at his parish of Elton in Huntingdonshire. At Northampton, while held up by officials and the crowd, they see the Queen and her retinue.

November

13 (Wed) W and MW return to Rydal.

17 Dora has another setback, and is to remain at RMt while Q and his daughters are on Belle Isle. They will all return to their Ambleside lodgings early in December.

December

18 (Wed) W writes on behalf of his son John, immediately on receiving a notice, dated 11 November but not delivered to the vicarage, Brigham, until 17 December (leaving only four days to make objections), of a railway which is scheduled from Cockermouth to Workington, and planned to pass through John's property, not many yards from his house.

25 HCR finds W and MW well, but Dora an invalid. (During his stay he finds that W is less impressed than he had been by

Tractarianism, and not upset by his own Unitarianism, though HCR can express his liberal views more freely at Mrs Fletcher's and Mrs Arnold's.)

1845

January

2   (Thurs) HCR plays whist with the Ws, as he does every *lawful* evening, as the Scots might say (i.e. excepting Sundays).

15 At Mr Davy's (he had settled at Lesketh How, Ambleside) W sits next to Harriet Martineau, and steers clear of mesmerism. (HM, who had just arrived at Ambleside, which she was to make her home, believed that she owed her recovery to mesmerism.) Another disbeliever present, besides W and Davy, is the latter's mother-in-law, the authoress Mrs Fletcher, who lives at Lancrigg, Easedale.

23 HCR leaves Rydal, and W hopes he will receive from the printer at Kendal, on his return journey, a few copies of the two letters on the Kendal–Windermere railway that he (W) has sent to *The Morning Post.*

February

1   (Sat) The Ws call on Harriet Martineau, who 'relates strong things of cures by Mesmerism'.

13 William, who has been ill again, must return to Carlisle from Rydal; the house taken for IF will be ready in a few days.

April

4   (Fri) Dr Davy, IF, and the Ws (MW reluctantly) have agreed that it would be wise for Quillinan to accept his brother's offer of a house at the mouth of the Douro for him and Dora. He is afraid of the voyage for her.

8   Dora gives up the idea of going to Portugal, for the sake of her mother.

10 W expresses a long-standing wish to publish his poems independently of his prose, the prefaces and supplement to be included in the prose volume which is being considered. John is expected home from Italy to attend to his parish and affairs.

18 W feels he must attend the Queen's Ball on the 25th, and will

leave with the Quillinans on the 23rd. Q is to attend his brother's wedding at Oporto, and Dora will accompany him for the sake of her health.

24 W is staying with the Moxons; he is to borrow Court dress (lent to Tennyson nearly six years later), bag-wig, and sword, from Rogers for the ball.

May

5 (Mon) After a period with the Moxons, W is at Hampstead with Mrs Hoare. HCR reports dining with them, and finding W in wretched spirits, anxious about Dora (who leaves for Lisbon on Wednesday), and suffering from eye-trouble. After two recent meetings, W and Tennyson are cordial at Moxon's dinner-party later this month.

12 At Rydal, W writes to thank Moxon, his wife, and his daughter, for their great kindness to him; he will always be grateful to Rogers for his care and concern. He was enchanted when he 'came into the Lake District a little above Bowness', his eyes better for the return journey, though he still needs an amanuensis.

June

2 (Mon) With Carter's help, he is now preparing for the new edition of his poems (a collected edition which the less affluent can afford).

6 He writes 'The Westmoreland Girl' for his grandchildren.

17 John W leaves RMt with his four boys, whom he is taking to their sick mother at Lucca, after his brief return to Brigham.

20 IF and Kate Southey return with the young Miss Arnolds from Furness Abbey with news of the navvies working on the railway that passes close by the east window. (W's sonnet 'At Furness Abbey', dated 21 June 1845, is based on what he was told.)

14 July In a letter to Moxon, he discloses that Dora has had a severe illness in Portugal. The American poet W. C. Bryant has called on him.

August

6 (Wed) John Monkhouse leaves RMt after a fortnight's stay.

7 MW is delighted with reports of Dora's improvement in

health; the reverse is true of John's wife Isabella. The youthful poetess Emmie Fisher is again at RMt; Charles W, his daughter, and three lady friends occupy the Quillinans' lodgings at Ambleside.

September
7   (Sun) John is expected back soon, to resume his duties at Plumbland.
18   W sets off with William for Brigham, to decide the site to which the parsonage is to be removed to make room for the railway.
23   W and MW leave to see Tom H at Brinsop Court (where they mean to stay a month, calling at York to see relatives, and at Leeds, on their return journey). They expect to be absent about six weeks.
29   From Brinsop W writes to Derwent Coleridge to condole with him on the loss of his mother, whom he had known more than fifty years.

28 October   He writes from York, where he had been anxious to see his oldest relative, a contemporary, Mrs Robinson. On the 30th he and MW will leave to visit the Marshalls at Headingly, Leeds.

November
4   (Tues) They leave Leeds and reach Rydal.
5   He sends a second letter to Moxon, eliminating his honours (Poet Laureate, etc.) from the title-page of his collected poems. All the prose is to be printed at the end.
25   W thinks the engravings of the Chantrey bust and of Rydal Mount, for the new edition of his poems, considerably improved. His son John is still at RMt, and in very good health.

December
9   (Tues) HCR receives the new edition of W's poems in a handsome volume. (Moxon had acted in accordance with W's suggestion of 14 July that it should be 'out against the time that Christmas presents are called for'.)
16   With reference to a report on education and related volumes sent by an Inspector of Schools, W thinks too much emphasis is placed on book-learning, not enough on outdoor pursuits

(this 'from one who spent half of his boyhood in running wild among the Mountains'), and too little on 'books of imagination which are eminently useful in calling forth intellectual power'.

19 HCR reaches Rydal, and has time to call with the Ws on IF and others at Ambleside.

24 News comes of the death of John's youngest son at Lucca; two children have been taken to Albano for change of air, and one remains, stricken with fever, with Isabella. The lost grandchild, W wrote (2 Jan 1846), 'was one of the noblest Creatures both in mind and body I ever saw'.

31 Harriet Martineau dines at RMt to meet Moxon, who is on a week's visit; she talks endlessly on mesmerism.

1846

January

1 (Thurs) In his eagerness to reach Rome, John passes in the mail without calling, but leaving a letter on the way; he purposes to bring his children back.

22 W's recent bereavement and fears are expressed in two sonnets: 'Where lies the truth?' (10 Jan) and 'Why should we weep or mourn, Angelic boy'. CW has been alarmingly ill, and is still very weak.

February

2 (Mon) He dies at his Buxted rectory.

A few days later W is suffering from his old eye complaint, and fears that his dear nephew John, now living at Ambleside, has not long to live. The Queen has sent him four portraits of her children in return for the presentation copy of his collected poems.

8 Miss Martineau says that W's mind is so fully occupied with whatever he is thinking of that he soon forgets his griefs. He goes every day, she continues, to IF, greets her with a smacking kiss, and sits down by her fire 'to open his mind'.

March

12 (Thurs) He thanks his nephew Charles for a copy of his Winchester farewell sermon; he cannot agree with his

encouragement of emulation, which is too close to envy, as he used to tell Dr Bell, in whose system it was a 'master-spring'. (C had been appointed Warden of Glenalmond School in Perthshire; he became Bishop of St Andrews.)

14   From Sir William Hamilton comes news that W has been made an honorary member of the Royal Irish Academy.

2 April   John and his children are expected to reach London in a day or two.

May
13   (Wed) John and two of his boys are still at RMt; the two eldest are at school near Fleetwood; Isabella, her doctor, and her mother are on their way home. Miss Martineau is happy in her new house. Depressed chiefly by public affairs, W finds pleasure among birds and flowers; he reads his own poetry less than any other, and often thinks his life 'in a great measure wasted'.

19   Archbishop Whateley of Dublin, who is staying with Mrs Arnold, calls on W. (A day or so earlier James had driven W, MW, and Jemima Quillinan to W's old haunts at Hawkshead, which he made a point of seeing every year; with no boys playing or roaming about the vale, the place has changed immensely from what it had been in his schooldays. The Quillinans are sight-seeing in Spain, *en route* for England.

June
22   (Mon) John, Isabella, and their four boys are at RMt. Dora and Q are now in the Isle of Wight with IF.

29   HCR meets the Quillinans at Mrs Hoare's, Hampstead, on their way to Rydal. Dora looks well.

July
18   (Sat) W acknowledges receipt of his Laureate's salary from Moxon (who collects it), and requests him to pay £5 into the Haydon fund; (H had shot himself on 22 June). Dora is back and 'gradually strengthening'. W hopes Moxon will enjoy his tour in Switzerland with Tennyson; but for his nephew's illness he would like to visit the Pyrenees (with MW).

30   The Qs now have a home, Loughrigg Holme by the Rothay

river; (the rent, £80 p.a. including servants' wages, is paid by the Ws).

August

17 (Mon) Q takes Dora and her parents for an evening drive; afterwards they have their first game of whist, in preparation for HCR's Christmas visit. William has been staying at Brighton with Miss Graham (whom he is to marry in February).

18 W's nephew John dies at Ambleside, in the presence of his mother and his cousin William.

(In a letter to Henry Taylor, written about this time, W asks him to tell IF that Q is busy with Portuguese literature; Kate Southey is still at RMt, and W's rheumatism does not allow him to ride in a carriage.)

October

1 (Thurs) Dora has almost completed the journal she kept in Portugal and Spain.

2 W sends his condolences to Catherine Clarkson on the death of her husband.

19 In his letter to IF, W refers to her intended gifts to William 'in four gilded frames'. Dora is 'wonderfully strong and well'. MW would like W to accompany her on a vist to IF at Bath in the winter; he would prefer to take them both abroad in the spring.

November (early) After having declined candidature, W has been proposed for the Lord Rectorship of the University of Glasgow; despite his majority of twenty-one votes, the deputy Lord Rector has decided in favour of Lord John Russell. Dora, with Q's assistance, has just concluded revising her journal, and W looks forward to hearing it read by MW.

14 December John is coming by coach, and his three boys will arrive (from school) on Wednesday; as they have lost so much education, W proposes to examine their progress. Moxon has made Dora a generous offer for her journal; (he published it in 1847).

1847

January

12   (Tues) HCR's visit is curtailed; he arrives late and, instead of the usual four, spends little more than two weeks at Rydal.

19   On the day of William's wedding at Brighton there is a tea-party of fifty, including the servants, at RMt.

30   HCR has more conversation with W than on any previous day since his arrival. His host is back to his 'usual flow', and criticizes Henry Hallam's judgment of taste and literature in 'his great history'. (HCR had found W less animated and talkative, willing to let heresies which he would not have tolerated earlier pass uncontradicted.) William arrives with his wife Fanny.

March

15   (Mon) At Bath (he and MW are staying at IF's, 8 Queen Square) W accepts a request from Prince Albert to compose an ode to be sung at his (the Consort's) installation as Chancellor of the University of Cambridge on 6 July.

19   HCR arrives, at IF's invitation.

April

8   (Thurs) The Ws leave Bath, and are met at the London railway station by Moxon; they proceed to Mrs Hoare's, Hampstead.

9   They expect to see Christopher and his wife about 1 p.m., and are most anxious to hear that Dora is better. (She had caught a cold before Christmas, on her way to Carlisle, to help William prepare his home; her lungs had been affected, and she never recovered.) Moxon is to call.

26   HCR visits W at his nephew's 'in the Westminster Cloisters', and sits with him while Wyon's son models his head for a bas-relief medallion. The sitting is interrupted by alarming news of Dora. In the evening W and MW leave for Rydal.

29   From Rydal W sends T. Attwood Walmisley of Trinity College, Cambridge, 'the promised Ode corrected as well as under distressing circumstances' he had been able to do it. (Just when it was written, its plan and composition being very largely Quillinan's, is not clear.) His nephew had

encouraged him to think the words would suit Walmisley's music.

May

5 (Wed) W writes in general agreement with Walmisley, and tells him to reject any alterations but one, to suit the music.

7 Dora has been moved to RMt for nursing, and MW writes to Lady Monteagle on her state. John W has left that morning after a three-day visit to his 'only beloved Sister and early companion'. (During the ensuing weeks he and William are at RMt whenever their duties permit.)

June

1 (Tues) Mrs Arnold writes to HCR on the 'composure and cheerful submission' of Dora, which teaches the Ws 'to bear the greatest sorrow which could have befallen them'. MW informs Lady Monteagle that W, 'not having the consolatory *duty* of nursing', suffers most.

8 W informs Mr Dawson that his daughter is 'wasting away in a pulmonary consumption', and thinks that the water-bed he lent them about the same time in 1846 for her cousin would give Dora relief.

July

1 (Thurs) John cannot leave his children at Plumbland; he has administered the Sacrament to Dora on three occasions.

9 Dora dies just before 1 a.m.

August

9 (Mon) An order by W for a copy of his poems, strongly and handsomely bound for use in a school, to be sent to the Revd Dr Woolley Rossall near Fleetwood, indicates the school to which John's sons have been sent.

12 Writing from RMt, IF tells HCR that she will speak 'of the blessed death of beloved Dora' when they meet. D is now W's chief employment; he attends her indoors and out. MW looks more aged and feeble than he.

21 September MW has taken W to the new vicarage at Brigham (Isabella is on the Continent, after leaving her daughter Jane at a school in Brighton). A drive to Whitehaven having done him good, she hopes she will prevail on him to spend time with William at Brisco near Carlisle before their return to RMt.

18 October   They are staying with Wm and Fanny at Brisco. W sleeps and walks a great deal. He is now at his last sitting with the miniature-painter Thomas Carrick, after hours every morning the previous week on this engagement.

December
 6   (Mon) W cannot remember whether he has written to IF since their return. He has seen Quillinan very little, partly because he cannot bear to cross the bridge and field that leads to Loughrigg Holme.
18   HCR arrives, bringing W's grand-daughter Jane and her cousin and school-friend Clara Curwen (on her way to Workington Hall); John's boys have left, after ten days at RMt on their way home.
24   HCR writes: 'Mr W sits generally alone. And whichever room I may be in, he goes into the other.' Whist is out of the question.
27   MW tells IF (at Kelston Knoll, near Bath) that HCR is in 'his usual redundant spirits'. His visit would be very dull, were he not such a welcome and cheerful visitor in the neighbourhood. She and W had derived great pleasure and comfort from the visit of Christopher and his wife (from Westminster), who had collected notes in preparation for his *Memoirs of William Wordsworth* (1851).
29   W tells Moxon that HCR is still with them, and will leave at the end of next week. 'Our sorrow, I feel, is for life.'

1848

January
 8   (Sat) HCR takes leave of W, who cannot speak for weeping. During the latter part of his stay HCR has persuaded him to walk with him every day the weather was favourable, and even to make calls, but MW had told him that afterwards he would return to his room and cry incessantly.
17   IF informs HCR that the notes which W dictated to her on his poems, and which she had intended for Dora, must now go

to Quillinan. She regrets to hear of the want of understanding between Q and the Ws.

1 February   Q tells HCR that W and he walk together 'a good deal now, and he seems to seek and take pleasure in my company'. He talks constantly of Dora, and comes to Q's house occasionally. William and Fanny leave Rydal for their new home; both think the Mount, like their previous house at Brisco, is too airless for F, who is delicate.

8 April   W and MW leave, expecting to be away four weeks, two with William and Fanny at Carlisle, followed by two at Brigham. (News comes to John W, after staying with them at Carlisle, of Jane's attempt to run away from her school at Brighton, and he has to bring her home.) From John's vicarage, W enjoys walks in the neighbourhood of his birthplace (by the Derwent river to Cockermouth).

20 May   He and MW return home after six weeks' absence.

June
  6   (Tues) W (Quillinan thinks) is less disposed 'to bear up when alone or only with his wife'; he needs company, and Kate Southey is with them; (Q had spent eight or nine days with them at Brigham).
  7   MW is glad to hear from HCR that IF seems to be in better health and spirits. She regrets that her daughter-in-law Fanny, who is now in Edinburgh with her father, seeking medical advice, is in a weak state. At Brigham all is as well as can be expected, with Isabella in Italy, and staying there with her brother for the winter, 'in search of health'.

23 July   Callers are good for W, Quillinan writes, though RMt does not have as many 'pilgrims' as in previous years, except the last. He has left the Ws at tea with his two girls, John Monkhouse (one of whose bull calves has won the £20 prize at York Agricultural Show), two of John's boys, Herbert Hill (Southey's son-in-law), one of his boys, and Hartley Coleridge. James Stephen (late of the Colonial Office) called on W yesterday. John's two boys' birthdays are today and tomorrow, and all the children in the neighbourhood and some adults have been invited to celebrate with them tomorrow evening.

August
2   (Wed) William and Fanny have stayed for a short period, after visiting a friend of hers near Manchester. MW is not looking forward to the tourist season; it seems as if 'America had broken loose', so many from that country, New York in particular, coming to see the poet, who receives all strangers cordially. She is interrupted as she writes by a group of young tourists who appear in front of the hall window.

5   W and MW go to visit Mrs Pollard (the late Mrs Marshall's sister) at Hallsteads, and perhaps Mrs Crackanthorpe. D is upset at his departure, for he spoils her, Quillinan says.

11   More than fifty train-trippers invade RMt, walking without leave over the terrace and garden, but doing no harm.

17   The Ws return; they have visited all their surviving Penrith friends, and the Crackanthorpes at Newbiggin Hall. John has removed his boys from Rossall's school, and sent them to Sedbergh.

29   It is not just Americans who call, MW writes, but bishops, including the Bishop of London and Mrs Blomfield; she is pleased that they divert W from his sad thoughts.

November
After the death of their mother in Italy, MW is anxious, early this month, to be with her grandchildren at Brigham, but it is difficult to get away with W, so much is he subject to D's wishes and 'waywardnesses'.

18   (Sat) W writes to John Peace from Brigham.

30   He returns with MW to RMt.

December
27   (Wed) HCR arrives before 9 a.m., after travelling by rail the previous day. Breakfast and the customary inquiries over, he and W call at Hartley Coleridge's cottage, to discover if there is any hope of his recovery.

28   HCR finds the Ws much more cheerful, and has had more conversation with W in two days than during the whole of his previous visit. Fox How, he writes, is the headquarters of Whiggery, as RMt is of High Churchism. (Earlier) in the year he recalled W's saying that he had 'no respect for the Whigs' but 'a great deal of the Chartist' in him.)

30   John leaves early with his two boys, who have been at RMt

from Sedbergh since before Christmas. Derwent Coleridge is MW's guest; he had come expecting to find his brother dead.

1849

January
7   (Sat) Hartley Coleridge dies.
11 He is buried at Grasmere, near the W graves. HCR takes his leave after the funeral. He has found W more calm and composed than he expected, D sunk further in insensibility, and Quillinan busy with his translation of Camoens' epic.
12 W walks through snow and sleet to visit Q, who finds him in 'his most cheerful mood', talk about his grandchildren recalling his own boyhood, then *the* STC. A day to 'Boswellize', Q thinks.

February
1   (Thurs) Mary Hutchinson is with the Ws at Rydal; (she and her crippled husband Tom now live with their son George at Mathon vicarage, West Malvern).
6   She and the Ws leave to call on Mrs Myers and Kate Southey at Keswick; (they are on their way to Brigham).

March
7   (Wed) MW writes from William's house at Carlisle, after their stay at Brigham, where Jane is teaching John's younger boys; she (Jane) is to go with Mary H to Mathon for a change.
26 The Ws and Mary H leave Carlisle, and spend the night with relatives at Penrith.

7 April   W thanks IF for her good wishes, and tells her what a great comfort it will be to have her once again under their roof.

May (late?)   The Ws visit Tom and Mary H at Mathon, and stay several weeks; they hope to meet IF at Malvern in June.

June
21 (Thurs) HCR goes with Moxon to Malvern, to spend a few days with W; IF is there.
24 W walks twice over Malvern Hill without difficulty. HCR

notices that, although in good health, W has lost his mental vigour.

30	The Ws leave Mahon and arrive home in the evening.

2 July	After attending two services, and receiving the Sacrament, the previous day, Tom H dies at 3 a.m. His son Thomas reaches RMt with the news at 10 p.m.

July (later)	Mrs Gaskell is in the Lake District; she and her two daughters have tea on the 11th with Quillinan, who persuades W to meet her and her husband.

16 August	Though nothing is said in Q's presence, it is not forgotten that this is MW's birthday and Dora's. Mr and Mrs Johnson (from London) spend part of the day at RMt, and John W arrives with his daughter Jane.

December
1	(Sat) HCR receives from W the first letter he has written him since Dora's death; it expresses a strong hope that he will make his customary Christmas visit. HCR intends to go, but not to stay as long as usual, partly because the Ws are not as active as they used to be, partly because old Mrs Fletcher and Harriet Martineau will not be in the vicinity. W acknowledges the receipt of a print of 'Our Lady of the Snow' on the Rigi (cf. 18–19 Aug 1820 and W's poem of that title in *Memorials of a Tour on the Continent, 1820*), and a basket of applies, from William Pearson.
18	HCR is unable to come owing to indisposition. Matthew Arnold is expected to arrive at Fox How.
29	HCR's friend, the American preacher J. C. Richmond, tells W that the six great English poets are Chaucer, Spenser, Shakespeare, Milton, Wordsworth, and Martin Tupper.

1850

January
2	(Wed) The Ws, including John, and Matthew Arnold and his wife, dine with Quillinan.

18 W writes to a lady, thanking her for a print of the Queen
    which she has sent in token of her visit.

2 February John's boys come for three days on their way to
Sedbergh School.

March
10 (Sun) W attends Rydal Chapel; in the evening he walks with
    his niece Elizabeth H (from Brinsop Court) to Grasmere.
12 He walks with MW to a cottage near White Moss Common.
14 He suffers an attack of pleurisy.

April
Early this month, after seeming to recover, W is exhausted and
has to spend most of his time in bed.
?8 (Mon) A copy of Charles's sermon arrives from Glenalmond,
    and MW reads it to W.
?9 She loses the hope of recovery which had come to her the
    previous evening.
23 Writing before noon, Quillinan reports that John and William
    are at RMt, as well as the two Miss Hutchinsons (Sarah had
    been there some time with Elizabeth; their mother Mary is
    expected daily). D has taken command of herself, and thinks
    of others' feelings. Christopher and his wife will arrive for
    three days at the end of the month; he will be 'tasked to write
    the Life even sooner perhaps than he expected'. W dies at
    noon, according to Harriet Martineau.
27 He is buried at Grasmere.

May MW, who gives the poem its title, sends *The Prelude* to Moxon
for publication.

June Quillinan checks the proofs.

July *The Prelude* is published.

Edward Quillinan, not yet sixty, dies unexpectedly on 8 July 1851,
after catching cold on a fishing expedition. D soon relapses after
W's death, and lives almost physically helpless, generally in a
world of illusion, until her death on 25 Jan 1855. Catherine
Clarkson and IF die in 1856. (Knowing that IF was too infirm to

travel north, MW went with her grand-daughter Jane, as autumn approached in 1853, to see her while she was staying with Henry Taylor in London. A few weeks later, on 7 Nov, she and Jane were taken by HCR to spend a few days with Mrs Clarkson at Playford Hall.) Although nearly blind in her last years, MW retains her faith and serenity; she dies on 17 Jan 1859.

Persons of Importance in Wordsworth's Life

(These sketches are not biographical digests; they present no more than backgrounds which illuminate W's relationships with people outside his own family and relatives. Well-known writers such as Coleridge, Scott, Southey, De Quincey, Hazlitt, and Keats are excluded.)

Sir George Beaumont, landscape painter and patron of art (1753–1827). Born at Dunmow, Essex; educated at Eton and New College, Oxford; succeeded to the baronetcy in 1762; married in 1778, and toured Italy with his wife in 1782; elected to Parliament in 1790. In 1800 he began the rebuilding of Coleorton Hall. He had been a close friend of Sir Joshua Reynolds, and was one of the first to detect the merits of Wilkie and Landseer. Among the artists and writers he befriended, in addition to Wordsworth, were Coleridge, Haydon, and the sculptor John Gibson. He admired the landscapes of Wilson and Claude, but his own work rarely rises above the mediocre. His collection began with drawings of English artists such as Wilson and Girtin, and was steadily and discriminatingly augmented with works of the old masters. One of his great ambitions was the establishment of a national gallery, to which he contributed conspicuously, after the purchase of Angerstein's collection by the State, by adding sixteen of his own pictures, including Claudes, Rembrandts, and Wilkie's 'The Blind Fiddler'.

Thomas Clarkson, anti-slavery agitator (1760–1846). Son of the headmaster of Wisbech Grammar School, he was educated at St Paul's School and St John's, Cambridge. The subject of his prize-wining Latin essay set the course of his life. Its translation made him many friends, and led to his acquaintance with William Wilberforce. After being appointed to the committee for the suppression of the slave trade, Clarkson stayed in Paris six months, unsuccessfully endeavouring to win the support of the French Government. His health undermined by extensive

223

travelling in England to collect evidence for his cause, he was compelled to retire in 1794. Nine years later he rejoined the committee, and the bill for the abolition of the slave trade was passed in January 1807, to receive the royal assent in March. In 1818 he interviewed the Emperor of Russia at Aix-la-Chapelle to secure his influence among the allied sovereigns at the forthcoming conference on ending the slave trade throughout their dominions. He and Wilberforce were made vice-presidents of the Anti-Slavery Society, but Clarkson was unable to play an active role in the movement which led to the passing of the 1833 bill for emancipating slaves within the British Empire. His health had suffered; after a period of total blindness, an operation restored his sight. He was awarded the freedom of the City of London. His last appearance on a public platform was at the Anti-Slavery Convention of 1840, a scene commemorated by the painter Haydon. He died at Playford Hall.

Derwent Coleridge (1800–1883): educated at St John's, Cambridge; ordained by the Bishop of Exeter in 1825, and soon afterwards made head of Helston Grammar School, Cornwall. His work *The Scriptural Character of the English Church* was published in 1839. In 1841 he was appointed principal of St Mark's College, Chelsea, newly founded by the National Society; here he placed great emphasis on choral services in the chapel. He was an accomplished linguist. He wrote a biography of his brother Hartley (1849), edited his poetry and prose, and (with his sister Sara) some of his father's works.

Hartley Coleridge, poet and periodical writer (1796–1849), was born at Clevedon, Somerset. From his earliest years he showed exceptional propensities for abstract thinking and romantic imaginings. After the separation of his parents, he was brought up in Southey's family, and spoilt by other occupants of Greta Hall. He became a shy young man of small physique, awkward, impatient of control, but a ready and engaging conversationalist. At Oxford the freedom of his views annoyed those in authority; his failure to win the Newdigate Prize did not improve his temperament. He was too partial to wine at parties to retain his Oriel fellowship; in compensation he was allowed £300 at the end of his probationary year. As a teacher at Ambleside, he failed to keep discipline; more self-disciplined in temporary posts at

Sedbergh, as teacher in 1837 and head in 1838, he worked more commendably. His main literary research was devoted to the works of Massinger and Ford, his edition being published with biographies in 1840. Two volumes of his poetry and prose were collected by his brother Derwent, and appeared in 1851.

(Sir) Humphry Davy, scientist (1778–1829), was born and educated at Penzance; he developed very early a love of literature and experimental science. His education was continued privately at Truro. After his father's death, he was apprenticed to a Penzance surgeon, with whom his experimental work continued. In 1798 he was appointed Dr Beddoes' assistant, and given charge of the Pneumatic Institution at Bristol. In 1801 he became assistant lecturer at the Royal Institution, London, director of its chemical laboratory, and editor of its journals. He was elected Fellow of the Royal Society in 1803, and its secretary in 1807. His discoveries, and the eloquence of his lectures, drew distinguished audiences. His fame became European; he won the Napoleonic Prize, and was awarded the honorary degree of LL.D. at Trinity College, Dublin. After being knighted in 1812 and marrying a lady of great wealth, his tastes and company became more aristocratic. He had recognised the talents of Faraday, and made him an assistant at the Royal Institution. His scientific work in a variety of fields continued to the end, though today he is remembered chiefly for his safety lamp in mines. In 1818 he was made a baronet, and in 1820 he succeeded Sir Joseph Banks as President of the Royal Society. An apoplectic attack followed by paralysis made him retire to Italy, to which he returned, after a period in England, in 1828. As he was dying (still interested in the electricity of the torpedo), his wife and brother joined him in 1829. He rallied at Rome, but died afterwards at Geneva.

Frederick William Faber, hymn-writer and leader of Catholic converts (1814–1863). Soon after Frederick's birth his father became secretary to the Bishop of Durham. F was educated at Bishop Auckland, Kirkby Stephen, Shrewsbury, and Harrow. After two years at Balliol he became a scholar of New College, Oxford, in 1834. He won the Newdigate Prize in 1836, and was made a Fellow of New College in 1837. He was a great admirer of Henry Newman. Ordained deacon in 1837, he took a small reading party to Ambleside, assisted the Revd John Dawes there, and became acquainted with W. In 1845, three years after being appointed rector of Elton, Huntingdonshire, he abjured Protestantism and was received into the Catholic Church. He formed a community of converts, which was transferred from Birmingham to Cotton Hall, thanks to the munificence of the Earl of Shrewsbury. From 1849 he was superior of the newly formed London Oratory, which was transferred in 1854 to Brompton, where he died. He is remembered chiefly for his hymns; among his poems will be found one on Loughrigg, and Brathay sonnets.

William Godwin (1756–1836), born at Wisbech, son of a Dissenting minister and educated at Hoxton Presbyterian College, became a 'complete unbeliever' in 1787, after five years in the ministry. He turned to literature, but it was not until *Political Justice* (1793) that he achieved fame and temporary fortune; he had read the manuscript of Paine's *The Rights of Man*, and become friendly with Thomas Holcroft and Horne Tooke. A rationalist, believing in the benevolence of mankind, he wished to sweep away the restraints of social institutions. Nevertheless, after living with the feminist Mary Wollstonecraft, he married her five months before she died in giving birth to their daughter, the future Mrs Shelley. After writing his wife's biography, Godwin produced numerous works, including novels, plays, essays, and a 'Life' of Chaucer. The bookshop which he set up in London in 1805 involved him in many difficulties. The most powerful and implicitly revolutionary of his novels is *Things as they Are, or the Adventures of Caleb Williams* (1794).

George Huntly Gordon (1796–1868) was prevented by deafness from entering the Church of Scotland. Sir Walter Scott, for whom he acted as amanuensis, found him a post in 1826 as private secretary to Stephen Rumbold Lushington, Secretary of the Treasury. Later he worked in the Stationery Office.

Benjamin Robert Haydon, historical painter (1786–1846), was born at Plymouth. From his grandfather and from his father, a printer and publisher, he inherited a love of painting which was stimulated by a Neapolitan who described works by Raphael and Michelangelo. Needing discipline, he was transferred from a grammar school at Plymouth to another at Plympton. In 1804, determined to be a painter, he left Plymouth for London, where he sought advice but worked under no master. Despite successes, and the interest and help of Sir George Beaumont, H quarrelled with the Academy, alienated friends, and accumulated debts. His 'Judgment of Solomon' (1814) restored confidence in him, without making him solvent. For six years the huge canvas of 'Christ's Entry into Jerusalem' was his major preoccupation. He married in 1821, but was continually harassed by creditors. After imprisonment for debt he endeavoured to make a living by portraits and small pictures; later he was more successful in London and northern towns and cities as a lecturer. He showed astonishing energy, but his works rarely equal his inspiration; both are to be found in his journals. His pride and overpowering feelings, coupled with disappointment and financial failure, proved too much for him in the end; he shot himself in his studio.

Maria Jewsbury (1800–1833), poet and sister of the novelist Geraldine, was born in Derbyshire. Her parents moved to Manchester in 1818; on the death of her mother soon afterwards, M took charge of her sister and three brothers. Alaric Watts persuaded her to adopt literature as a profession in 1824. In 1832 she married the Revd W. K. Fletcher, a chaplain in the East India Company; she died of cholera at Poonah less than a year after reaching India. Her health was delicate, but she had a vivacious personality and quick powers of perception; cf. W's note to 'Liberty', a sequel to his poem on the vase of gold and silver fish which she presented to the Ws in 1829.

John Kenyon, poet and philanthropist (1784–1856), was born in Jamaica. His parents died while he was at school in Bristol; his education continued at Charterhouse and, after some dabbling in science, at Peterhouse, Cambridge, which he left without a degree in 1808. After his marriage, he settled at Woodlands between Nether Stowey and Alfoxden, where he became friendly with Thomas Poole, and through him with Coleridge, Lamb, Wordsworth, and Southey; his philanthropy was of great benefit to STC's family. Rich and without ambition, he lived for society and travel. The discovery that Robert Browning's father was one of his school-fellows led to an unbroken friendship with the Brownings; when they visited England, his house was their home. He was a genial host and gastronome. The wealthy brother of his second wife, who died in 1825, left him most of his property in 1849. The largest of his many legacies, £10,000, went to Browning.

Charles Lloyd, poet (1775–1839), eldest son of the Birmingham Quaker banker and philanthropist. His first volume of poetry was published in 1795, the year in which he met STC (who had come to Birmingham to find subscribers for *The Watchman*). Lloyd was so impressed by his knowledge and eloquence that he engaged to live with him at £80 p.a. in return for three hours of daily instruction. This began at Kingsdown, Bristol, and continued at Nether Stowey, where Lloyd had alarming fits. After a period in London, where he became friendly with Lamb, he returned; a breach followed when STC heard of his mischievous gossip with Lamb. Lloyd's novel *Edmund Oliver* drew on STC's life in the Army but was principally intended as an attack on Godwin's marriage views. After his marriage in 1799, he lived first at Barnwell near Cambridge, then at Low Brathay, Ambleside. In 1811 he began to suffer auditory illusions. He escaped from the Retreat, York, in 1818, suddenly appearing at De Quincey's cottage. During his temporary recovery he lived with his wife in London. He died in an asylum at Chaillot near Versailles. His verse, which includes a number of translations, shows descriptive talent, but is weak in expression and technique. Talfourd thought his conversation revealed fine analytical perceptiveness.

John Gibson Lockhart (1794–1854), son of a Scottish minister, attended Glasgow High School and University, and proceeded early to Balliol, where he gained a first class in Classics in 1813. After a visit to Germany, where he met Goethe at Weimar, he studied law at Edinburgh, but turned to literature, and became a leading, often caustic, contributor to *Blackwood's Magazine*. He played no small part in attacking the 'Cockney School' of poets. He met Scott in 1818, married his daughter Sophia in 1820, wrote novels, and continued to support Blackwood. When Murray made him editor of *The Quarterly Magazine* in 1825 at £1000 p.a., he moved to London. It is to his credit that he sent the profits from his greatest work, the biography of Scott, to pay Sir Walter's creditors. Reserved and proud, he left an impression of coldness which often belied him; his last years were saddened by his isolation. He went to Italy in search of health, and returned, like Scott, to die at Abbotsford.

Harriet Martineau (1802–1876), writer and sister of the theologian James M, was born at Norwich in a Unitarian family of Huguenot descent. She was educated, first at home, then in a Norwich school where she learnt French and Latin. Afterwards she became deaf for life, and suffered frequently from poor health. Writing became a serious exercise when her father's camlet-manufacturing business failed in 1829. Soon, influenced by the Society for the Diffusion of Useful Knowledge, she began to enjoy success as a writer of tales laced with political economy. From the proceeds she made an investment which was to provide an annuity of £100 from 1850. Acting on medical advice, she travelled in 1834 to America, where she did not conceal her anti-slavery feelings. After her return in 1836 she wrote *Society in America* and *Deerbrook*, a novel. Her health at Tynemouth from 1839 to 1844 was poor until she was regularly mesmerized by Spencer T. Hall and Mrs Wynard. She then moved to Ambleside, and at Clappersgate bought land for her new home 'The Knoll' (completed in 1846), and sufficient for a small farm, which she developed with the aid of a Norfolk labourer. Her visit to Egypt and Palestine followed. *Letters on the Laws of Man's Social Nature* (1851), an agnostic correspondence with H. G. Atkinson, created considerable offence, and alienated her brother James. Enthusiasm for Comte led to her abridgment of his *Positive Philosophy* (1853) and to the visit of Marian Evans (the future George Eliot) in October 1852, when her model cottages were highly admired; (Charlotte Brontë had stayed with her in December 1850). She contributed to periodicals and wrote a guide to the Lakes. When she died her *Autobiography* had reached 1855; she was buried at Birmingham.

Thomas Poole of Nether Stowey (1765–1837) was brought up to follow his father's tannery business (which he inherited in 1795), and educated largely as a result of his own initiative. He remained unmarried. He gave STC financial support after the failure of his politically progressive publication *The Watchman*, and introduced him to Thomas Wedgwood and his brothers. In 1809 he advanced money for *The Friend*. Hartley Coleridge stayed with him during Oxford vacations. Poole became actively interested in the poor laws and in the Sunday School movement. (See Mrs Henry Sandford, *Thomas Poole and his Friends*, 1888.)

Henry Crabb Robinson (1775–1867) was born at Bury St Edmunds;

after being articled to an attorney at Colchester, he entered a London solicitor's office. The death of an uncle in 1798 brought him an annual income of £100, which enabled him to travel. As a result he became proficient in German, met Goethe and Schiller in 1801, and settled at Jena, where he became acquainted with Mme de Staël. The Napoleonic war enforced his return to England in 1805, and he became foreign correspondent of *The Times*, later foreign editor. During the Spanish insurrection against the French he was its special correspondent in the Peninsula, returning with Sir John Moore's army after the battle of Corunna. After observing his terms in the Middle Temple, he was called to the bar in 1813, when he joined the Norfolk circuit, from which he retired in 1828. His friends were notable and numerous not only in England but also in western Europe. He was a founder of the Athenaeum Club and of University College, London. He is remembered chiefly for his diaries, which are characterized by shrewd, liberal judgment.

Samuel Rogers, poet (1763–1855), entered his father's City bank after being privately educated, and became head of the firm in 1793, a year after the publication of *The Pleasures of Memory*, the poem which made him famous. In 1803 he resigned from his bank with an income of £5000 p.a., to remain a devotee of the arts, a bachelor host at 22 St James's Place, and a generous patron. His taste was fastidious; his conversation, shrewd and often tart. His art collection was sold at his death for £50,000; three of his pictures – a Titian, a Guido Reni, and a Giorgione – were bequeathed to the National Gallery.

Hugh James Rose, classical scholar and theologian (1795–1838), was educated at Uckfield school, Sussex, where his father, a local curate, was master, and at Trinity College, Cambridge. He won the first Bell scholarship at the University in 1814. Missing a Fellowship, he was ordained deacon in 1818, and became curate at Buxted, Sussex, then vicar of Horsham. He spent a year in Germany for the sake of his health, and on his return delivered, as select preacher at Cambridge (a position he held for a number of years), four sermons directed against the rationalization of theology in Germany. A conference which took place at Hadleigh, Suffolk, when he was rector there in 1833, may be regarded as an early stage in the Tractarian movement. After being compelled by ill-health to resign the Professorship of

Divinity at the University of Durham in 1834, Rose became domestic chaplain to Archbishop Howley. In 1836 he became Principal of King's College, London. He had hardly begun his duties when he was stricken with influenza, from the effects of which he never recovered. He left in October 1838 to winter in Italy, and died at Florence in December.

Richard ('Conversation') Sharp (1759–1835), son of an English officer, was born at the British garrison, Newfoundland. After partnership in a West India trading firm in London, he set up business as a hat-manufacturer at the same address. He was keenly interested in politics and literature, and knew Johnson and Burke. His friendship with Samuel Rogers began in 1792. He was an original member of the literary society which was founded in 1806. As an M.P., he was elected to important committees. At Fredley Farm, Mickleham, near Dorking, he met the chief persons of his day. He often travelled on the Continent, and frequently visited the Lake District. Wordsworth said that he did not know anyone with a greater knowledge of Italy. In 1828 Sharp issued privately his anonymous *Epistles in Verse*. He died unmarried at Dorchester on his way to London, his ward and adopted child Maria Kinnaird inheriting the bulk of his property.

(Sir) John Stoddart, journalist and advocate (1773–1856), born at Salisbury, educated at Salisbury Grammar School and Christ Church, Oxford. His *Remarks on the Local Scenery and Manners of Scotland* was published in two volumes in 1801, the year in which he became a member of the College of Advocates. From 1803 to 1807 he was the King's and the Admiralty advocate in Malta. After being a leading writer for *The Times*, he started a rival newspaper, *The New Times*, in February 1817. In 1826 he was appointed Chief Justice of the Admiralty Court in Malta, and knighted by George IV at St James's Palace.

Daniel Stuart, journalist (1766–1846), was born in Edinburgh, and sent to London in 1778 to join his brothers in a printing business. In 1788 he and one of his brothers undertook the printing of *The Morning Post*, which they acquired in 1795 for £600. In Daniel's hands it became a leading, Tory-inclined daily. Eight years later he sold this paper for £25,000, and concentrated on *The Courier*, an evening paper which he acquired in 1796. It was a great success, particularly among the clergy. After withdrawing from *The Courier* in 1822, he bought Wykeham Park, Oxfordshire.

Thomas Noon Talfourd, judge and author (1795–1854), was born at Reading, where he was educated after a period at Mill Hill. He read law with Joseph Chitty, but gave much time to literature and politics. His friendship with Charles Lamb began in 1815. His taste in poetry changed under the influence of Wordsworth's, on which he wrote an enlightened essay in *The New Monthly Magazine*. He married in 1822, soon after becoming a barrister. The demands of his legal profession did not turn him from literature. The best of his tragedies is *Ion*, which, with its première on Talfourd's birthday, 26 May 1836, scored a brilliant success. He is remembered more for his memoirs of Charles Lamb. He was returned three times as M.P. for Reading, and gained much distinction in the House by his handling of the Copyright Bill.

John Thelwall, reformer and lecturer on elocution (1764–1834), was the son of a London mercer. Distaste for the business and for the family discord which followed his father's death made him look elsewhere for employment. After serving as a tailor's apprentice, and studying law and divinity, he published two volumes of poetry in 1787. Idealistic and independent-minded, he became intoxicated with French revolutionary doctrines, and was such an eloquent demagogue that Horne Tooke offered to send him to a university. In 1791 he married, began the study of medicine, and joined the Society of the Friends of the People. On the evidence of Government spies he was arrested in 1794, and sent to the Tower with Horne Tooke and Thomas Hardy; at the end of the year he was acquitted. He left London, and for almost two years remained a public critic of the Government. The desire for a more peaceful life led to his settling as a farmer near Brecon. In 1800 he began his career as a highly gifted and popular lecturer on elocution. His interest in the cure of stammering increased, and in 1809 he began such a practice in Lincoln's Inn Fields. In 1818 he turned to parliamentary reform, but the failure of his journal *The Champion* made him return to elocution, on which he lectured in various parts of the country. He was a man of sanguine temperament and integrity who held fast to his democratic convictions.

John Wilson, author (1785–1854), the 'Christopher North' of *Blackwood's Magazine*, was born at Paisley, where he attended school. From Glasgow University he proceeded to Magdalen College, Oxford, in 1803. An athlete of amazing strength, he won the Newdigate Prize (for poetry) in 1806. After purchasing a cottage and land at Elleray, with a superb view over Windermere, he settled there, and dedicated himself to poetry and sport. Four years after his marriage in 1811 he lost his inherited fortune as a result of his uncle's dishonesty. He was received by his mother in Edinburgh, and, with J. G. Lockhart, became the foremost of Blackwood's writers at a time when high-spirited insensitivity could turn into malignity for the entertainment of readers with a limited range. When Lockhart moved to London in 1825, Wilson became virtually editor of *Blackwood's*. With no real qualifications he was elected for political motives to the Chair of Moral Philosophy at Edinburgh University in 1820. Better qualified in literature, he revealed himself at his best in his numerous contributions to the series of *Noctes Ambrosianae* which lasted from 1822 to 1835. He returned to Elleray for holiday periods, but life was saddened for him by the death of his wife Jane in 1837.

Bibliography

The Wordsworth letters are by far the most important source of information for Wordsworth's life as a whole, especially as edited in the revised edition of the first six volumes of *The Letters of William and Dorothy Wordsworth* (previously arranged and edited by Ernest de Selincourt), Oxford:

1. 1787–1805, revised by C. L. Shaver, Oxford, 1967.
2. 1806–1811, revised by Mary Moorman, Oxford, 1969.
3. 1812–1820, revised by Mary Moorman and Alan G. Hill, Oxford, 1970.
4. 1821–1828, revised by Alan G. Hill, Oxford, 1978.
5. 1829–1834, revised by Alan G. Hill, Oxford, 1979.
6. 1835–1839, revised by Alan G. Hill, Oxford, 1982.

Ernest de Selincourt's edition has been used for the remaining letters:

7. 1831–1840, Oxford, 1939.
8. 1841–1850, Oxford, 1939.

For particular periods (at Alfoxden and Grasmere, the 1803 tour in Scotland, and the 1820 tour on the Continent) the most descriptive and detailed accounts will be found in Dorothy's journals:

Ernest de Selincourt (ed.), *Journals of Dorothy Wordsworth* (2 vols), London, 1941.

Three supplementary volumes of letters are recommended:

Kathleen Coburn (ed.), *The Letters of Sara Hutchinson*, London, 1954.
Mary E. Burton (ed.), *The Letters of Mary Wordsworth* (selected), Oxford, 1958.
Beth Darlington (ed.), *The Love Letters of William and Mary Wordsworth*, London, 1982.

To these should be added the letters of S. T. Coleridge, especially the first three volumes, and those of John Wordsworth:

Earl Leslie Griggs (ed.), *Collected Letters of Samuel Taylor Coleridge* (6 vols, issued in pairs), Oxford, 1956, 1959, 1971.
Carl H. Ketcham (ed.), *The Letters of John Wordsworth*, Ithaca, N.Y., 1969.

The diarist Henry Crabb Robinson is one of the most rewarding sources:

Thomas Sadler (ed.), *Diary, Reminiscences, and Correspondence of Henry Crabb Robinson* (2 vols), London and New York, 1872.
Edith J. Morley (ed.), *The Correspondence of Henry Crabb Robinson with the Wordsworth Circle* (2 vols), Oxford, 1927.
Edith J. Morley (ed.), *Henry Crabb Robinson on Books and their Authors* (3 vols), London, 1938.

Of contemporary records which have more incidental relevance, four are specially recommended: the letters of Charles Lamb and John Keats, and

Kathleen Coburn (ed.), *The Notebooks of Samuel Taylor Coleridge* (3 vols), London, 1957, 1962, 1973.
Willard Bissel Pope (ed.), *The Diary of Benjamin Robert Haydon* (5 vols), Cambridge, Mass., 1960 and 1963.

Much valuable information will be found in Mary Moorman, *William Wordsworth, A Biography* (2 vols):

The Early Years, 1770–1803, Oxford, 1957.
The Later Years, 1803–1850, Oxford, 1965.

The most exhaustive chronological study is by Mark L. Reed; it is probably too acronymic and conjectural for all but those who wish to specialize in Wordsworth biography. Two volumes have appeared:

Wordsworth: The Chronology of the Early Years, 1770–1799, Cambridge, Mass., 1967.
Wordsworth: The Chronology of the Middle Years, 1800–1815, Cambridge, Mass., 1975.

For guidance on the dates of many of Wordsworth's poems, the notes which he dictated to Isabella Fenwick (and which are usually provided in editions of his collected poems), though not always reliable, contain useful information additional to that found elsewhere. Almost all of this relevant evidence is provided in the notes of Ernest de Selincourt's edition of *The Poetical Works of William Wordsworth,* Oxford: vol. i, 1940: vol. ii, second edition, 1952; vols iii–v, 1946, 1947, 1949.

General Index

Coleorton Farm   63, 67, 68
Coleridge, Berkeley (son)   32
Coleridge, Derwent (son)   40, 56,
    58, 64, 69, 72, 76, 85, 117, 153,
    163, 210, 219, 224, 225
Coleridge, Edward (nephew)   127
Coleridge, Hartley (son)   23, 43,
    58, 69, 70, 155, 169, 183–4, 190,
    218, 219, 224–5, 229
  at school   76, 85, 91, 93
  at Oxford   96, 97, 224
  teaching   121, 123, 125, 134, 184
  at the Ws'   43, 72, 76, 128, 183,
    217
  drunkenness   136, 149, 152, 153,
    156, 173
Coleridge, Henry Nelson
    (nephew)   155, 169
Coleridge, (Sir) John Taylor
    (nephew)   105, 177, 183, 203
Coleridge, Samuel Taylor   21–57
    passim, 97–8, 104, 124, 127,
    157, 168, 169, 229
  Mediterranean period   59–67
    passim
  return   67–8, 68ff
  London lectures   72, 73, 86, 87
  at Allan Bank   75–80 *passim*
  quarrel with W   81, 83, 85–7, 90
  Rhineland tour with W and
    Dora   144
  poems: The Ancient Mariner
    27, 30, 36; Christabel   30,
    40; Dejection: An Ode   46,
    47; The Eolian Harp   25;
    Hexameters   34; This Lime-
    tree Bower   26; The
    Wanderings of Cain   27;
    William Wordsworth, To
    69–70, 97
  Biographia Literaria   23, 104
  The Friend   76–80 *passim*, 229
  Osorio   25–6, 30
Coleridge, Mrs (Sara)   24, 26, 42,
    50, 58, 59, 61, 65, 68, 72, 109,
    132, 148, 153, 156, 179, 210
Coleridge, Sara (daughter)   50, 58,
    76, 88, 107, 109, 125, 132, 143,
    148, 150, 156, 179, 183, 191, 224

Collins, William (painter)   107
Collins, William (poet)   145, 146
Colthouse   4, 6, 7, 7–8
Como, Lake   9, 114–15, 181
Coniston   3, 122
Coniston Water   5, 110, 125, 153,
    192
Constable, John   68, 176
Cookson, Ann   *see* Wordsworth,
    Ann
Cookson, Christopher (Uncle Kit)
    5, 8, 13; *see* Crackanthorpe
Cookson, Elizabeth (daughter of
    Mrs C. of Kendal)   188
Cookson, Mrs (of Kendal)   91,
    103
Cookson, Revd William (W's
    uncle)   5, 6, 12, 15, 23, 49, 66,
    85, 105, 189
Cottle, Joseph   21, 22, 28, 30, 31,
    31–2, 32, 33, 34, 36, 143, 150
The Courier   76, 77, 231–2
Coventry   171
Cowper, William   194
Coxe, William   8, 10
Crabbe, George   76
  his son   175
Crackanthorpe, Christopher   36,
    38
  his wife   17
Crosthwaite, Samuel   166
Crowcombe   31
Cruikshank, Mr and Mrs   29, 30
Crummock Water   37, 101
Crump, Mr (and his family)   60,
    71, 78, 83, 94, 127, 129, 154
Cunningham, Allan   121, 127, 135,
    142, 168
Curwen, Clara   216
Curwen, John   154, 182, 202
Curwen, Isabella   154, 155; *see*
    Wordsworth, Isabella

Darwin, Erasmus   30, 32
Davy, (Sir) Humphry   38, 39, 58,
    63, 86, 159, 163, 225
Davy, Dr John   159, 182, 183, 189,
    202, 204, 208

Index to Wordsworth's Poetry and Prose

DATE DUE

may			

GAYLORD   PRINTED IN U.S.A.